W9-CAO-037

v. 1

NATIVE NORTH AMERICAN BIOGRAPHY

Wapiti regional library

NATIVE NORTH AMERICAN BIOGRAPHY

Volume I
A–I

Edited by Sharon Malinowski
and Simon Glickman

PAPL
DISCARDED

U·X·L

An imprint of Gale Research,
An ITP Information/Reference Group Company

I(T)P

Changing the Way the World Learns

NEW YORK • LONDON • BONN • BOSTON • DETROIT
MADRID • MELBOURNE • MEXICO CITY • PARIS
SINGAPORE • TOKYO • TORONTO • WASHINGTON
ALBANY NY • BELMONT CA • CINCINNATI OH

NATIVE NORTH AMERICAN BIOGRAPHY

Sharon Malinowski and Simon Glickman, *Editors*

Staff

Sonia Benson, *U·X·L Developmental Editor*
Carol DeKane Nagel, *U·X·L Managing Editor*
Thomas L. Romig, *U·X·L Publisher*

Shanna P. Heilveil, *Production Associate*
Evi Seoud, *Assistant Production Manager*
Mary Beth Trimper, *Production Director*

Michelle DiMercurio, *Art Director*
Cynthia Baldwin, *Product Design Manager*

This publication is a creative work fully protected by all applicable copyright laws, as well as by misappropriation, trade secret, unfair cooperation, and other applicable laws. The editors of this work have added value to the underlying factual material herein through one or more of the following: unique and original selection, coordination, expression, arrangement, and classification of the information. All rights to this publication will be vigorously defended.

Copyright © 1996
U·X·L
An Imprint of Gale Research Inc.

All rights reserved, including the right of reproduction in whole or in part in any form.

  ™ This book is printed on acid-free paper that meets the minimum requirements of American National Standard for Information Sciences—Permanence Paper for Printed Library Materials, ANSI Z39.48-1984.

ISBN 0-8103-9821-4 (Set)
ISBN 0-8103-9816-8 (Volume 1)
ISBN 0-8103-9817-6 (Volume 2)

Printed in the United States of America

I(T)P™   U·X·L is an imprint of Gale Research Inc.,
an International Thomson Publishing Company.
ITP logo is a trademark under license.

CONTENTS

CONTENTS

ENTRIES BY
TRIBAL GROUPS/NATIONS

Abenaki
Alanis Obomsawin

Apache
Cochise (Chiricahua)
Geronimo (Bedonkohe Chiricahua)

Blackfeet
James Gladstone
Jamake Highwater

Cherokee
Louis W. Ballard
Elias Boudinot
Wilma Mankiller
John Rollin Ridge
Will Rogers
Sequoyah
Nancy Ward

Cheyenne
Ben Nighthorse Campbell (Northern)
Dull Knife (Northern)

Chippewa
Louise Erdrich
Pontiac

Choctaw
Phil Lucas

Comanche
LaDonna Harris
Quanah Parker
Sanapia

Cree
Harold Cardinal
Elijah Harper
Buffy Sainte-Marie

Creek
Mary Bosomworth
Chitto Harjo
Joy Harjo (Muscogee)
Will Sampson, Jr.

Dakota
Hank Adams
Charles A. Eastman (Santee)
John Trudell (Santee)
Rosebud Yellow Robe

Delaware
Delaware Prophet
Hanay Geiogamah

Dene
Ethel Blondin-Andrew

Duwamish
Seattle

Hopi
Frank C. Dukepoo
Ramona Sakiestewa

Huron
Deganawida

Inuit
William L. Hensley
Kenojuak
Peter Pitseolak

Kansa
Charles Curtis

Kiowa
Hanay Geiogamah
N. Scott Momaday

Kwakiutl
Mungo Martin

Lakota
Amos Bad Heart Bull (Oglala)
Black Elk (Oglala)
Mary Brave Bird
Crazy Horse (Oglala Brulé)
Tim Giago (Oglala)
Russell C. Means
Billy Mills (Oglala)
Leonard Peltier
Red Cloud (Oglala)
Sitting Bull (Hunkpapa)
Rosebud Yellow Robe (Brulé/Hunkpapa)

Lehmi
Sacagawea

Maidu
Frank Day

Menominee
Ada E. Deer

Métis
Tantoo Cardinal
Gabriel Dumont
Louis Riel

Micmac
Anna Mae Aquash

Modoc
Captain Jack
Michael Dorris

Mohawk
Joseph Brant
Molly Brant
Hiawatha
Emily Pauline Johnson
Robbie Robertson
Jay Silverheels
Kateri Tekakwitha

Nakota
Hank Adams (Assiniboine)
Gertrude Simmons Bonnin (Yankton)
Ella Cara Deloria (Yankton)
Vine Deloria, Jr. (Yankton)
Vine Deloria, Sr. (Yankton)

Navajo
Barboncito
Harrison Begay
Carl Nelson Gorman
R. C. Gorman
Manuelito
Peterson Zah

Nez Percé
Joseph

Nisqually
Billy Frank, Jr.

Numu (Northern Paiute)
Sarah Winnemucca
Wovoka

Ojibway (Ojibwa)
Dennis J. Banks (Anishinabe)
Clyde Bellecourt
Norval Morrisseau
Leonard Peltier

Omaha
Susan La Flesche Picotte

Oneida
Graham Greene

Onondoga
Hiawatha

Osage
Charles Curtis
Maria Tallchief

Ottawa
Pontiac

Pequot
William Apess

Pima
Ira Hayes

Powhatan-Renapé
Pocahontas
Powhatan

Pueblo
Paula Gunn Allen (Laguna)
Frank C. Dukepoo (Laguna)
Maria Martinez (Tewa/San Ildefonso)
Nora Naranjo-Morse (Tewa)
Leslie Marmon Silko (Laguna)

Quapaw
Louis W. Ballard

Salishan
Sherman Alexie
    (Spokane/Coeur d'Alene)
Dan George (Squamish)
Seattle (Suquamish)

Sauk and Fox
Black Hawk
Jim Thorpe

Seminole
Betty Mae Tiger Jumper

Seneca
Handsome Lake
Ely S. Parker

Shawnee
Tecumseh

Shoshone
Sacagawea

Sioux
Paula Gunn Allen
Louis W. Ballard

Wampanoag
Massasoit
Squanto

Wanapam
Smohalla

Washo
Datsolalee

Yahi
Ishi

Yakima
David Sohappy, Sr.

READER'S GUIDE

Native North American Biography profiles 112 Native North Americans from the United States and Canada, both living and deceased, who are notable in their achievements in fields ranging from civil rights to sports, politics and tribal leadership to literature, entertainment to religion, science to military. The entries focus on the political, social, or historic environment in which these individuals have lived, as well as on their childhoods, family backgrounds, education, and the achievements and contributions for which they are known. A black-and-white portrait accompanies most entries, and a list of sources for further reading or research is provided at the end of each entry. Cross references to other profiles in these volumes are noted in bold letters within the text. The volumes are arranged alphabetically and conclude with an index listing all individuals by field of endeavor.

Related reference sources:

Native North American Almanac features a comprehensive range of historical and current information on the life and culture of the Native peoples of the United States and Canada. Organized into 24 subject chapters, including major culture areas, activism, and religion, the volumes contain more than two hundred black-and-white photographs and maps and a cumulative subject index.

Native North American Chronology explores significant social, political, economic, cultural, and educational milestones in the history of the Native peoples of the United States and Canada. Arranged by year and then by month and day where applicable, the chronology spans from prehistory to modern times and contains more than 70 illustrations and maps, extensive cross references, and a cumulative subject index.

Native North American Voices presents full or excerpted speeches, sermons, orations, poems, testimony, and other notable spoken works of Native Americans. Each entry is accompanied by an introduction and boxes explaining terms and events to which the speech refers. The volume contains pertinent black-and-white illustrations and a cumulative subject index.

Comments and Suggestions

We welcome your comments on *Native North American Biography* as well as your suggestions for people to be featured in future editions. Please write: Editors, *Native North American Biography,* U•X•L, 835 Penobscot Bldg., Detroit, Michigan 48226-4094; call toll-free: 1-800-877-4253; or fax: 313-961-6348.

PICTURE CREDITS

The photographs and illustrations appearing in *Native North American Biography* were received from the following sources:

Cover: Sitting Bull: **The Bettmann Archive;** Louise Erdrich: **Photograph by Michael Dorris;** Graham Greene: **© Barry King 1992/Gamma-Liaison.**

UPI/Bettman: pp. 1, 22, 35, 144, 150, 227, 246, 248, 251, 254, 277, 309, 321, 367, 372, 395; **Photograph by Tama Rothchild, Courtesy of Paula Gunn Allen:** p. 6; **The Granger Collection, New York:** pp. 19, 43, 62, 87, 131, 208, 236, 266, 284, 288, 296, 301, 304, 330, 340, 355, 360, 384, 388; **Mike Okoniewski/The Image Works:** p. 24; **AP/Wide World Photos:** pp. 26, 92, 112, 118, 156, 210, 239, 352, 378; **The Philbrook Museum of Art, Tulsa, OK:** pp. 32, 83; **Western Historical Manuscript Collection:** p. 39; **The Bettmann Archive:** pp. 45, 182, 231, 243, 270, 311, 315, 345, 358; **Bruguier Collection:** p. 49; **Archive Photos:** pp. 54, 74, 124; **Courtesy of Library of Congress:** pp. 58, 146, 264, 317, 333, 342, 364; **Reproduced by permission of Richard Erdoes:** pp. 67, 68; **Reuters/Bettmann:** p. 70; **Canapress Photo Service:** pp. 78, 176; **Photograph by Brian Willer, Toronto, Canada:** p. 80; **© M. Bernsau/The Image Works:** p. 89; **© 1994 Walter Bigbee:** pp. 100, 173, 178; **Photograph by Felix Farrar, Courtesy** of Frank Dukepoo: p. 121; **Courtesy of the Royal Ontario Museum:** p. 127; **Photograph by Michael Dorris:** p. 135; **Courtesy of Hanay Geiogamah:** p. 142; **Courtesy of R. C. Gorman Navajo Gallery, Taos, NM:** pp. 159, 160, 161; **© Barry King 1992/ Gamma-Liaison:** p. 163; **Courtesy of New York State Library:** p. 166; **Archives and Manuscripts Division of the Oklahoma Historical Society:** p. 168; **National Archives of Canada/Neg. No. C85125;** p. 204; **McCord Museum of Canadian History. All Rights Reserved:** pp. 213, 281, 282; **Reproduced by permission of West Baffin Eskimo Cooperative Ltd.:** p. 215; **Archives and Special Collections on Women in Medicine, Medical College of Pennsylvania:** p. 217; **Courtesy of Phil Lucas Productions, Inc.:** p. 222; **The *Toronto Star*/J. Goode:** p. 257; **Glenbow Archives, Calgary, Canada, NA-1039-1;** p. 258; **Photograph by Mary Fredenburgh, Courtesy of Nora Naranjo-Morse:** p. 260; **Photograph by Rafy, Courtesy of National Film Board of Canada:** p. 262; **Archive Photos/American Stock:** p. 294; **Glenbow Archives, Calgary, Canada:** p. 306; **© Copyright 1975. The Saul Zaentz Company. All Rights Reserved:** p. 325; **The Image Works:** p. 331; **Photograph by Robyn McDaniels:** p. 334.

Hank Adams

Assiniboine/Dakota Sioux activist
Born May 16, 1943, Fort Peck Indian
Reservation, Montana

In the early 1960s, Hank Adams and other Indians argued that the treaties signed in the 1850s still guaranteed them the right to fish at traditional sites.

Hank Adams

Hank Adams was one of the leaders in the struggle over Indian fishing rights in the Northwest. He helped raise public awareness of Native Americans' struggles through his political work, first by appealing to the government, later by engaging in protest actions. A tireless activist, he once took a bullet for his cause; he soon recovered from this setback and returned to the fight. His efforts helped increase Indians' control over their lives and livelihoods.

Adams was born in 1943 at a place known as Wolf Point, or Poverty Flats, on the Fort Peck Indian Reservation in northeastern Montana. He grew up, however, on the Quinault Indian Reservation on Washington's Olympic Peninsula. Adams attended Moclips High School, where he was student body president, editor of the school newspaper and annual, and a member of the football and basketball teams.

After graduating in 1961, Adams studied communications skills at the University of Washington from 1961 to 1963. He then moved to California, where he became involved in politics and the Democratic party. He supported President John F. Kennedy and later, during the 1968 Democratic primary, worked on Robert F. Kennedy's presidential campaign. From 1965 to 1967, Adams worked with citizens' rights advocate Ralph Nader and the staffs of U.S. senators, including Robert F. Kennedy, acquainting Congress with Indian issues. A result of his work was the creation of the Select Senate Subcommittee on Indian Education.

Fights for treaty and fishing rights

In the early 1960s, Adams's activism grew more militant when he became involved in the growing Red Power movement and joined the National Indian Youth Council, an organization created by Native American college students. Many of the young, college-educated Indian leaders who emerged during the 1960s and 1970s were members of the council. After receiving his draft notice in April 1964, Adams refused to serve in the U.S. Army, declaring that he would not join the military until Indian treaty rights were recognized. His protest failed, however, and he did a term of military service. After leaving the army, Adams plunged right into the fight for Indian fishing rights in the Northwest. As chair of the National Indian Youth Council's Washington State Project, Adams organized fish-ins and demonstrations protesting the state's policies on Indian fishing rights.

Many of Washington's Natives live on small, widely scattered reservations in the Puget Sound lowlands. Traditionally fishing folk with villages on the rivers and along the coasts, the Indians gave up most of their land when they signed treaties in the 1850s. But they did retain their right to fish at their usual and accustomed places. In the early 1960s, Adams and other Indians argued that the treaties signed in the 1850s still guaranteed them the right to fish at traditional sites. When state officials and sport and commercial fishermen disagreed, fishing rights battles followed.

In 1964, Adams helped organize a march on the Washington state capital in Olympia. The march included actor Marlon Brando and over 1,000 Indians. It captured the public's attention and was followed by other marches and fish-ins (a form of protest similar to the "sit-ins" of the 1960s). In 1968, Adams became the director of the Survival of American Indians Association, a western Washington organization primarily concerned with Indian fishing rights.

Fishing rights struggle turns violent

Throughout the late 1960s and into the mid-1970s, Adams continued to campaign against state regulation of Indian fishing at traditional sites. Two of the best-known sites of protest in western Washington were on the Nisqually River near a place called Frank's Landing, and on the Puyallup River near the city of Tacoma. Frank's Landing, a six-acre tract on the Nisqually River below the small Nisqually Indian Reservation south of Puget Sound, had been purchased by Willie Frank (the last known full-blooded Nisqually) to replace lands he lost in the government's Fort Lewis acquisition. Frank's Landing became the scene of fish-ins and sometimes violent confrontations between state officials and Nisquallis. Violence also erupted between Indians and police at fishing sites on the Puyallup River.

From 1968 to 1971, Adams was regularly arrested and jailed for his role in the fishing rights battles on these two rivers. In January 1971, he and a colleague, Michael Hunt, were fishing on the Puyallup River, where battles between police and Indian fishermen had recently taken place. Sometime after midnight, while watching a net for a friend, Adams was shot in the stomach. He claimed two white men had shot him, but police disputed his account and the assailant was never found. After recovering from the gunshot wound Adams continued to fight for Indian fishing rights.

During the same period Adams worked to establish tribal fishery programs, requesting technical assistance, management services, and funding for these programs from the federal government. Adams argued that federally funded Indian fishery programs should be included in the economic development plans of Northwest Indian tribes. He also advocated hiring Native American fishery biologists and enforcement officers to administer the fisheries.

The struggle to gain recognition of Indian treaty fishing rights was strengthened with a decisive victory in 1974, when Federal Judge George Boldt ruled in favor of the Indians in the landmark decision *U.S. v. Washington*. Judge Boldt ruled that treaty Indians were entitled to 50 percent of the commercially harvested fish in Washington. Boldt's decision forced the state of Washington to recognize Indian treaty fishing rights.

Adams's role as a political activist, organizer, and leader helped bring about the recognition of Indian treaty fishing rights in the Northwest. He called for tribal involvement in off-reservation fishery management at a time when Indian tribes had no such role off their reservations. Tribal, federal, and state comanagement of natural resources has now become accepted practice.

Adams has had numerous articles published in newspapers and journals, and his views have also been expressed in films and on television. He has been involved in monitoring and lobbying the Washington state legislature; he has twice entered primary elections as a congressional candidate; and in 1973 he served as a special liaison between the White House and the Indians occupying Wounded Knee, South Dakota—the site of the 1890 massacre of Sioux men, women, and children by U.S. soldiers—helping to negotiate a settlement.

Further Reading

Cohen, Fay G., *Treaties on Trial: The Continuing Controversy over Northwest Indian Fishing Rights,* Seattle: University of Washington Press, 1986.

Native North American Almanac, edited by Duane Champagne, Detroit: Gale Research, 1994.

Steiner, Stan, *The New Indians,* New York: Dell, 1968.

Uncommon Controversy: Fishing Rights of the Muckleshoot, Puyallup and Nisqually Indians, Seattle: University of Washington Press, 1970.

Sherman Alexie

Spokane/Coeur d'Alene writer
Born 1966

"Survival = Anger x Imagination. Imagination is the only weapon on the reservation."

Sherman Alexie is, according to many readers and critics, one of the most exciting young Native American writers of the 1990s. While still in his early twenties he began publishing poems and within a few years he had captured the attention of a large and prestigious readership and won several distinctive awards for his work. Although he now lives in Spokane, Washington, Alexie visited the reservation where he spent his childhood several times while a student. Life there, with all its richness, humor, and complexity—including problems like poverty and alcoholism—has been a frequent subject in his poetry and fiction.

Alexie is the son of a Spokane father and a part-Coeur d'Alene mother. He grew up on the Spokane Indian Reservation in Well-

Sherman Alexie

pinit, Washington. When he was eighteen years old he went off to college at Gonzaga University in Spokane, but after two years he transferred to Washington State University in Pullman, where he majored in American Studies. Alex Kuo, his creative writing teacher at Washington State, encouraged him to try to publish his writing.

Success comes quickly

Alexie's first published poems began appearing in magazines in 1990. These publications had a fairly small readership. But by 1993 he had earned praise from numerous well-known writers and critics—including those in such magazines as *Esquire* and *Vanity Fair*—and he was championed as an important young Native American writer. In the years in between he won several prizes, including a 1991 poetry fellowship from the

Washington State Arts Commission and a creative writing fellowship from the National Endowment for the Arts in 1992. Alexie assembled a small collection of poems, also known as a chapbook, entitled *I Would Steal Horses,* which won the fifth annual chapbook contest sponsored by the Slipstream Press. In only two years, four of Alexie's books were published.

Alexie's journey from unknown writer to critics' favorite is a remarkable one. A rave notice in the *New York Times Book Review,* in which reviewer James R. Kincaid called Alexie "one of the major lyric voices of our time," is just one example of the reception that greeted his first collection of fiction and poetry, 1992's *The Business of Fancydancing.* Yet Alexie has made as important a contribution to publicizing his books as have his favorable reviewers. Between 1992 and 1993 alone he presented over 290 readings of his works to audiences ranging in size from six people to 1,000.

Alexie entered the literary world at a time the reading public wanted to hear from Native American writers. His early career coincided with the five-hundredth anniversary, or quincentennial, of explorer Christopher Columbus's arrival in the so-called New World. Although U.S. history books claimed for years that Columbus had "discovered" the Americas and that he was welcomed by the Native peoples, many Native American writers have pointed out that a land with people on it doesn't need to be "discovered." More importantly, they insist, Columbus and his men murdered and enslaved the Indians they met while looking for gold. This anniversary sparked a lot of controversy about the way European-based culture has remembered the history of the

Americas, glorifying the conquest of a land while at the same time ignoring the violence and deprivation suffered by its inhabitants during the conquest.

Alexie's writings helped to express in powerful new ways the anger so many people felt about the quincentennial. His book *Old Shirts & New Skins* is, among all his writings to date, the most militant and direct in addressing the oppression and hardship that "New World" natives have endured. One poem, "Postcard to Columbus," answers the quincentennial celebrations with a single blast. Alexie also addresses such painful issues as the nineteenth-century Sand Creek massacre (a unprovoked army attack on a Southern Cheyenne and Arapaho camp during the Civil War, in which an estimated 500 Native Americans were brutally massacred), the stereotyped portrayal of Native Americans in Hollywood movies, and harsh conditions on the reservation.

The element of humor

In *The Lone Ranger & Tonto Fistfight in Heaven,* Alexie's collection of short fiction published in 1993, he writes: "Survival = Anger x Imagination. Imagination is the only weapon on the reservation." Yet another survival tool, one that Alexie uses in his work, is humor. His comic view, even in the face of misery and pain, is part of all of his books. He is considered the first major Native American writer to work everyday humor consistently into his work, using laughter to address subjects as difficult as racist state troopers, the shady dealings of the U.S. Bureau of Indian Affairs with Native people, and cancer.

In 1994 and 1995, Alexie published his first novels, *Coyote Springs* and *Reservation Blues.*

Further Reading

(all by Sherman Alexie)

The Business of Fancydancing (poetry and short stories), Brooklyn, NY: Hanging Loose Press, 1992.

Coyote Springs (novel), New York: Atlantic Monthly Press, 1994.

I Would Steal Horses (poetry), Slipstream Chapbook, 1992.

The Lone Ranger and Tonto Fistfight in Heaven (short stories), New York: Atlantic Monthly Press, 1993.

Old Shirts & New Skins (poetry), Los Angeles: UCLA American Indian Studies Center, 1993.

Reservation Blues (novel), New York: Grove Atlantic, 1995.

Salmontraveling (poetry), Brooklyn: Hanging Loose Press, 1993.

Paula Gunn Allen

Laguna Pueblo/Sioux writer, poet, and educator
Born 1939, Albuquerque, New Mexico

"Sometimes I get in a dialogue between what the Church taught me, the nuns taught me, and what my mother taught me, what my experience growing up where I grew up taught me. Often you can't reconcile them."

Paula Gunn Allen is one of the foremost scholars of Native American literature as well as a talented poet and novelist. A collector and interpreter of Native American mythology, she describes herself as a "multicultural event," citing her

Paula Gunn Allen

Pueblo/Sioux/Lebanese/Scottish-American ancestry. She also uses her experience as a woman—and as a lesbian—to offer fresh perspectives to her readers.

Allen was born in Albuquerque, New Mexico, and grew up in Cubero, New Mexico, a Spanish-Mexican land grant village near the Laguna and Acoma reservations and the Cibola National Forest in the north central part of the state. She attended mission schools in Cubero and San Fidel, but received most of her schooling at a Sisters of Charity boarding school in Albuquerque, from which she graduated in 1957. Several of her works, including her 1983 novel *The Woman Who Owned the Shadows* and some of her poetry, draw upon her experiences in this Catholic environment.

Studied Indian and Anglo-American culture

Allen became interested in writing in high school, after discovering the writings of American modernist (a writer who has rejected artistic or literary forms of the past and seeks new forms of expression) Gertrude Stein and such English Romantic (a nine-teenth-century literary movement that emphasized imagination and emotion) poets as Percy Bysshe Shelley and John Keats. Though she began her university studies at Colorado Women's College, she received both her bachelor's degree in English and her master of fine arts degree in creative writing from the University of Oregon. Allen received her doctorate in American studies with an emphasis on Native American litera-ture from the University of New Mexico, and it was there that she began to think of herself as a poet. Although she considered herself a prose writer at first, she attended a class taught by Robert Creeley, who introduced her to the work of poets Charles Olson, Allen Ginsberg, and Denise Levertov, all of whom would have a profound influence on her.

Allen has three children and is divorced. She is recognized as a major scholar, literary critic, and teacher of Native American litera-ture. She has taught at San Francisco State University, the University of New Mexico, Fort Lewis College in Durango, Colorado, the University of California at Berkeley, and the University of California at Los Angeles, where she was a professor of English. Her work explores the function that rituals serve in Native American literature, much of which has been handed down as storytelling and is called "oral tradition." Allen's belief that oral tradition has the power to aid healing and survival can be traced through all of her work.

Explored mixed background in work

Allen is sensitive to the conflicting influences in her background: Catholic, Native American, Protestant, Jewish, and Maronite (a Lebanese sect of Catholicism). In an interview with Joseph Bruchac for *Survival This Way,* Allen says: "Sometimes I get in a dialogue between what the Church taught me, the nuns taught me, and what my mother taught me, what my experience growing up where I grew up taught me. Often you can't reconcile them." The main character in her novel *The Woman Who Owned the Shadows* attempts to sort through the varying cultural influences in her life to reclaim a Native American women's spiritual tradition. On her journey, she uses traditional Laguna Pueblo healing ceremonies as well as psychotherapy (the treatment of mental or emotional disorders by psychological methods), the Iroquois story of Sky Woman, and the aid of a psychic Euro-American woman.

Allen writes from the perspective of a Laguna Pueblo woman, in whose culture women are accorded great respect. In the Laguna Pueblo society, women own houses, children inherit their mothers' names—this is known as matrilineal descent—and the major deities, or gods, are female. Two other writers from Laguna Pueblo are related to Allen— her sister, Carol Lee Sanchez, and her cousin, **Leslie Marmon Silko** (see entry). Allen's writings try to recover and describe this woman-centered culture. Her work explores women's relationship to the sacred, as well as the plight of contemporary Native American women, many of whom have lost the respect they were granted in the past.

Female focus

Allen says that she focuses on women in her work to show her Euro-American readers, especially female ones, that women have not always been placed in inferior or subservient roles in all cultures. Even so, Allen has admitted to mixed feelings about the feminist movement. This is because of the superior attitude some Euro-American women have about their culture, and their assumption that in Native American societies women are subservient. Such beliefs have been personally hurtful to her and other Native women. Overall, however, she says that feminists provide the best audience for her work and have given her much support. In her family, the woman-centered tradition was so strong that her grandfather wanted to name her mother Susan B. Anthony.

Native American contributions to democracy and feminism have also been among Allen's favorite subjects. Her writings challenge the popular idea that societies in which women enjoyed equality with men never existed. She has also worked hard to restore the place of gay and lesbian Native Americans in the community, presenting her ideas in works like 1981's ground-breaking essay "Beloved Women: Lesbians in American Indian Cultures."

Variety of awards and activities

Allen was awarded a National Endowment for the Arts writing fellowship in 1978, and she received a postdoctoral fellowship grant from the Ford Foundation-National Research Council in 1984. Around this time she also served as associate fellow at the Stanford Humanities Institute, coordinating the "Gynosophic [woman-knowledge] Gathering, a Woman Identified Worship Service," in Berkeley. She has also been active in the antinuclear and antiwar movements as well as the feminist movement.

Allen won an American Book Award in 1990 for *Spider Woman's Granddaughters: Traditional Tales and Contemporary Writings by Native American Women,* her attempt to remedy the lack of stories by and/or about Native women in literature collections. In her 1991 *Grandmother of the Light: A Medicine Woman's Sourcebook,* Allen further probes the ritual experiences of women in traditional stories. She traces the stages in a woman's spiritual path using Native American stories as models for walking in the sacred way.

With her multicultural background and diverse tastes, Allen writes her poetry by drawing on different rhythms and structures from such diverse sources as country-western music, Pueblo corn dances, Catholic masses, the compositions of Mozart, Italian opera, and Arabic chanting. Critics have praised her powerful descriptions of landscape, as well as her purity of language and emotional intensity.

Allen's 1982 *Shadow Country* received an honorable mention from the National Book Award Before Columbus Foundation. In this collection Allen uses the theme of shadows—the not dark and not light—to explore her mixed heritage. The poems are filled with spirits common to Native American literature, but represent her multicultural heritage as well. She also uses her poetry to deal with personal issues, such as her mother's suffering with lupus in the poem "Dear World" and the death of one of her twin sons in "On the Street: Monument."

Paula Gunn Allen has said that her work has a "haunted" quality and is often filled with the sadness of being split into many differing identities. Like her cultural background, Allen's work is a rich and diverse tapestry. The range of her experience, imagination, and compassion has helped her to make a rich contribution to Native American literature as a scholar, writer, and educator.

Further Reading

(all by Paula Gunn Allen)

The Blind Lion, Berkeley, CA: Thorp Springs Press, 1974.

A Cannon Between My Knees, New York: Strawberry Hill Press, 1981.

Coyote's Daylight Trip, Albuquerque, NM: La Confluencia, 1978.

Grandmothers of the Light: A Medicine Woman's Sourcebook, Boston: Beacon Press, 1991.

Indian Perspectives, Southwest Parks and Monuments Association, 1992.

The Sacred Hoop: Recovering the Feminine in American Indian Traditions, Boston: Beacon Press, 1986.

Star Child, Marvin, SD: *Blue Cloud Quarterly,* 1981.

Shadow Country, Los Angeles: University of California Indian Studies Center, 1982.

The Woman Who Owned the Shadows, San Francisco: Spinsters/Aunt Lute Books, 1983.

Wyrds, San Francisco: Taurean Horn, 1987.

Skin and Bones, Albuquerque, NM: West End Press, 1988.

William Apess

Pequot minister, activist, and writer
Born January 31, 1798, Colrain, Massachusetts
Died April 1839, New York City

As far as history can demonstrate, William Apess's A Son of the Forest *was the first published full-length personal narrative written by an American Indian.*

W illiam Apess was the most prolific Indian writer in the English language in the nineteenth century and the first Native American to write and publish his own autobiography, *A Son in the Forest*. After early sufferings in his life, Apess converted to Christianity, in which he found a strong identity and a political path he believed in. During his life, Apess had witnessed racism, exploitation, and inhumane behavior on the part of many Christian ministers, but he did not follow in the footsteps of their hypocrisy. His distinguished and well-researched writings on Christianity and his activism on behalf of Native American rights demonstrated that profound faith, intelligence, and humanitarian deeds can always work together.

Apess was a Pequot, once one of the most powerful tribal groups in New England. When the Puritans began to settle in the Northeast, exerting authority over Natives and demanding Pequot land, relations between the Puritans and Pequots became hostile. In 1637, Pilgrims, Puritans, and their Indian allies set fire to the Pequot fort at Mystic River, killing 700 people. The massacre, commonly called the Pequot War, nearly wiped out the Pequot as a group. Survivors of the conflict were sold into slavery in the West Indies or scattered to live a hidden existence in southeastern Connecticut. By the late eighteenth century, the remaining Pequots lived on two reservations, where they took care of their families mostly through day labor and domestic work. Their defeat by the settlers and the lowly status forced upon them in a Europeanized society damaged their strength as a cultural group. Individual Pequots seeking comfort or escape often became vulnerable to alcohol abuse and depression.

During the eighteenth and early nineteenth centuries, a large part of the Native American population, including the Pequot, responded strongly to evangelical Christianity (a form of the Christian faith that stresses converting others and spreading the word of the gospel). Apess was just one of several Native Americans who became prominent as ministers, and he remains outstanding for his many thoughtful writings.

Suffered in childhood

Apess was born on January 31, 1798, in Colrain, Massachusetts. His father, William, a half-blooded descendant of Wampanoag chief King Philip, was a shoemaker by trade. His mother, Candace, was a Pequot who may have had some African ancestry. Nineteenth-century records show that the spelling of the surname was *Apes* with one "s" until son William added the second "s" for his later publications.

Apess's parents had moved to Colrain from Colchester, Connecticut. They may have moved to escape Candace Apes's slave master, who did not free her until 1805. Eventually, the family returned to its former home. Apess's parents separated while he was still young, and he then lived with his maternal grandparents. The young boy suffered much abuse during this period, including a severely broken arm. He was placed in neighboring households as an indentured servant—a position similar to slavery for a set amount of time—and frequently tried to run away from his harsh circumstances. Apess received little formal schooling as a child.

Captivated by Christianity

Around 1809, at the height of the Second Great Awakening, a religious revival movement that had begun at the end of the previous century, Apess began attending revivalist meetings. He was powerfully affected by the teachings of Calvinists—followers of theologian John Calvin—about Christian salvation. Calvinism argued that humans were steeped in sin. They believed that salvation could not be achieved merely by doing good deeds, but only through God's intervention.

After learning what he could from the Calvinists, the youthful Apess found himself even more drawn toward what he called the "noisy Methodists." He was attracted to their fervor, finding that spontaneous expression in worship was more appealing to him than silence and solemnity. The Methodists' teachings contributed to his belief in the loving grace of Christ as the savior of mankind. Notably, the teachings also led to his strong conviction that Native Americans were among the Ten Lost Tribes of Israel mentioned in the Bible.

Apess's religious zeal and isolation from other Indians sometimes confused his identity as an Indian. Berry-picking one afternoon, he encountered sun-tanned white women. He thought they were the cruel Indians he had heard so much about and fled in fear. But his involvement in Christianity didn't prevent the various masters to whom he was indentured from flogging him. These masters sometimes gave Apess permission to attend Methodist meetings—but at other times they prevented him from doing so.

Fell into "wickedness," returned to faith

In early 1813 Apess finally ran away to New York City with another indentured youth and, prodded by unscrupulous, drinking soldiers, enlisted in the army as a drummer. Though he at first resisted the un-Christian habits of his companions, he soon fell in with their ways. He wrote in his autobiography, *A Son of the Forest*: "In little time I became almost as bad as any of them, could drink rum, play cards, and act as wickedly as any. I was at times tormented with the thoughts of death, but God had mercy on me and spared my life."

Apess's militia unit marched to Plattsburgh, New York, to prepare for a siege of Montreal. Although he was officially a drummer as well as being under the legal age for army service, Apess saw action in a few battles. After being discharged from his militia, he traveled and worked in southern Canada, socializing with several Native American families there, and eventually worked his way southward, through Albany, New York, and home to Connecticut.

By age 19 Apess resumed his earnest attendance of religious meetings. One crucial experience confirmed his Christian faith: leaving the southeastern Connecticut home of maternal relatives to visit his father, who had resettled in Colrain, Apess became lost one night in a swamp. This experience was a turning point in his beliefs. The swamp may have symbolized for him the mire of sin, or the wilderness where spiritual quests in the Bible took place. In any case, he felt himself called to preach the gospel and increasingly, even before his baptism in 1818, told congregations of Native Americans, whites, and blacks to repent and seek salvation. Although at this time he was legally forbidden to preach without a license, he taught his Christian message throughout Connecticut and in the Albany area.

In December 1821 Apess married Mary Wood of Salem, Connecticut, a woman ten years his senior whom he described as "of nearly the same color as myself." His religious work and the need to support his wife and growing family forced him into lengthy separations from them. Only on a few occasions, such as one preaching tour in the Albany area, was his family able to be near him. Apess preached to worshippers throughout New York, on Long Island, in New York City, in the Albany-Troy region, in Utica, and also in southern and coastal New England. In 1829, after the Methodist Episcopal church refused to ordain him, he was befriended by the Protestant Methodists who performed his ordination.

Writing, preaching, and activism

In 1829 the first edition of Apess's autobiography, *A Son of the Forest,* was pub-lished, recording his life up to that time. The story was done in a form called a "conversion narrative" or "testimony," in which a personal story is used as a kind of spiritual memoir that describes how the author has reached a state of grace (a state of divine assistance and blessing bestowed by God). Apess drew upon this tradition by showing how his childhood hardships and later misbehavior paved the way for his baptism and quest for salvation.

Apess's literary style is similar to that of other religious and political writers of his time. Its maturity and clarity are remarkable for someone who attended school for a mere six years, and then only during the winter months.

As far as history can demonstrate, *A Son of the Forest* was the first published full-length personal narrative written by an American Indian. Its title appealed to the non-Native book-buying public in a variety of ways. Those who found literacy among peoples of color in the United States as exotic relished the opportunity to read a "savage" tale. Readers interested in reforming savages, meanwhile, took the work as proof that Native Americans and African Americans were capable of becoming "civilized" according to European-based standards. Even while it played on such stereotypes, the book expressed some revolutionary ideas about the spiritual and political lives of Indians.

Apess came to preaching and writing in an era when white politicians, educators, and religious leaders intensely debated the fate of the Indian and the slave. Such figures often came up with schemes for Indian removal from the South and the return of slaves to Africa. Apess was aware that his congregations included as many curious onlookers who simply wanted to witness an Indian preacher as repentant sinners.

A Son of the Forest includes a lengthy appendix in which Apess rearranged and paraphrased much of the text of a book entitled *A Star in the West,* published in 1816 by Elias Boudinot (not the Cherokee writer-editor of the same name). The book demonstrated some striking similarities between the customs and character traits of biblical Hebrews and those of Native Americans. Apess used this text because he agreed with its argument that American Indians belonged to the Ten Lost Tribes that scattered from Israel after it was overrun by the Assyrians in the eighth century before Christ.

In the 1830s Apess wrote a great deal about religious, historical, and political issues. *The Increase of the Kingdom of Christ: A Sermon* was printed in 1831 with an appendix entitled *The Indians: The Ten Lost Tribes.* John the Baptist, the preacher in the wilderness and forerunner of Jesus of Nazareth, is the model for *The Increase,* in which Apess presented a detailed and well-organized argument showing Native Americans as one of God's chosen groups.

Pioneering "oral history"

Another book, *The Experiences of Five Christian Indians of the Pequot Tribe,* was published in 1833, revealing Apess's skills as a writer, historian, and editor. It is mainly comprised of five testimonies from different people that confront the Pequots' sad legacy. Apess's personal statement, opening this collection, condenses the experiences he had related in *A Son of the Forest* while force-fully challenging whites about their racism. In the second testimony, his wife Mary describes her parents and presents her own thoughts about the advantages of piety, or religious devotion.

In another testimony in the book, "The Experience of Ann Wampy," Apess describes Wampy's life and reproduces her style of speech. This is an early example of oral history, which faithfully presents a written record of the spoken word. The first edition of *Experiences* also includes Apess's militant essay "An Indian's Looking-Glass for the White Man." Here Apess attacks the racial hypocrisy of white Christians who live in a world largely populated by peoples of color. He also reminds Christians of the non-white identity of Jesus. This daring essay recalls the *Appeal to the Colored Citizens of the World* (1829) by abolitionist David Walker, and prefigures some statements by black activist Malcolm X in the twentieth century.

Imprisonment and a new publication

After hearing rumors about harsh conditions under which the Mashpee Wampanoag Indians on Cape Cod lived, Apess visited their community in 1833. He quickly became embroiled in the "Mashpee Revolt" against the Commonwealth of Massachusetts. That state worked to deny the tribe any form of self-government and representation; at the same time it quietly encouraged corruption and greed by white landowners and squatters—those who claimed land by occupying it. Apess served a 30-day jail sentence for leading a group of Indian men in removing timber from a trespassing white man's wagon. Apess was probably not the revolt's architect, though he played an important role in advancing Indian rights in this conflict.

After a peaceful solution was achieved, Apess compiled a documentary history of the incident, *Indian Nullification of the Unconstitutional Laws of Massachusetts Relative to the Mashpee Tribe; or, The Pretended Riot Explained.* Published in 1835, it combined his observations with reprinted letters, depositions and petitions to governing officials by the Wampanoag representatives, and letters reprinted from regional newspapers. The *Indian Nullification* is one of the outstanding law-related documents by a private individual in the nineteenth century.

The final surviving work by Apess, *Eulogy on King Philip, as Pronounced at the Odeon, in Federal Street, Boston,* was first printed in 1836. By this time, he had begun to use the additional 's' in documents for his name. The *Eulogy* is a long speech comparing seventeenth-century Wampanoag leader King Philip to a martyred American patriot slain in the process of defending his country from invaders.

For many years, Apess scholars could only speculate about his fate after 1838. The only written record about him at that time that survives is an inventory of his household goods resulting from a debt action in Barnstable, not far from the Mashpee community in Massachusetts. However, in recent years a published obituary came to light describing Apess's death from "apoplexy" in late April 1839, in New York City. Details of his autopsy suggest a head injury possibly related to alcohol, which he had managed to avoid for two decades. Whatever the fatal circumstances, William

Apess in his last years saw precious little evidence that Native Americans would receive justice in their native land.

Further Reading

Apess, William, *On Our Own Ground: The Complete Writings of William Apess, a Pequot,* edited by Barry O'Connell, Amherst: University of Massachusetts Press, 1992.

Ruoff, A. LaVonne Brown, "Three Nineteenth-Century American Indian Autobiographies," in *Redefining American Literary History,* edited by A. LaVonne Brown Ruoff and Jerry W. Ward, New York: Modern Language Association, 1990.

Anna Mae Aquash

Micmac political activist
Born March 27, 1945, near Shubenacadie,
    Nova Scotia, Canada
Died c. 1976, South Dakota

The murder of Anna Mae Aquash remains unsolved, but she is remembered as a powerful symbol of an era of Native rights activism.

From the era of Native American political activism and militancy during the early 1970s, there is no more haunting figure than Anna Mae Pictou Aquash. An active American Indian Movement (AIM) member, as well as mother, wife, social worker, and day care teacher, she is remembered as much for her untimely death as for her life's work. Found murdered on the Pine Ridge Reservation during a time of tremendous social and political upheaval, she has become a symbol of the movement for Indian rights.

Childhood on a Micmac reserve

Aquash was born on March 27, 1945, to Mary Ellen Pictou and Francis Thomas Levi, both Micmac Indians. She came into the world in a small Indian village just outside the town of Shubenacadie, in Nova Scotia, Canada. Levi left before Anna Mae was born, and Mary Ellen's third grade education didn't provide her the skills required to support her children. Still a young woman herself, Mary Ellen Pictou admitted to being a little too unsettled to offer her girls much in the way of discipline. Aquash spent her early years in an atmosphere of poverty and uncertainty.

Aquash's mother married Noel Sapier, a Micmac traditionalist, in 1949. A strong believer in the preservation of what was left of the Micmac culture and religion, Sapier brought discipline and emotional security to the family. He moved them to Pictou's Landing, another small Micmac reserve, and tried to make a living between seasonal farmhand jobs and traditional craftwork. Although they were still very poor, Aquash learned a great deal about the richness of her people's culture at this time.

Poverty often breeds disease, and conditions were very poor at Pictou's Landing. In 1953, Aquash was plagued with recurrent eye infections. By the time an Indian Department physician recognized the signs of tuberculosis of the eye, Aquash had already developed tuberculosis of the lung. She recovered but was physically weak for some time afterward.

In 1956, Noel Sapier died of cancer, and a new phase of Aquash's childhood began. Until then, she had encountered racism mostly during trips to nearby towns. After Sapier's death she went to an off-reserve school and was shocked by the way she was treated there. Although reserve schools were notoriously below standard, Aquash had always maintained an A-average. By the end of her first year at the new school, however, she was failing all her subjects. In later years, she would often talk about how constant jeers, racial slurs, and lewd comments had ruined her school years. Aquash was not alone; many Micmac youth followed the same pattern of failure when they enrolled in off-reserve schools.

Aquash's difficulties with verbal and sometimes physical threats from classmates continued in high school. She steadily performed at lower and lower grade levels, but she stayed in school, something that many of her Indian classmates had not done. Her school problems were compounded when her mother ran away to another reserve to get married again. Aquash and her siblings came home to find that they had been abandoned. Because it was common for Micmacs to work as migrant farmhands throughout the Maritime Provinces and New England, and Aquash herself had worked summers as a harvester, she dropped out of school and turned to the only profession she knew, working the potato and berry harvest.

New life in Boston

At the age of 17, Aquash decided to move to Boston to seek her fortune. Reportedly on something of a dare, she went there with Jake Maloney, a young Micmac she knew but had never dated. They found themselves in Boston in 1962—a strange, noisy, bustling world for people used to reserve life. The presence of many other Micmacs who had also moved there made the transition somewhat easier, though, and the couple soon settled in.

Aquash began working in a factory and set up house with Jake. They considered themselves married and started a family. In 1964 and 1965, Aquash gave birth to daughters Denise and Deborah. Just after Deborah's birth, the couple married in New Brunswick and moved to another Micmac reserve. Although they had enjoyed life in Boston, they had mixed feelings about raising their daughters in such a big city, and they moved back and forth between Boston and the Maritime Provinces in Nova Scotia several times. During their stays in Canada, they immersed themselves in Micmac tradition, learning much from Jake's step-uncle, one of the few remaining Micmacs at that time who kept to the old ways.

Becomes a community organizer

In 1968, Natives were calling for equal rights, cultural recognition, and the fulfillment of promises made in treaties. Aquash worked as a volunteer in the Boston Indian Council's headquarters while holding down her factory job. Her council work centered on helping young, urban Natives develop self-esteem, a technique that seemed to help them avoid alcohol abuse. It was a topic close to Aquash's own life. At this time she and Jake Maloney had broken off their marriage and, for a short period after the breakup, she frequently drank too much. She

had also seen the havoc created by heavy drinking in Indian communities.

At the Indian Council Aquash heard about a planned protest by AIM. A number of New England AIM members were joining with national leader **Russell Means** (see entry) to protest the "official" version of Thanksgiving by converging on the Mayflower II, a reconstruction of the ship that carried the Pilgrims to America. The traditional story behind Thanksgiving was that the Pilgrims were greeted by—and shared a feast with—welcoming Indians. This version, according to AIM, neglected to mention the legacy of conquest and slaughter that Europeans brought to the New World. Aquash participated in the protest and the event made her even more determined to work for Native rights.

Aquash, along with her daughters, moved to Bar Harbor, Maine, to work in the Teaching and Research in Bicultural Education School Project (TRIBES). The girls attended the school and Aquash taught. The curriculum there consisted of conventional subjects as well as Indian history, values, and beliefs to foster pride in the students. Although the project was successful, it was closed in 1972, when funding was cut. The family returned to Boston, where Aquash enrolled in the New Careers program at Wheelock College. This program included both classroom instruction and community work. Aquash's assignment was teaching at a day care center in Roxbury, a predominately African American section of Boston. She excelled in the program and in her work, and was eventually offered a scholarship to attend Brandeis University in Massachusetts. Aquash declined the offer, preferring to continue her work in the black and Indian communities.

The Trail of Broken Treaties march

Around this time, she met and began a relationship with Nogeeshik Aquash, a Chippewa artist from Ontario. Together, they raised her daughters and became more involved in the growing Indian rights movement. In 1972 the couple participated in the march on Washington, D.C., called the Trail of Broken Treaties. Originating with AIM, the march included Indians from all over the country who converged on the capital to draw attention to Indian issues. The group took over and occupied the Bureau of Indian Affairs building and then presented a list of 20 civil rights demands. After a week of occupation, the government promised to review their demands, point by point—a great victory marking the first time a national organization of Indians had faced a confrontation as a united people.

Several months later, in April 1973, a group of 200 Indians led by AIM congregated at the site of the 1890 Wounded Knee massacre (in which 500 army soldiers opened fire on a group of Minneconjou Ghost Dancers, killing 300 men, women, and children). Wounded Knee, located near the Pine Ridge Reservation in South Dakota, was chosen as the place for protest because of its painful historical significance. AIM wished to draw public attention to its efforts against the reputedly corrupt administration of the tribal chair of the Oglala Sioux, Richard "Dick" Wilson, who used beatings and intimidation to rule the reservation.

As hostilities increased, Wounded Knee was occupied by 2,000 Indians in a siege lasting 70 days. When word of the occupation and resulting siege by federal troops reached Boston, Anna Mae and Nogeeshik left for South Dakota. Arriving several days later, they immediately busied themselves by sneaking food and medical supplies to the occupiers. Initially, they camped at Crow Dog's Paradise, the home of medicine men Henry Crow Dog and Leonard Crow Dog. Later, inside one of the stores at Wounded Knee, Aquash helped deliver Pedro, the first son of **Mary Brave Bird** (see entry), who would soon marry Leonard Crow Dog. On April 12, 1973, Anna Mae married Nogeeshik Aquash in a traditional Lakota (Sioux) ceremony presided over by Nicholas Black Elk and Wallace Black Elk.

The standoff at Wounded Knee ended with the indictment of AIM leaders **Dennis Banks** (see entry) and Russell Means. The Aquashes returned to Boston, where they continued their work for the movement. Aquash was on her way to becoming a national AIM leader. In 1974, she moved to St. Paul, Minnesota, to work in the AIM office there. Within a year, she was involved in the Menominee Indian takeover of an abandoned Alexian Brothers Catholic Monastery in protest of the termination of their federal Indian status. The conflict in Gresham, Wisconsin, ended peacefully, but from that time on, Aquash was constantly under Federal Bureau of Investigation (FBI) observation.

Back to Wounded Knee

During the summer of 1975, Aquash and AIM security chief **Leonard Peltier** (see entry) attended an AIM conference in Farmington, New Mexico, to lend support to Navajo protests over mining in the Four Corners area. From there, they were called back to Pine Ridge to help organize security for Lakota traditionalists and AIM supporters who were being attacked by Wilson's provisional police force. They camped on the property of the Jumping Bull family. On June 26, 1975, a fight broke out between two FBI agents and AIM members. Two agents and a young Indian were killed. AIM members scattered as an international manhunt began for the FBI agents' killers. Peltier was later arrested, charged, and convicted of the murders of the two FBI agents.

Three months later, in September 1975, Aquash was arrested with several others during a raid on the Rosebud Reservation in South Dakota. Fearing the worst, she jumped bail and went "underground" (hid from the law). In November, she was leaving the Port Madison Reservation in Washington state when federal agents began watching the two vehicles in the AIM caravan. In Oregon, just one mile short of the Idaho border, state troopers stopped the group and Aquash was again arrested. She was extradited to South Dakota in handcuffs to face charges from the raid at Rosebud, as well as federal charges of transporting and possessing firearms and dangerous weapons, including dynamite. Since she had not been indicted on the earlier charges, the South Dakota judge released her on bail; she fled again on November 24, 1975.

On February 24, 1976, a Lakota rancher found Aquash's dead body while riding the perimeter of his property. Her body's deteriorated condition indicated that she had been dead for some time. The corpse was initially taken to the Pine Ridge Public Health Service for an autopsy. Her cause of death was listed as exposure, and since no one was able to identify her, she was buried as a "Jane Doe"—an anonymous corpse. Her hands were cut off and sent to FBI headquarters in Washington, D.C., for possible identification, and a week later, Aquash was identified. When her family was informed, they called on AIM to help them secure a second autopsy. On March 11, 1976, another postmortem revealed a .32 caliber bullet hole at the base of Anna Mae's skull. Her death was then officially designated a homicide. Aquash was reburied with traditional rites, and the investigation of her murder began.

When Leonard Peltier was arrested for the murder of the two FBI agents at Pine Ridge, the FBI based part of their case against him on the account of a witness. A Lakota woman, Myrtle Poor Bear, claimed she had seen Peltier commit the murders. She later changed her story, saying that she had been coerced into identifying Peltier as the killer by an FBI agent, who had said she might meet the same end as Anna Mae Aquash. Aquash, whose murder had taken place right after Peltier's arrest, had earlier told the FBI she knew nothing about the murders of the agents and would not cooperate with them.

Although two senators brought the matter before Congress and the Department of Justice, and although Canadian authorities demanded full accounting for the murder of one of their citizens on the federal land of a friendly neighboring country, the investigation never went far. The murder of Anna Mae Aquash remains unsolved, but she is remembered as a powerful symbol of an era of Native rights activism.

Further Reading

Brand, Johanna, *The Life and Death of Anna Mae Aquash*, Toronto: James Lorimer, 1978.

Matthiessen, Peter, *In the Spirit of Crazy Horse*, New York: Viking Books, 1983.

Native American Women, edited by Gretchen M. Bataille, New York: Garland Publishing, 1993.

Amos Bad Heart Bull

Oglala Sioux artist and tribal historian
Born 1869
Died 1913

"Without doubt, the Amos Bad Heart Bull picture history is the most comprehensive, the finest statement as art and as report of the North American Indian so far discovered anywhere."—Mari Sandoz

A self-taught artist who told the story of his Oglala Sioux tribe in pictographs (a way of using pictures rather than words to tell a story), Amos Bad Heart Bull left behind a priceless record of his people. His pictographs describe much of the cultural life of the proud Plains warriors as well as the story of their defeat and removal onto reservations.

Helen Blish, a teacher and art historian, rescued 400 of Bad Heart Bull's pictographs, having them photographed before their burial with his sister's body. Thanks to Blish's efforts, *A Pictographic History of the Oglala Sioux* was published in 1967. The book combines her scholarly writings about the drawings with photos of the pictographs themselves. The illustrations from this book have been featured in every television documentary about the Ghost Dance, the defeat of U.S. General George Armstrong Custer, and the deaths of warrior chiefs **Sitting Bull** and **Crazy Horse** (see entries). The artist's pictures of Crazy Horse, his cousin, are the only surviving likenesses of him, since Crazy Horse reportedly never allowed himself to be photographed.

Blish was able to interview two of Bad Heart Bull's uncles, He Dog (Sunka Bloka) and Short Bull (Tatanka Ptecela), on the Pine Ridge Reservation in South Dakota, to learn a little about the artist's life. Short Bull and He Dog told her that Bad Heart Bull's father, Amos Bad Heart Bull the Elder, had been a band historian, and had created a chronicle on animal hide. This hide recorded the outstanding single event of each year. Since he died young, the task of bringing up his son fell to Short Bull and He Dog, and to their brothers, Little Shield and Only Man. The uncles told the boy stories of the battles they had fought in and observed his interest in collecting treaties and other documents about Indian encounters with whites.

Self-taught artistry

Without any formal instruction, Bad Heart Bull began creating annotated drawings, illustrations combined with explanatory writing. He taught himself to write using a system invented by missionaries to write the Lakotan language. He also learned

Pictograph by Amos Bad Heart Bull of the leaders at the Battle of the Little Bighorn: George A. Custer, Crazy Horse, and Sitting Bull.

English from the soldiers at Fort Robinson, in northwestern present-day Nebraska, where he had enlisted as a scout for the U.S. Army in 1890.

From a clothing dealer near the fort in Crawford, Nebraska, Bad Heart Bull bought a used ledger, in which he began his 415 drawings using black pen, indelible pencil, blue, yellow, green, and brown crayons, and red ink. In some instances he painted with a brush so fine that the strokes can be seen only under magnification. Some of the pictures are touched with a gray or brown wash in places. He worked at this project for about two decades, recording the civic, religious, social, economic, and military life of the Oglala.

His techniques allowed Bad Heart Bull to present several perspectives of an event at once. He used a sweeping overview to portray masses of people engaged in dramatic actions. Depicting large scenes of battle, religious ceremonies, or processionals to a buffalo hunt from above, he captured tribal activities in a way that might remind modern viewers of long shots in movies. Then, he would render close-ups of some aspect of the scene on the same page, framed and set off to one side, so that one could compare the long view of the event to the impact on an individual participant. He also experimented with other techniques such as full-face depictions, rear-views, scenes of wounded horses viewed from below, or dancers in three-quarter view. These perspectives added drama and realism to his pictures.

Told epic story with drawings

Each set of Bad Heart Bull's drawings tells part of a heroic epic. The first group shows tribal events before 1856. The councilmen (*wakicunza*) and their marshals (*akicita*) are shown deliberating in the camp council, then at a buffalo hunt and a sun dance, and the eight warrior societies are shown in their ceremonial clothes. The next set of pictures tells the story of the conflicts between the Oglala Sioux and the Crow, their hereditary enemies on the Plains, in skirmishes from 1856 to 1875. The third set narrates the Battle of the Little Bighorn in Montana, where General Custer and his men were defeated and killed.

The next group of pictures shows the reorganization of Oglala society as it was forced to accept reservation existence. It opens with the ceremonies: the Sacred Bow, the Victory Dance, the Dance of the Black Tailed Deer, the Horse Dance, and the Vision Quest. These are followed by eight depictions of courting scenes, and ten of games. This section closes with the transition to farming. The next to last set depicts the Ghost Dance—a late nineteenth-century ritual intended to bring back the slaughtered buffalo and other lost elements of Plains life—and the Battle of Wounded Knee, in which the U.S. cavalry massacred over 300 Sioux. The final set shows the Fourth of July being celebrated in 1898 and in 1903 on the Pine Ridge Reservation. By grouping his pictures in these narrative sequences and preserving the most minute details of daily life, he told the history of his band over 60 years and created a unique historical record.

Rescued for posterity

In 1926 Helen Blish was a graduate student at the University of Nebraska searching for examples of Plains art. From W. O. Roberts of the Pine Ridge Agency, she learned about Bad Heart Bull's drawings, which had been given, after the artist's death in 1913, to his sister, Dolly Pretty Cloud. Blish, a teacher in a Detroit high school, spent her summer vacations studying Bad Heart Bull's pictographs, which were kept in a trunk on the dirt floor of Pretty Cloud's one-room cabin on the reservation. It was only after much persuasion that Blish was permitted to rent these works of art for a modest annual fee and to analyze them for her master's thesis under the noted art historian, Hartley Burr Alexander.

Following Lakota custom, the prized ledger book was buried with Pretty Cloud upon her death in 1947. Fortunately, though, Blish's work had been given to the American Museum of Natural History in New York City before her death in 1941. In 1959, the University of Nebraska Press decided to publish Bad Heart Bull's pictorial history and tried without success to get permission to have the ledger removed from the grave. However, researchers found that Alexander had photographed the priceless document page-by-page in 1927.

These illustrations were interwoven with Blish's manuscript and published in book form. Mari Sandoz, the biographer of Bad Heart Bull's cousin, Crazy Horse, supported the project from the beginning and wrote the introduction to the book in the last year of her life. She said, "Without doubt, the Amos Bad Heart Bull picture history is the most comprehensive, the finest statement as art and as report of the North American Indian so far discovered anywhere."

Further Reading

Blish, Helen H., *A Pictographic History of the Oglala Sioux,* Lincoln: University of Nebraska Press, 1967.

Dockstader, Frederick J., *Great North American Indians,* New York: Van Nostrand Reinhold, 1977.

The Indians' Book, edited by Natalie Cirtis Burlin, New York: Harper, 1923.

Sandoz, Mari, *Crazy Horse: The Strange Man of the Oglalas,* Lincoln: University of Nebraska Press, 1942.

Louis W. Ballard

Quapaw-Cherokee music educator and composer
Born July 8, 1931, Miami, Oklahoma

Louis W. Ballard's initial goal was to foster greater appreciation for the music of his people. As his career developed, he began wanting to bring Indian music into the mainstream through American folk music.

L ouis Wayne Ballard is one of the most celebrated Native American composers. He has worked in a variety of musical styles but has always worked Native American themes into his compositions. As a specialist in the gathering of music for edu-

cation—or music curriculum—for the U.S. Bureau of Indian Affairs, Ballard also has been a pioneer in developing educational materials centering on different cultures. He has traveled extensively, establishing bicultural music programs, which add Native American music to the curriculum in schools, and he has lectured on Indian art and music at colleges around the United States.

Ballard was born in Miami, Oklahoma, in 1931. His mother was of Quapaw-French ancestry, while his father was of Cherokee-Scot heritage. Ballard was surrounded by music from a very young age. He learned Native songs and dances as a youth attending tribal ceremonies, for example, and his mother, a pianist, wrote children's songs. As he matured, his grandmother encouraged him to learn to play piano, and he soon began taking lessons at a mission chapel near her home. A talented student, Ballard began writing out his own musical ideas and composing not long afterward.

Ballard studied music at Bacone College and Northeast Oklahoma Agricultural and Mechanical College, and went on to earn his bachelor's degree from the University of Tulsa, in Tulsa, Oklahoma. During his undergraduate years, he held various jobs— janitor, dishwasher, ambulance driver, drugstore clerk, and waiter—to help finance his education. He also worked as a nightclub pianist and a singer.

While at the University of Tulsa in the early 1950s, Ballard discovered the music of Hungarian composer Béla Bartók. Ballard was strongly influenced in his own writing by Bartók's use of Hungarian themes. In fact, he became determined to weave ethnic elements into his own work by using Indian

Louis W. Ballard

tribal themes and recurring elements. His initial goal was to foster greater appreciation for the music of his people. As his career developed, he began wanting to bring Indian music into the mainstream through American folk music. In 1967, Ballard completed his master's degree in music at the University of Oklahoma, where he had been awarded the F. B. Parriott fellowship for his accomplishments.

Earned recognition for compositions

A versatile composer, Ballard has written many types of music for nearly all instruments, from ballet to choral arrangements, including chamber and orchestral works. Though he has won a number of prestigious awards for different styles, he has enjoyed notable success with ballet. *Koshare*—a ballet based upon an ancient Hopi creation story—premiered in Barcelona, Spain, in 1960 and was first performed in the United States seven years later. Also in 1967, his ballet *The Four Moons* was featured in the celebration of the state of Oklahoma's sixtieth anniversary. Ballard's instrumental piece *Mid-Winter Fires* highlighted the White House Conference on Children and Youth in 1969 and the University of Colorado Conference on American Indian Music in 1971.

In 1969, Ballard won the Marion Nevins MacDowell Award for his woodwind quartet *Ritmo Indio,* and was later nominated for a Pulitzer Prize for his piece *Desert Trilogy.* In 1972 he became the first professional musician to be awarded the Indian Achievement Award created by the Indian Council Fire. Two of his most popular pieces are his cantata based on the life of actor-humorist Will Rogers, *Portrait of Will,* and his choral work *Scenes from Indian Life.*

During the mid-1970s, Ballard served as the music department dean for the Institute of American Indian Arts in Santa Fe, New Mexico. He also became the music curriculum specialist for the U.S. Bureau of Indian Affairs, where he oversaw the program development for all reservation schools. In this role, he insisted that all students be introduced to Indian instruments and compositions to learn culture and the unique musical style of each tribe. As a result, he became known for emphasizing cultural identity, or ethnicity, in music education.

Over the years, Ballard has collected a great number of ceremonial and dance songs, Indian lullabies, and love songs. He also created classroom educational materials in the form of a film and a phonodisc recording. *American Indian Music for the Classroom* includes a spoken introduction by the composer, a teacher's guide, an Indian land areas map, study photographs, and an 18-page bibliography.

Ballard also acts as music consultant and president of First American Indian Films, Inc. The company has released a film entitled *Discovering American Indian Music,* which includes a composition by Ballard and discusses the social and ceremonial functions of music. The film provides examples of traditional tribal music and dance and also touches on modern issues. Ballard lives in Santa Fe, New Mexico, with his wife, a concert pianist, and three children.

Further Reading

Native North American Almanac, edited by Duane Champagne, Detroit: Gale, 1994.

Wilets, Bernard, *Discovering American Indian Music* (motion picture), BFA Educational Media, 1971.

Dennis J. Banks

Anishinabe Ojibway activist, teacher, and author
Born April 12, 1937, Leech Lake Indian Reservation, Minnesota

Dennis J. Banks has been a tireless activist for Native rights, often in the face of outright hostility and violence.

A founder and current field director of the American Indian Movement (AIM), Dennis J. Banks has been a tireless activist for Native rights, often in the face of outright hostility and violence. An actor

Dennis J. Banks

years as a fugitive before serving more time in prison. He later became involved in international sacred runs—marathons designed to heighten spiritual awareness and draw worldwide attention to the plight of Indians.

Banks was born on the Leech Lake Indian Reservation in northern Minnesota in 1937. At the U.S. government's Bureau of Indian Affairs (BIA) boarding schools, he and his younger brother, Mark, lost their Native language. He entered the U.S. Air Force in 1953, serving in Japan. The ties he forged with the Japanese people, and the alliances he formed with Buddhist leaders, led later to his sponsoring sacred runs in Japan and publishing his award-winning autobiography, *Sacred Soul,* there in 1988.

The founding of AIM

Unable to find steady employment in the Minneapolis-St. Paul area after his discharge from the service in the late 1950s, Banks began to drink heavily. Apprehended in a grocery-store robbery, he was imprisoned for more than two and a half years; his white accomplice was freed. He was released in 1968, and by July of that year he, George Mitchell, and **Clyde Bellecourt** (see entry) had formed the American Indian Movement in Minneapolis to assist Indians in exercising their civil rights, improving their economic and social conditions, and reclaiming their Indian traditions.

In November 1969, Banks and 200 other AIM members participated in the occupation of Alcatraz Island, the former site of a notorious prison in San Francisco Bay. They demanded that all surplus federal land be

and university lecturer—and the first Indian university chancellor—he has lectured regularly around the United States. As a young man Banks was often in trouble, and he was once imprisoned for robbing a grocery store. While in prison he formed AIM with two other Indian prisoners. As a leader of the organization, he was at the head of some of the major revolutionary actions of the 1970s, such as an occupation of Alcatraz and the 1973 takeover of the town of Wounded Knee. In trouble with the law again, this time for his political activities, Banks spent several returned to the control of Indians and wanted the island turned into a cultural center for Native Americans. Indians from many different tribes held the island for 19 months, attempting to negotiate with the government and broadcasting key issues about the treatment of Native Americans on Radio Free Alcatraz. The occupation ended when the government used arm force to evict the protestors, but AIM had drawn a great deal of public attention to Indian causes and enlisted a spirited group of new members. A new era of activism had begun.

On Thanksgiving in 1970, AIM sponsored a day of mourning at Plymouth, Massachusetts, hoping to show that the holiday's myth of Indians welcoming and feasting with whites covered up the reality of violence and exploitation Native Americans endured. In the spring of 1971, the group set up camp at Mount Rushmore—a peak in the Black Hills in South Dakota where images of past U.S. presidents engraved in the rock form a monument to American government—to dramatize Lakota claims to the Black Hills.

Protests turn to battles

The fall of 1972 saw Banks, Bellecourt, Mitchell, and Mad Bear Anderson leading the Trail of Broken Treaties march across the United States to Washington, D.C. This symbolic march followed the legacy of broken promises made to Indians by the American government. Although meetings with the administration had been prearranged, federal officials refused to talk with AIM leaders. Since they were also denied appropriate housing, which had been promised them, they went to the BIA building to protest. When riot squads tried to evict them, they occupied the offices for five days. Treated poorly and never given a fair hearing in Washington, the group was blamed for damages to the BIA building and paid to leave town. After they left, they became the targets of the Federal Bureau of Investigation (FBI), which used spy tactics to impede AIM's activities.

On February 28, 1973, the historic takeover of Wounded Knee began. At this location in southwestern South Dakota the U.S. Cavalry had massacred hundreds of Sioux men, women, and children in 1890. AIM was called upon for help by the Sioux traditionalists in South Dakota, who were demonstrating against the alleged corruption of Richard Wilson, the elected council head of the Pine Ridge Reservation. In the occupation that followed, 2,000 Indians under the leadership of AIM withstood tanks, heavy artillery, helicopter strafing, and roadblocks. The siege did not end until May 9. At the national convention in White Oak, Oklahoma, that year, Banks—widely recognized for his charisma and communication skills—was elected leader of AIM.

On February 6, Sarah Bad Heart Bull requested the help of AIM at the Custer courthouse in South Dakota. When she protested the release of the murderer of her son, Wesley Bad Heart Bull, police clubbed her. Two hundred AIM protestors, angered after the mother of the victim was allegedly pushed down a flight of stairs, set fire to some cars and a building; 37 Indians were arrested, Banks among them. On February 12, 1974, an eight-month trial began. Banks was acquitted of the ten felony changes lodged against him because the prosecution had used illegal wiretaps to listen to private

Banks leads march in Rapid City, South Dakota, February 1973

phone conversations as well as falsified documents and perjured—that is, deliberately lying—witnesses.

Banks urged AIM members to discipline themselves so as not to discredit the movement. His efforts were thwarted by the FBI. Bad publicity about Banks was deliberately instigated by Douglass Durham, an infiltrator who had attached himself to Banks as his pilot and bodyguard. Durham admitted on March 5, 1975, in Des Moines, Iowa, that he was an informant for the FBI. The leaders of the FBI had worked tirelessly to undercut Indian rights activism.

On March 12, Durham identified the agents to whom he had reported and admitted he had instigated crimes and then released denunciations to the press. However, on July 26, 1975, a South Dakota court found Banks guilty for his involvement in the Custer courthouse riot. Rather than serve a 15-year sentence, he fled to California.

Governor Edmund G. Brown granted him amnesty until his term expired in 1983.

Banks earned an associate of arts degree at the University of California, Davis, and began teaching at Deganawida-Quetzecoatl (DQ) University. There he served as the first American Indian university chancellor. He also taught at Stanford University in Palo Alto, California, and has lectured worldwide about Native American issues and culture.

In March of 1983, Banks was granted sanctuary on the Onondaga Reservation near Syracuse, New York. There he ran six miles a day, coached young runners, chopped firewood, and conducted drives for food and clothing donations. A year later, he surrendered himself and was sentenced to three years in the South Dakota penitentiary.

Serves Pine Ridge Reservation

Upon his parole on December 9, 1985, Banks worked at the Loneman School as an alcoholism counselor, hosted a weekly show on the radio station KILI, sponsoring talks against drug use, and tried to find jobs for the unemployed by luring businesses to the reservation. In 1987, he was successful in having the offense of grave desecration—the destruction or other damaging of Indian burial sites—upgraded from a misdemeanor to a felony in Kentucky and Indiana. He coordinated reburial ceremonies for 1,200 disturbed sites in Uniontown, Kentucky.

In 1991, Banks moved to northern Kentucky, where he assumed leadership of Sacred Run, an organization he had founded in 1978. As director and coach, he had led spiritual runs totaling 43,000 miles as of the fall of 1993. In 1988, Banks led runners 3,600 miles across North America and then ran 2,000 miles through Japan, beginning in Hiroshima on the forty-third anniversary of the dropping of the atomic bomb. In 1990, Sacred Run ran across Europe through 13 countries from England to Moscow in the former USSR.

In 1991, Sacred Run crossed Canada from Vancouver, British Columbia, to Kahnawake, Quebec. Over the next two years, they ran from Alaska to New Mexico, ran 6,000 miles in Australia, and then traveled to New Zealand's North Island to run another 1,000 miles. In 1994, Banks led the Walk for Justice from California to Washington, D.C., to plead for the liberation of Indian political prisoner **Leonard Peltier** (see entry)—who was jailed after a gun battle at Pine Ridge Reservation between Oglala Sioux and FBI agents—as well as to draw attention to a variety of other Native issues.

Banks has also appeared in three movies: *War Party* in 1988, *Thunderheart* in 1991, and 1992's *The Last of the Mohicans*. He has also produced a tape recording featuring Native American music, *Still Strong*.

Further Reading

Contemporary Newsmakers, Detroit: Gale, 1986.

Crow Dog, Mary, *Lakota Woman,* New York: Harper Perennial, 1991.

Matthiessen, Peter, *In The Spirit of Crazy Horse,* New York: Viking, 1983.

Printup, Wade, "Run for Land and Life: Japan," *Turtle Quarterly,* winter-spring 1989, pp. 4-14.

Barboncito

Navajo leader, ceremonial singer, and war chief
Born c. 1820, Canyon de Chelly (now northeast-
ern Arizona)
Died 1871, Canyon de Chelly
Also known as Little Bearded One, Daagi'i or
Hastiin Bidaghaa'i ("The One [or Man] with
the Mustache"), Hashke yich'i' Dahilwo'
("He Is Anxious to Run at Warriors"),
Bisahalani ("The Orator"), and Hoozhooji
Naata ("Blessing Speaker")

*"I will not go to the Bosque. I will never
leave my country, not even if it means that I
am killed."*

Barboncito was a Navajo war chief who headed the Navajo resistance to U.S. attempts to gain tribal lands in the mid-1860s. He shared the resistance leadership with his brother, Delgadito, and with **Manuelito** (see entry), another Navajo war chief. A firm but peaceful opponent of the United States' encroachment onto his people's homelands, Barboncito was beloved by his people for his eloquence, his leadership skills, and his inspirational role as a religious singer. He is remembered for signing the 1868 treaty with the U.S. government ensuring the Navajos, or "the Diné" ("the people," as they call themselves), the lands on which they still live today.

Barboncito was born to the Ma'iideeshgi-izhnii ("Coyote Pass") clan at Canyon de Chelly, in present-day northeastern Arizona. The mountains of this area provided the Navajos a strong defensive position. He quickly rose to become one of the council chiefs of the Navajo people.

Signed first treaty

Around the time of the Mexican War, in which the United States and Mexico competed for land in the Southwest, the U.S. Army occupied Santa Fe, in north central New Mexico Territory. With the army in Santa Fe, the Navajo signed their first treaty, the Doniphan Treaty of 1846, with the white settlers. Barboncito was one of the chiefs to sign the treaty, agreeing to peaceful relations and beneficial trade with the whites. Despite the treaty, fighting continued between the Navajo and whites because Doniphan had failed to get the signatures of all the Navajo chiefs. Furthermore, the U.S. Army lacked the military strength to prevent hostilities between the Navajo and nearby Spanish-Mexicans, who sought to enslave the Indians. Leaders on both sides tried without success to put an end to this warfare. Attacks and negotiations by U.S. troops sent mixed signals to the Navajo, who believed the Anglo-American settlers were unlawfully seizing Indian land.

Barboncito, also known as "The Orator" and "Blessing Speaker," did not participate in these skirmishes. In the late 1850s, he acted as a mediator between the Navajo and the whites and argued for ending the warfare. Navajos and whites fought over the grazing lands of Canyon Bonito near Fort Defiance, located in what is now the eastern part of the state of Arizona. The Navajo had let their horses graze in these pastures for centuries, but the settlers also wanted the lands for their horses. In 1860 U.S. soldiers slaughtered a number of Navajo horses, leading the Navajo to raid army herds to replenish their losses. The United States responded by destroying the homes, crops, and livestock of the Navajo people.

Retaliated against white aggression

The Anglo-American attack on the Navajo forced Barboncito to action. He soon earned the war name Hashké yich'i' Dahilwo' ("He Is Anxious to Run at Warriors"). With the help of Manuelito, he led over 1,000 Navajo warriors in a retaliatory attack on Fort Defiance. The great war skills of Barboncito and Manuelito nearly won them the fort, but they were eventually driven off by the U.S. Army and pursued into the Chuska Mountains of northeastern Arizona. In the mountains, the U.S. troops were unable to withstand the Navajo hit-and-run attacks.

With neither side emerging as the winner, Indians and whites sat down at a peace council once again. Barboncito, Manuelito, Delgadito, Armijo, Herrero Grande, and 17 other chiefs met Colonel Edward R. S. Canby at Fort Fauntleroy, 35 miles south of Fort Defiance. They all agreed to the terms of a treaty in 1861. For a time, the Navajos and whites got along peacefully, but distrust between the two groups continued.

When the U.S. military diverted most of its forces east for the Civil War, the Navajo increased their efforts at what the whites called "cattle-rustling and general marauding." The United States then led an extensive campaign to "burn-and-imprison" the Navajos. This was spearheaded by Colonel Christopher "Kit" Carson and mercenaries from the Ute people, traditional enemies of the Navajo. Barboncito made peaceful overtures to General James H. Carleton, Carson's commanding officer, in 1862, but the assault against the Navajo people dragged on.

When this ruthless practice proved unsuccessful, Carleton ordered Carson to move the entire nation of Navajo clans from their homes in the Arizona area to a region known as Bosque Redondo, in the arid lowlands of southeastern New Mexico—all despite protests from the Indian Bureau and Carson himself. Carleton said that he aimed to transform the Navajos from "heathens and raiders" to "settled Christians" under the watchful eye of troops stationed at nearby Fort Sumner.

Carleton met with Barboncito and other chiefs in April 1863. He told the Navajo that they could prove their peaceful intentions by going to Bosque Redondo. Barboncito replied, as quoted in *Bury My Heart at Wounded Knee*: "I will not go to the Bosque. I will never leave my country, not even if it means that I am killed." And despite the U.S. Army's efforts to force him from his home, Barboncito stayed.

Last holdout in resistance movement

Barboncito led the resistance movement at Canyon de Chelly against Carson and the whites with the aid of Delgadito and Manuelito. Again Carson launched a scorched-earth campaign against the Navajo and it's Dinetah ("Navajo Land"), destroying fields, orchards, and hogans (earth-covered Navajo dwellings) and confiscating cattle from the Continental Divide to the Colorado River. Though only 78 of the 12,000 Navajo people were killed, Carson's efforts crushed the Navajo spirit. By 1864 the troops had devastated Canyon de Chelly, hacking down thousands of peach trees and obliterating acres of cornfields. Eventually, a shortage of food and supplies forced the Navajo to surrender their sacred stronghold.

That same year, the "Long Walk" began, in which eight thousand Navajo people—two-thirds of the entire tribe—were escorted by soldiers across 300 miles to Bosque Redondo in the arid lowlands of eastern New Mexico. About two hundred Indians died during the journey. The remaining Navajos escaped west with Manuelito, who eventually surrendered in 1866 (two months before Barboncito). Barboncito was the last Navajo chief to be captured and led to Bosque Redondo. When he found conditions there worse than he imagined, he escaped and returned to Canyon de Chelly, but he was recaptured.

The Long Walk to Bosque Redondo was horrifying and traumatic for the Navajo people. They had to contend with disease, blight, grasshoppers, drought, supply shortages, infertile soil, and quarrels with Apaches. An estimated 2,000 people died of hunger or illness at the relocation settlement. As a ceremonial singer with knowledge of his people's ancient beliefs, Barboncito knew that tradition forbade the Navajo to leave their sacred lands, to cross the rivers, or to abandon their sacred mountains and shrines. Being forced to do so, and to become dependent on whites for food and other supplies, was spiritually destructive for the Navajo and for Barboncito. He stayed as long as he could in the sacred lands, but on November 7, 1866, he, too, led his small band of 21 followers to Bosque Redondo.

During their stay there, Barboncito led ceremonies that the Navajo believed would help them to return home. The most frequently practiced ceremony of that time was called "Ma'ii Bizee naast'a" ("Put a Bead in Coyote's Mouth"). According to historical records, the Indians formed a large circle with Barboncito and a female coyote, who faced east, in the center. Barboncito caught the coyote and placed in its mouth a white shell, tapered at both ends with a hole in its center. As he set the coyote free, she turned clockwise and walked westward. This was seen as a sign that the Navajo people—the Diné—would be set free.

Negotiated for final, lasting peace

In 1868 Barboncito, Manuelito, and a delegation of chiefs traveled to Washington, D.C., after General Carleton had been transferred and could no longer inflict his policies on the Navajo. Barboncito was granted great status by U.S. officials—more authority than tribal custom would have accorded him. He played a leading role in negotiations with General William Tecumseh Sherman and Colonel Samuel F. Tappan, telling them that the creator of the Navajo people had warned the tribe never to go east of the Rio Grande River. He explained the failures of Bosque Redondo: even though they dug irrigation ditches, the crops failed; rattlesnakes did not warn victims away before striking as they did in Navajo Country; people became ill and died. Barboncito told the white negotiators that the Navajo wished to return home.

But the U.S. government was not inclined to return all of "Navajo country" to the Navajos. Sherman gave Barboncito and the other chiefs three choices: to go east to Oklahoma (then known as Indian Territory), to relocate in New Mexico and be governed by the laws of that territory, or to return to a small portion of their original lands. The Navajos chose the last option. On June 1, 1868, the Navajo leaders, including Barboncito, signed a treaty with the U.S. government. The agreement begins: "From this day forward all war between the parties to this agreement shall forever cease." The treaty established the Navajo Reservation in present-day New Mexico and Arizona, which is today the largest Native nation in the United States, both in territory and population.

Although he was the last to surrender, Barboncito was the first to sign the document with his "X." He died on March 16, 1871, at Canyon de Chelly, having established himself as a distinguished chief and a skillful negotiator.

Further Reading

Brown, Dee, *Bury My Heart at Wounded Knee,* New York: Holt, 1970.

Handbook of the North American Indians, edited by William C. Sturtevant, Washington, DC: Smithsonian Institution, 1983.

Insight Guides: Native America, edited by John Gattuso, Boston: Houghton Mifflin, 1993.

The Native Americans: An Illustrated History, edited by Betty Ballantine and Ian Ballantine, Atlanta: Turner Publishing, 1993.

Native North American Almanac, edited by Duane Champagne, Detroit: Gale, 1994.

Harrison Begay

Navajo artist
Born November 15, 1917, White Cone, Arizona
Also known as Haskay Yah Ne Yah ("Warrior Who Walked Up to His Enemy")

Among Navajo traditions is a belief that there is or can be an orderly balance of all the conflicting forces of the world. This belief finds expression in Harrison Begay's style, which is at once serenely still and vitally active.

Harrison Begay is one of the most famous of all Navajo painters. His widely collected watercolors and silkscreen prints have won many major awards. Noted for its fine detail, restrained color, and elegance of composition, his work has become a major influence among painters. Students of his art say that by studying his paintings one learns not only technique but also religion. Among Navajo traditions is a belief that there is or can be an orderly balance of all the conflicting forces of the world. This belief finds expression in Begay's style, which is at once serenely still and vitally active.

Herds family's sheep

Begay was born in 1917 at White Cone, Arizona, to Black Rock and Zonnie Tachinie Begay. His mother belonged to the Red Forehead clan, and his father adopted the Zuni Deer clan. His father was said to be related to Manuelito, the esteemed Navajo medicine man. As a boy Begay herded his family's flock of sheep near Greasewood, in northern

Night Chant by Harrison Begay

Arizona, where he still lives. In 1927, he was sent to school at Fort Wingate, but he ran away to spend the next four years at home, studying alone as he tended the sheep. In 1934, he attended Fort Defiance Indian School and later Tohatchi Indian School in northwestern New Mexico. He graduated from high school in 1939 as salutatorian, one of the highest achievers in his class, and gave an address at commencement.

The institution that conferred distinction upon him as an artist was Dorothy Dunn's studio at the Santa Fe Indian School. Dunn was a non-Native American who had a great influence on Southwest Indian art. In her studio, which was active from 1910 to 1960,

the Southwest style of art developed. Among Begay's classmates at Dunn's studio were Navajo painters Gerald Nailor, Quincy Tahoma, and Andy Tsinajinnie. They were taught to depict pastoral landscapes and tribal traditions, such as ceremonial dances, hunting scenes, and household activities. These were painted in a flat, two-dimensional style, usually in pale colors.

Begay's work was described as realistic and full of energy, while his quiet manner concealed his seemingly boundless talent. In 1940, Begay attended Black Mountain College in Blueridge, North Carolina, to study architecture for one year. That same year he married Ramona Espinosa, whom he would divorce five years later. In 1941, he enrolled in Phoenix Junior College in Arizona.

Serves in the U.S. Army

Begay was one of the 21,767 Native American veterans of the U.S. Army in World War II. From 1942 to 1945 he served in the signal corps. He participated in the Normandy campaign, the land and sea assault by the Allied powers (chiefly the United States, Great Britain, and the Soviet Union) that led to the defeat of the European axis powers (Germany and Italy). He was stationed in Iceland and in Europe. Upon his discharge from the army, Begay moved to Colorado, where he stayed until September 1947. While there, he was briefly tutored by an artist in Denver. The army had trained him to be a radio technician, but his artistic talent enabled him to make a living as a full-time painter after his return.

Works in arts and crafts shops

Begay was given space to paint at Clay Lockett's Arts and Crafts Shop in Tucson, Arizona. He also painted in Parkhurst's Shop in Santa Fe, New Mexico, and in Woodard's Shop in Gallup, New Mexico. He cofounded TEWA Enterprises, which made silkscreen prints of his work. This method of duplication also made his work affordable to the general public. Begay has specialized in sensitive renditions of animals such as fawns, antelope, deer, sheep, and horses. He is also fond of depicting looms as subjects, as in his often reproduced painting, *Two Weavers,* of 1946.

In 1959, the artist had an Enemyway chant performed for him, a ceremony to pro-tect warriors from the ghosts of slain enemies. As payment to the singer who conducted the rite, Begay presented a set of three paintings of the Navajo sacred mountains. A similar set of the four sacred mountains, each associated with a different color and a different direction, is now owned by the Museum of Northern Arizona at Flagstaff. In order to compose these paintings, Begay studied the Navajo origin traditions.

Begay prefers to work in watercolors because oil painting takes too long. He regularly exhibits at the Philbrook Art Center each May, and at the Gallery in New Mexico, which sponsors exhibits for five days in August each year at the Intertribal Indian Ceremonials. He won two grand awards at the Intertribal festivities and has been a consistent winner at state and tribal fairs. In addition to Begay's considerable achievements in the art world, he is the state champion long distance runner, having broken the record in the mile race.

Further Reading

Dockstader, Frederick J., *Indian Art in America,* Greenwich, CT: New York Graphic Society, 1966.

Dunn, Dorothy, *American Indian Painting,* Albuquerque, NM: University of New Mexico Press, 1968.

Wade, Edwin L., *The Arts of the North American Indian: Native Traditions in Evolution,* New York: Hudson Hills Press, 1986.

Clyde Bellecourt

Ojibway activist
Born 1939, White Earth Reservation, Minnesota

To Clyde Bellecourt, the 1972 Trail of Broken Treaties march seemed the fulfillment of an Ojibway prophecy that one day all the tribes on the Turtle Continent—as many Indians call North America—would unite in brotherhood.

C lyde Bellecourt, one of the co-founders of the American Indian Movement (AIM), has been one of the most effective activists for Indian rights in the modern era. Thanks in part to his efforts, AIM actions such as the 1973 occupation of the Wounded Knee massacre site and the Trail of Broken Treaties march drew mainstream attention to Native issues. Bellecourt has also attempted to put Indian juveniles back in touch with their heritage. A staunch opponent of violence, he survived an attempt on his life, cleared himself of criminal charges associated with earlier AIM activities, and continued with his work.

He grew up on the White Earth Reservation in Minnesota with seven sisters and four brothers, none of whom ever had enough to eat. In the ninth grade, unable to tolerate the racist attitudes in the public school he had been forced to attend, he dropped out of school. At the age of 15, he looked for jobs in the city when work was unavailable on the reservation. Unable to find employment in the city, he became involved in robberies and burglaries and eventually found himself in prison.

Begins hunger strike in prison

Sentenced to Minnesota's Stillwater State Prison, Bellecourt began a hunger strike, determined to die. A fellow inmate, Eddie Benton Benai, tried unsuccessfully to get him to eat by dropping a candy bar into his cell every day. Bellecourt refused to touch them, and they piled up. Then one day Benai brought him a book about his Ojibway heritage. The story revived his will to live and restored his pride in being an Indian. In 1962, Bellecourt began educating his fellow inmates about their distinguished traditions. This process, he reflected later, was a humble version of the Native American Studies programs that would develop at universities years afterward.

Released from prison in 1964, Bellecourt tried to organize the "Red Ghetto" of Minneapolis—Indian people in the city who were humiliated in the schools, harassed by police, discriminated against by employers, and unfairly treated by the courts—to protest for their civil rights. In July 1968, Eddie Benton Benai, George Mitchell, **Dennis Banks** (see entry), and Clyde's brother Vernon journeyed with Bellecourt to form a coalition called Concerned Indian Americans (CIA) by incorporating a nonprofit organization with an all-Indian board and staff, which elected Vernon Bellecourt the national director.

The group disliked the abbreviation CIA, since it was the same as America's Central Intelligence Agency, which often supported repression in other countries. A respected elder suggested that since they were always talking about what they aimed to do, they should call the organization "aim." A veteran suggested that they take as their symbol

Clyde Bellecourt at Wounded Knee, 1973

an upside-down American flag since this is an internationally recognized distress symbol. They also determined to grow their hair and wear it in braids to signify their warrior status. They relinquished their neckties and adopted wooden chokers. To symbolize their reborn pride, they wore red jackets with thunderbird emblems on the back.

With a small grant from the Urban League, funds from church groups, and a donation from the Northern State Power Company for which Bellecourt worked, he bought two-way radios to monitor police calls, and cameras and tape recorders to obtain evidence of the violent treatment Indians received at the hands of police. After recording vicious beatings, AIM began filing suits against the police department, and had attorneys and bondsmen waiting at the police station when these situations arose. Bellecourt's street patrol advised Indians who had been arrested that they were entitled to legal defense and to a jury trial and that they need not let themselves be pressured into pleading guilty. His vigilance dramatically reduced the number of arrests, but he himself was beaten more than 30 times by angry police.

AIM "survival schools"

With the support of Minnesota's judicial system, AIM was able to offer Indian juvenile offenders an alternative to reform school. An intensive course in Indian heritage was begun in 1970, designed to counteract the misinformation these youngsters had been given in conventional history books. They learned the truth about their heroic leaders and were spiritually fortified by learning the traditional stories of their own culture.

The old ceremonies, which had been outlawed for years, were revived. The Bellecourt brothers visited medicine man Leonard Crow Dog, and through him met other Lakota holy men such as Lame Deer, Frank Fools Crow, and Pete Catches, who still practiced the sun dance and the pipe ceremony, and still remembered the traditional songs and taught the power of the drum. Through this exchange, the elders were able to transmit the old ways to the young; and they, infused with these values, became involved with tribal people whenever they were in trouble.

The occupation of Alcatraz Island

From November 1969 to June 1971, AIM members occupied the abandoned federal penitentiary on Alcatraz Island in San Francisco Bay. About 200 Indians participated and issued a proclamation stating that they claimed it "by the right of discovery" and that they wanted to use it as a cultural center. They read a sarcastic list of the ten ways in which it was suitable for an Indian reservation: first, it was isolated; second, it had no fresh water; third, it had no sanitation facilities; fourth, it had no means of employment; fifth, it had no health care facilities; sixth, the soil was rocky; seventh, there were no plants or game animals; eighth, there were no educational facilities; ninth, the population exceeded the land base; and, tenth, Indians have always been treated as prisoners.

During this symbolic 19-month takeover, Indian activists broadcast on Radio Free Alcatraz. Instead of negotiation, armed force was used to evict them as trespassers. But the action enlisted new members to their cause, such as **John Trudell** and **Russell Means** (see entries), who subsequently founded an AIM chapter in Cleveland. Other demonstrations followed at symbolically important American locations such as Mount Rushmore in South Dakota and Plymouth Rock in Massachusetts, as well as at the site of a fishing rights struggle in the Pacific Northwest. Wherever treaty rights had been violated, these young militants staged symbolic protests. Bellecourt said that the drum that had been silenced for so long was now being heard from coast to coast.

The Trail of Broken Treaties march

From across the country, a four-mile-long procession of Native people arrived in Washington, D.C., on November 3, 1972, just before the presidential election, to dramatize the U.S. government's unkept promises from more than 300 treaties made with Indians. To Bellecourt, this seemed the fulfillment of an Ojibway prophecy that one day all the tribes on the Turtle Continent—as many Indians call North America—would unite in brotherhood.

The activists had not intended to take over the government's Bureau of Indian Affairs (BIA) building, but had simply gone there to apply for decent housing for their holy men who had come with them. Instead, riot squads broke in to drive them out. Their attempts to deal as representatives of sovereign nations over denied treaty rights was turned into a confrontation, which was misrepresented in the media. President Richard M. Nixon never gave them a hearing, even though a polite reception had been promised before they set out. The damage done to the building by armed federal agents was blamed on the Indians, who were accused of vandalism.

In the wake of this incident, the BIA Commissioner and his staff were fired, and the government paid the Indians $66,000 to leave Washington. From then on, the Federal Bureau of Investigation (FBI) targeted AIM, using a variety of secretive tactics to thwart the organization's efforts. On January 11, 1973, a Nixon aide informed them that the government would not make treaties with its own citizens. Counterintelligence agents were sent to infiltrate AIM meetings.

Wounded Knee II

At Wounded Knee, the site of the mass grave of the ghost-dancers shot down by U.S. troops in 1890 in Pine Ridge, South Dakota, the poorest tribe in the United States declared itself the Independent Oglala Nation on February 28, 1973, and invited AIM to help them take their stand. The government sent tanks, paramilitary units, and heavy artillery; road blocks went up around the reservation. On March 13, a federal grand jury issued indictments against Clyde Bellecourt and others; a group of attorneys in St. Paul formed a legal defense fund on March 22 to assist and filed a suit on April 16 stating that the military siege was attempting to starve the people into submission. In response, the government tightened the blockade, turned off the water, and arrested anyone attempting to bring medicine or food into Wounded Knee.

Unlike the more militant AIM members, Bellecourt was so opposed to violence that he had not carried a weapon at Wounded Knee. He had always counseled pacifism, and still sought a peaceful solution. He was shot in the stomach by an advocate of violence, Craig

Camp, whom Russell Means believed the FBI had paid for his services. Bellecourt's life was saved by John Fire Lame Deer's doctoring. Bellecourt ennobled himself by refusing to testify against his attacker in court. After extended litigation, the charges against Bellecourt for his participation at Wounded Knee were finally dismissed.

Targeted sports and gaming interests in 1990s

Bellecourt has remained active in the ensuing years, though his focus has changed. In the 1990s, he turned his attention toward America's leisure activities and their effect on Native Americans. With his National Coalition on Racism in Sports and the Media, he led numerous protests against the use of mascots and team names—such as the Washington Redskins, Cleveland Indians, and Kansas City Chiefs—that he and other Natives considered racist. One early victory scored by the organization was a decision announced by the *Oregonian* newspaper not to print any longer the names of such teams, but only the cities for which they played.

Bellecourt also spoke out against white firms that he believed exploited tribal gambling. Since tribes were able to set up gaming institutions outside U.S. jurisdiction (legal authority), they were often subject to unscrupulous and opportunistic money interests. He decried the debt and drug abuse that often resulted from such transactions, and led numerous protests against Buffalo Brothers, a white-owned firm that he and others accused of draining profits from Indians without making any contribution to Native American life. The protests included an occupation of a casino. Bellecourt's targets may have shifted

through the years, but his commitment to active dissent has not wavered.

Further Reading

Matthiessen, Peter, *In the Spirit of Crazy Horse,* New York: Penguin, 1983.

Native American Testimony: A Chronicle of Indian-White Relations from Prophecy to the Present, 1492-1992, edited by Peter Nabokov, New York: Penguin, 1992.

The Sporting News, February 3, 1992, p. 13.

Black Elk

Oglala Lakota Sioux spiritual leader
Born c. 1863, Little Powder River, Montana or Wyoming
Died August 17, 1950

Black Elk's spiritual power was energetic and broad enough to span the two distinct religious traditions of Sioux spirituality and Catholicism. He learned the intricacies and contemplated the mysteries of both traditions with the zeal of someone with true spiritual thirst, the same thirst that prodded him never to forget his great vision and always to seek to decipher it.

Nicholas Black Elk, more widely known simply as "Black Elk," was a Lakota Sioux spiritual leader of the Oglala band. He started as a traditional Lakota holy man, or *wicasa wakan,* and went on to spend the greater part of his life as a devout Roman Catholic. Those close to him considered him a truly spiritual figure.

"Black Elk before the Six Grandfathers," illustration by Standing Bear, in John Neihardt's *Black Elk Speaks*

He is often remembered in connection with the 1932 book by the poet John Neihardt, *Black Elk Speaks*. In this book he remembered pre-reservation Sioux spiritual life and spoke at length about his boyhood and young adulthood. The biography ends his narrative at about age 25, when he witnessed the U.S. Cavalry's 1890 massacre of hundreds of Sioux at Wounded Knee, South Dakota. Yet Black Elk lived well past 80 years of age, and although the image presented to the world in *Black Elk Speaks* has strongly influenced non-Indian depictions of Sioux culture, it does not reflect the way Black Elk is remembered in his own community. He again explained traditional Sioux religious life in Joseph Epes Brown's 1953 book *The Sacred Pipe*.

Early life and faith

Black Elk witnessed many dramatic events during his childhood and young adulthood. Although there is some doubt as to his actual date of birth, he told Neihardt he was born in December 1863 on the Little Powder River, which runs through eastern Montana and Wyoming. Black Elk's concern for matters of the spirit followed that of his father, also called Black Elk, who was a medicine man. In 1866, when his son was a toddler, the elder Black Elk was wounded at the Fetterman Fight, in which a U.S. Cavalry unit was routed by their Sioux, Arapaho, and Cheyenne opponents under the leadership of the great Oglala chief **Red Cloud** (see entry). Black Elk claimed to be a cousin of another great Oglala chief, **Crazy Horse** (see entry).

In May 1876, Black Elk's father lost faith in Red Cloud and took his family to join the Oglala leader Crazy Horse. This enabled the young Black Elk to witness and participate in U.S. Cavalry General George Armstrong Custer's defeat at the battle on the Little Bighorn River in June. After the murder of Crazy Horse in 1877, Black Elk's band was among those who fled to Canada and joined **Sitting Bull** (see entry). In the years afterward, Black Elk witnessed the extermination of the buffalo and the beginning of the reservation era. He joined Buffalo Bill's Wild West Show and toured the United States and Europe. Later he became involved in the Ghost Dance movement, which sought to use ritual to bring back to life dead warriors, slaughtered buffalo, and other casualties of westward expansion by whites. Some Sioux Ghost Dancers spearheaded a resistance that led to the 1890 massacre of Sioux men, women and children at Wounded Knee, South Dakota.

Spiritual vision and conversion

The most influential event of the young Black Elk's life, however, was the vision he experienced when he was nine years old. This great vision was his spiritual calling, a calling that led him first to learn the traditional role of a *wicasa wakan,* then to become a Ghost Dance adherent and leader, and finally to become a devout spiritual adviser in the Catholic community.

An important part of his vision was the instruction of the Six Grandfathers that he should lead his people down the good road of life, peace, and prosperity by nurturing the sacred tree and keeping the nation's hoop intact. The description of this vision that appears in the Neihardt book is long and complex, and Black Elk struggled to understand and fulfill his vision throughout his long life.

A later major formative experience in Black Elk's life occurred in 1904. He was called to doctor a sick boy and had begun traditional healing rituals when a Catholic priest arrived at the scene and ejected him, throwing his drum and rattle from the room and saying, "Satan, get out!" Black Elk remained outside and waited for the priest. When he was leaving, the priest invited Black Elk to accompany him to Holy Rosary Mission. Black Elk stayed at the mission, desiring to be baptized. He accepted the Catholic faith on December 6, 1904, the feast day of St. Nicholas, and from that day on he was called Nicholas or "Nick" Black Elk.

Shortly after his conversion, Black Elk became a catechist, instructing new converts to the Christian religion, preaching, and, if the need arose and no priest were present, administering the sacraments. In this capacity he was a member of the Society of St. Joseph, an organization of Catholic men who sponsored prayer meetings and an annual summer conference, the Catholic

Sioux Congress. He learned his Bible well, often citing Bible stories and verses. He was enthusiastic and energetic in winning over new souls to the Catholic faith.

In the years following his conversion, Black Elk did not dwell on or even discuss his pre-Christian life and occupation. It is likely that he considered traditional Sioux and Christian spiritualities quite compatible. According to his daughter, Lucy Looks Twice, Black Elk applied the term *wicasa wakan* to Catholic priests as well as to medicine men and women.

By the time John Neihardt arrived at Black Elk's door to record his "life story," Black Elk had not been a practicing medicine man for almost 30 years. After *Black Elk Speaks* was published in 1932, Black Elk and some of those close to him—most notably his Jesuit priest friends—seemed to have had serious objections to the book. Like many "as told to" books about Indian and other notable figures, it presented the story in the customary Western manner: in chronological order, emphasizing childhood events. The book ends with Black Elk's words, "And I, to whom so great a vision was given in my youth—you see me now a pitiful old man who has done nothing, for the nation's hoop is broken and scattered. There is no center any longer, and the sacred tree is dead." Yet Black Elk had accomplished a great deal since his youth, and he wrote an angry letter criticizing the white man's description of him and insisting that Catholicism had made him a better man.

Black Elk died on August 17, 1950. He had told Joseph Epes Brown that there would be unusual phenomena in the sky on the day that he died, and those present at the wake reported seeing falling stars and unusually bright northern lights. Some also reported seeing symbols in the sky, including a figure eight and a hoop. In the words of his old friend and fellow Catholic organizer, John Lone Goose, "Maybe the Holy Spirit shined upon him because he was such a holy man."

Black Elk's spiritual power was energetic and broad enough to span two distinct religious traditions. He learned the intricacies and contemplated the mysteries of both traditions with the zeal of someone with true spiritual thirst, the same thirst that prodded him never to forget his great vision and always to seek to decipher it. He will be remembered and revered in a universal sense as a holy man, a *wicasa wakan,* of merging cultures in a changing America.

Further Reading

Neihardt, John, *Black Elk Speaks,* Washington Square Press, 1959.

Steltenkamp, Michael F., *Black Elk: Holy Man of the Oglala,* Norman: University of Oklahoma Press, 1993.

Black Hawk

Northern Sauk (or Sac) and Fox resistance leader
Born 1767, present-day Rock Island, Illinois
Died October 3, 1838, Iowaville, Iowa
Also known as Black Sparrow Hawk and Ma-ka-
      tai-me-she-kia-kiak

"I fought hard, but your guns were well aimed. The bullets flew.... My warriors fell around me; it began to look dismal. I saw my evil day at hand. The sun rose dim on us in the morning, and at night it sank in a dark cloud, and looked like a ball of fire. That was the last sun that shone on Black Hawk. His heart is dead, and no longer beats in his bosom. He is now a prisoner to the white men." —From Black Hawk's surrender speech, August 27, 1832

Black Hawk's attempt to resist U.S. settlement in the homelands of the Algonquian tribes in northwestern Illinois and southern Wisconsin may not have succeeded, but his attempt to muster a confederacy of these tribes was historic. When the government encroached upon the Algonquian lands, certain tribal leaders ceded the territories through treaties. Black Hawk's Northern Sauk and Fox band was unrepresented in the negotiation of these agreements, and so he began to resist. In 1832, he led a series of ill-fated battles with U.S. forces, known as Black Hawk's War, that ended in defeat for his people. Though Black Hawk himself became something of a celebrity, he ended up without power or influence. The Sauk and Fox people, meanwhile, lost their ancestral land and were relocated several times.

Black Hawk was born into the Thunder Clan in 1767 in Sauk Sautenuk/Saukenuk, Virginia Colony (now Rock Island, Illinois). He developed into a brave warrior, taking his first scalp at the age of 17 in war parties against the Osage (Wazhazhe) and Cherokee to the south. He married a woman named Assheweque ("Singing Bird"), with whom he had three children, including his son Whirling Thunder.

Military defeats and alliances

The chain of events that would make Black Hawk a resistance leader began in 1804, when the leaders of the southern Sauk and Fox of the Missouri—under the influence of alcohol that government representatives brought to negotiations—signed the Treaty of St. Louis, handing over all tribal lands east of the Mississippi—50,000,000 acres—to the United States.

Black Hawk claimed that these tribal leaders did not speak for or represent the *northern* Sauk and Fox of the Mississippi, a separate tribal group. He refused to move to Iowa from his territory in Illinois and Wisconsin. Before the United States could take action against him, Black Hawk became a supporter of Shawnee tribal leader **Tecumseh**'s idea of a Native tribal confederacy, an alliance of tribes who would protect one another's interests, especially from the whites. Like Tecumseh, Black Hawk sided with the British against America in the War of 1812, which was fought over international trading rights. America was victorious, however, and, in response to Black Hawk's hostile actions, the U.S. government began to hold discussions with Keokuk, a younger rival chief of the Fox clan.

These two military and political losses put Black Hawk even more at odds with both the United States and Keokuk, and over the next decade the situation got worse. In 1816 the U.S. Army—foreseeing a need to protect new white settlers—built Fort Armstrong at Rock Island, Illinois, within Black Hawk's traditional homeland. Two years later, the Illinois Territory became the twenty-first state. During the 1820s, while the state still had a small population, Black Hawk strengthened his ties with the British empire by making frequent trading trips back and forth to Canada. Because of this, he and his followers were sometimes called the "British Band."

Keokuk continued to negotiate with the U.S. government for Sauk and Fox land. In 1829, he advised peace to his people and surrendered to the United States as a neutral. In company with two other Sauk and Fox chiefs, Keokuk gave up the Rock River land area to the United States in exchange for land west of the Mississippi in what is now Iowa and an annuity—an ongoing regular payment—for the tribe. He also warned the U.S. government of Black Hawk's warlike intentions. Black Hawk's band returned from their winter hunt in the spring of 1829 to Saukenuk, their Rock River village, to find their land and homes occupied by white squatters. Shocked and enraged, Black Hawk and his followers nonetheless stayed and shared their village with the newcomers for the remainder of that summer and for the next two years.

Black Hawk, painting by George Catlin, 1832

Black Hawk's War

Black Hawk's attempt to preserve the Sauk homeland from white settlers had failed. In the summer of 1831, the U.S. government sought to make the invasion complete. On June 26, army troops bombarded Saukenuk to force the 2,000 dwellers of Black Hawk's village across the Mississippi in accordance with Keokuk's agreement. Warned in advance of the attempt, however, Black Hawk and his villagers had escaped the previous night into Iowa and remained there through the following March. Black Hawk received spiritual and political support for his resistance from the Winnebago prophet White Cloud, and counted more than 2,000 people, including 600 warriors, among his followers. However, he received no aid in the struggle from the British.

On April 5, 1832, Black Hawk's band of 1,000 crossed the Mississippi River back into Illinois and headed north, trying to win support from other tribes in the area. The Winnebagos and Potowatomis, however, declared their neutrality and refused to support Black Hawk. Meanwhile, the U.S. Army and state militias were called up. Among the volunteers to fight were such future political notables as Abraham Lincoln, Zachary Taylor, Jefferson Davis, and Daniel Boone's son, Nat. A month later, Black Hawk was ready to admit defeat and surrender.

On May 14, 1832, as his truce party approached the U.S. troops under a white flag, nervous soldiers fired on them. His warriors retaliated and won the battle, which became known as Stillman's Run, after the panicked flight of Major Isaiah Stillman's men. Happy in their victory, but cautious about reprisals, Black Hawk and White Cloud headed back north to Wisconsin. For the next two months, however, the combined U.S. forces kept Black Hawk's band on the run with minor skirmishes along the way. With no aid from other tribes, lacking food, and losing troops to desertion, Black Hawk continued to press north into Wisconsin.

On July 21, 1832, the U.S. Army and Wisconsin militia, aided by Winnebago informers, attacked Black Hawk in the Battle of Wisconsin Heights, near present-day Sauk City, northwest of Madison. Many Natives were killed, but others escaped by raft across the Wisconsin River, pushing westward toward the Bad Axe River that flows into the Mississippi. On August 1, 1832, the U.S. steamship *Warrior,* supported by cannon and soldiers on the riverbank, attacked Natives at the mouth of the Bad Axe River who were trying to convene under a truce flag. About 28 Natives were killed.

The following day Black Hawk argued for a northward march to the land of the Anishinabe and the Chippewa. Most of his band refused to follow him, so Black Hawk left with White Cloud and around 50 followers. On August 3, 1832, the 1,300-man U.S. Army attacked with cannon, artillery, and sharpshooters, slaughtering the 300 natives who had stayed behind. Dakota tribesmen killed those Sauk, Fox, and Winnebago who reached the western bank of the Mississippi. This fight became known as the Massacre at Bad Axe River.

Exhausted and demoralized, Black Hawk, White Cloud, and the remaining resistance fighters surrendered at Fort Crawford (present-day Prairie du Chien), Wisconsin, on August 27, 1832. In his surrender speech, Black Hawk stated, "I fought hard, but your guns were well aimed. The bullets flew.... My warriors fell around me; it began to look dismal. I saw my evil day at hand. The sun rose dim on us in the morning, and at night it sank in a dark cloud, and looked like a ball of fire. That was the last sun that shone on Black Hawk. His heart is dead, and no longer beats in his bosom. He is now a prisoner to the white men."

Prisoner of war

From Wisconsin, Black Hawk was taken to Jefferson Barracks, Missouri, and then held as a prisoner of war in Fort Monroe, Virginia. In 1833 he was taken to Washington, D.C., to meet President Andrew Jackson, and he later toured cities in the eastern United States. In the end, Black Hawk was allowed to return to Iowa as a hostage under

Black Hawk's surrender

the trusteeship of Keokuk, the U.S.-recognized leader of the Sauk. This, coupled with an injunction against assuming a leadership role, was the ultimate humiliation.

Black Hawk became something of a celebrity after his surrender. His portrait was painted by the famous painter of Native Americans, George Catlin, in 1832. It now hangs in the National Museum of American Art, which is part of the Smithsonian Institution in Washington, D.C. A great many authors wanted to write his life story; he ultimately dictated *Life of Ma-ka-tai-me-she-kia-kiak: The Autobiography of Black Hawk* to the trader Antoine LeClaire in 1833. In 1833 and 1837 Charles Bird King painted two more portraits of Black Hawk, which were

widely distributed. Black Hawk died, in his own words, "an obscure member of a nation that formerly honored and respected [his] opinions," on October 3, 1838, at Iowaville on the Des Moines River, at the age of 71.

The Sauk and Fox tribes suffered the fate that Black Hawk had foreseen for them. In the peace treaty of 1832 to 1833 that ended Black Hawk's War, America—with Keokuk's cooperation—took the remaining 6,000,000 acres of Sauk and Fox lands in Illinois and eastern Iowa, as well as Winnebago lands in southern Wisconsin. By 1837, all their neighboring tribes had escaped to lands west of the Mississippi. In 1842, the Sauk and Fox ceded away all land in Iowa, and accepted a smaller reservation in Kansas. Six years after that,

Keokuk died there in disgrace. The Sauk ceded away their Kansas lands in 1867 and accepted a smaller reservation in Oklahoma Indian Territory.

Black Hawk himself was not allowed to rest in peace in the land to which his people had fled. His remains were stolen from his burial ground and obtained by the governor of the Iowa Territory, who displayed them in his office. They were later recovered and placed on display in the Burlington Historical Society, Illinois, which burnt to the ground in 1855.

Further Reading

Brown, Dee, *Bury My Heart at Wounded Knee,* New York: Holt, 1970.

Native North American Almanac, edited by Duane Champagne, Detroit: Gale, 1994.

Waters, Frank, *Brave Are My People: Indian Heroes Not Forgotten,* New York: Clear Light, 1993.

Ethel Blondin-Andrew

Dene cabinet minister
Born March 25, 1951, Fort Norman, Northwest
    Territories, Canada

Despite her lack of political experience and money, as a Liberal party candidate Blondin-Andrew defeated her two male opponents by a landslide in the 1988 election.

Ethel Blondin-Andrew, a Dene Indian from the Arctic, was the first Native woman to sit in Canada's House of Commons. Elected by a landslide victory in 1988 to represent the Western Arctic, Blondin-Andrew was named secretary of state for youth and training by Prime Minister Jean Chrétien in November 1993. A high-profile cabinet minister, Blondin-Andrew has been outspoken in campaigning for aboriginal (native) rights.

Blondin-Andrew described herself to *HomeMaker's* as a "snotty-nosed kid from the bush." She was born in Fort Norman, Northwest Territories, in 1951 to a young, unmarried mother, Cecilia Modeste. At three months, Blondin-Andrew was custom adopted by her aunt and uncle, Joseph Blondin and Marie Therese (Tatti), and raised with their children. The relative Blondin-Andrew credits most with shaping her determination to succeed in life, however, is her grandmother, Catherine Blondin. "Because of my grandmother's influence, I always felt that I was equal to anybody," Blondin-Andrew commented.

As a youngster, Blondin-Andrew spent several happy years in the family's bush camp. At the age of nine, however, she was sent away to boarding school in Inuvik, in the extreme northwestern section of the Northwest Territories, near the border with the Yukon Territory. Three years later, she was diagnosed with tuberculosis of the spine and moved to a sanatorium in Edmonton, Alberta. When she recovered, Blondin-Andrew returned to the family's new home, purchased for $80, in the isolated community of Fort Franklin near Great Bear Lake in the Northwest Territories. She later reflected that these years in a poorly heated house without electricity or running water, though difficult, made her stronger and gave her perspective.

At the age of 14 Blondin-Andrew was selected for leadership training and sent to Grandin College, a coed high school in Fort Smith at the Alberta-Northwest Territories border. Her achievements there seemed threatened when she found herself pregnant and unmarried at age 17. Sent to a home for unwed mothers, Blondin-Andrew stubbornly refused to give up her son. By age 21, she had married and was studying at the University of Alberta while raising her three children, Troy, Tanya, and Tim Townsend. Graduating with a bachelor of education degree in 1974, Blondin-Andrew taught in remote Native communities around the Northwest Territories for several years. She was appointed an aboriginal languages specialist for the Department of Education in Yellowknife, Northwest Territories. Her first marriage ended in divorce.

Elected to Parliament by landslide victory

Blondin-Andrew became a senior civil servant in the mid-1980s when she was appointed manager and then acting director of the Public Service Commission of Canada's indigenous (native) development program in Ottawa, which trained Natives for government jobs. When the program ended, she returned to Yellowknife to become assistant deputy minister in the territorial government's Department of Culture and Communications. But Blondin-Andrew decided the best way to implement real change for her people was to run for elected office as a representative of the Western Arctic in the House of Commons. Despite her lack of political experience and money, as a Liberal party candidate Blondin-Andrew defeated her two male opponents by a landslide in the 1988 election.

Blondin-Andrew was named aboriginal affairs critic for the Liberal opposition government and quickly earned widespread respect and media attention for her sharp questioning of Prime Minister Brian Mulroney during the Mohawk land dispute at Oka, Quebec. (The Mohawk set up a blockade in 1990 to protest construction of a golf course on land they claimed was theirs. The 78-day armed standoff with police and soldiers drew worldwide attention.) Blondin-Andrew also chaired her party's Western/ Northern caucus and cochaired the party's leadership convention. When the Liberals were elected to office in 1993, Blondin-Andrew was given the junior cabinet post of secretary of state, responsible for youth and training.

In August 1993 she took time from her political duties to marry Leon Andrew, a Fort Norman trapper. Five months later, Blondin-Andrew charged her husband with two counts of spousal assault, stating that while she was sympathetic to her husband's problems, women could not allow themselves to be victimized. The couple reconciled while Andrew served his jail sentence. As a cabinet minister, Blondin-Andrew has continued working to legislate change for Canada's Native peoples.

Further Reading

Calgary Herald, January 13, 1991, p. A8.

Canadian Parliamentary Guide, edited by Kathyrn O'Handley, Toronto: Globe and Mail Publishing, 1994.

Canadian Who's Who, edited by Kieran Simpson, Toronto: University of Toronto Press, 1993.

HomeMaker's, January/February 1993, pp. 84-90.

Gertrude Simmons Bonnin

Yankton Sioux writer, educator, musician,
  and activist
Born February 22, 1876, Yankton Reservation,
  South Dakota
Died 1938, Washington, D.C.
Also known as Zitkala-Sa

Gertrude Bonnin's life serves as an example of the hardship educated Indians faced trying to live in both the red and the white worlds.

Strongly independent, a talented writer and musician, and an activist for Native American rights, Gertrude Simmons Bonnin was one of the most dynamic Native Americans of the first quarter of the twentieth century. Her spirit encouraged other prominent Native Americans of her time, such as **Charles Eastman** (see entry), Carlos Montezuma, and Arthur C. Parker. As a writer she shared her storytelling traditions with young readers; her essays and personal reflections voiced her anger at the suffering of Native people caused by elements of white society. Her life serves as an example of the hardship educated Indians faced trying to live in both the red and the white worlds.

Scholars have gathered a handful of facts about Bonnin's life: her mother, Tate I Yohin Win ("Reaches for the Wind"), also known as Ellen, was a Yankton Sioux of the Nakota cultural and linguistic group. Ellen was married three times to white men; her husband Felker was Gertrude's father. Before Gertrude's birth on February 22, 1876, on the Yankton Reservation in South Dakota, Felker abandoned his wife, who then returned to the Yankton Agency, where she eventually married John Haysting Simmons. Young Gertrude grew up as a Simmons. As a young woman she gave herself the name Zitkala-Sa, which means "Red Bird" in the Lakota language.

As a child at the Yankton Agency, Gertrude listened to the traditional stories about the various characters and animals that she would write about in her first book, *Old Indian Legends*. She lived according to traditional Yankton ways as much as was possible on the reservation. In 1884, she took the opportunity to get an education usually offered only to white children by attending White's Manual Labor Institute in Wabash, Indiana. This began a lifelong struggle between traditional and modern ways.

Ellen Simmons distrusted missionaries' efforts to educate Indian children and fiercely opposed her daughter's decision to go to a school "in the land of red apples"—as Indians who were "white on the inside" were known. When Gertrude returned from White's Institute and announced her decision to again leave the reservation to continue her schooling, she and her mother grew further apart. In 1888 and 1889 she attended the Santee Normal Training School in Nebraska, but returned to White's before moving on to Indiana's Earlham College in 1895.

At Earlham she applied herself vigorously to studying music, becoming a respectable violinist. In early 1896 her speech "Side by Side" gained her second place in statewide oratory honors among students, and was printed in the March issue of *The Word Corner,* the school paper at the Santee Agency. Gertrude also studied briefly in Boston at the New England Conservatory of Music. By the end of the century she was teaching at the Carlisle Indian School in Pennsylvania, performing along with the many Sioux musicians in its orchestra.

First collection of stories published

Despite the strained relations with her mother, Bonnin frequently returned home, wishing to stay in touch with her heritage. She dedicated herself to recalling and preserving her Nakota culture, and in 1901 Ginn and Company, located in Boston, published 14 of her stories as *Old Indian Legends,* under her chosen name of Zitkala-Sa. Meanwhile, her essays and reflections were published in such periodicals as *Atlantic Monthly, Harper's Magazine, Everybody's Magazine,* and *Red Man and Helper.*

Her magazine writings gave her a chance to expose to a great many readers not only the inaccuracies spread by whites about Indian education but also the bitter experiences schools created for Indian youngsters. She disagreed with Carlisle founder Richard Henry Pratt, who believed in teaching Indians agrarian, or farming, skills and domestic responsibilities. Her position, which was that Indian youths should be taught academic subjects, was remarkably similar to that of her African-American contemporary, scholar and educator W. E. B. DuBois. Both Bonnin and DuBois argued that minority children must excel in their studies if their people were to escape poverty and discrimination.

Gertrude Simmons Bonnin

Sometime also in 1900 Bonnin met activist and physician Carlos Montezuma, who despite his nickname "the fiery Apache" was actually a Yavapai Indian from Arizona and an 1889 graduate of the Chicago Medical College. Montezuma was so impressed by her that in 1901 he asked her to marry him. Both were strong-willed individuals, and although they broke the engagement that summer, they continued corresponding—sometimes with fierce debate—for decades. For instance, Bonnin rebuked Montezuma's idea of creating an all-male Indian organization.

Bonnin's letters to Carlos Montezuma are in his collected papers at the State Historical Society of Wisconsin, but none of his letters to her seem to have survived. The letters convinced Montezuma biographer Peter Iverson that Bonnin's indecision about marriage had more to do with marriage itself than with the man in her life. Yet he also believes she wanted to marry a man who shared her Yankton cultural heritage. On a visit to her mother in late 1901, she met Captain Raymond Bonnin, a Nakota like herself who was on the staff of the Indian Bureau. They married in 1902, and the following year their son, Raymond Ohiya Bonnin, was born. (Ohiya in the Nakota dialect means "Winner.")

The active writing and musical career of Zitkala-Sa, as she had begun signing her books, received less of her attention for several years as she and her husband worked on various reservations, including the Uintah and Ouray Reservation in Utah, between 1903 and 1916. She did, however, take time in 1913 to collaborate with classical music composer William Hanson on an opera, *Sun Dance,* that premiered in Vernal, Utah that year. Indians and non-Indians alike greatly enjoyed this opera, and it was occasionally performed elsewhere in Utah and in neighboring states. After being ignored for nearly two decades, *Sun Dance* was premiered by the New York Light Opera Guild in 1937, which selected it as its American opera for that year. Operas about American folk life gained popularity during the 1920s and 1930s, yet none about Native Americans except this one were coauthored by a Native American.

Bonnin's activism and organizations

Gertrude Bonnin was not a founding member of the Society of American Indians (SAI), a self-help organization that began in 1911 at Ohio State University. But she became one of its earliest supporters and active correspondents, rising eventually to positions on its staff. The organizers of the SAI, the most important of the pan-Indian groups—that is, groups open to all tribes—wanted a forum that would reach beyond issues affecting individual tribes; they saw themselves as advocates for issues affecting many different Indian reservation and community populations.

The SAI began publishing a quarterly journal, *The American Indian Magazine,* in 1916, and Bonnin's poem, "The Indian's Awakening," appeared in it. At the organization's conference in Cedar Rapids, Iowa, that September, she was elected secretary. She also began corresponding with Arthur C. Parker, the Seneca ethnologist, or cultural anthropologist, who was SAI's president. Bonnin also joined non-Indian organizations such as the League of American Pen Women and the General Federation of Women's Clubs.

Bonnin's work in Native American issues proved exciting, useful, and challenging for her. She joined those—both Indian and white—who opposed the use of peyote, a drug taken from a cactus that possesses hallucinogenic qualities and is used in many native rituals. Indian religious traditionalists, white anthropologists, and others argued for the merits of the plant, which had become a vital force in the cultural life of the Plains tribes. The plant had been in use for some time in religious ceremonies, and was said to have healing and as well visionary properties.

While in Utah, Bonnin opposed the use of peyote as a spiritual practice. In keeping with this position, Bonnin supported the Congressional Indian bill of 1918, which was designed for the suppression of the plant. The defenders of peyote seemed to have lost when the bill was passed, but enforcement of the bill proved weak. Eventually, peyote usage brought about the establishment of the Native American Church, which used and defended peyote as a sacred medicine.

Another endeavor that Bonnin began while living in Utah was her support for both the Indian Service and the Community Center movement. The Indian Service was run by Native Americans, many of whom were educated in mission and trade schools on or off reservations, who worked on the reservations or in other Indian communities performing the kind of support services work that Bonnin and her husband were doing. These Indians could have achieved greater material success by following a different path, and Bonnin sympathized with, praised, and encouraged their devotion to their communities and their career sacrifices.

Bonnin also believed that community centers such as the one at Fort Duchesne in Utah could contribute to the improvement of Indians if Indians themselves, along with white educators and missionaries, were willing to work together. She encouraged nonpartisanship, or the refusal to split into separate groups with varying and conflicting interests, at the centers. The movement failed as tribalism—loyalty to individual tribes rather than to Indians in general—increased and attempts to bring tribes together under the banner of pan-Indianism fell by the wayside.

With Gertrude's role in the SAI, the Bonnins relocated in 1916 to Washington, D.C. There "Gertie," as she was affectionately called, continued to help Native Americans make adjustments to white society. Although she was a respected leader, she continued experiencing the distrust of reservation Indians because she was part of both the Native American and white communities.

Bonnin faced several challenges in 1918. One involved her role in the peyote controversy, while the other had to do with differences with Marie Baldwin (Ojibway), the SAI treasurer. At the SAI's annual meeting, where Bonnin was reelected as secretary in addition to being elected treasurer, she joined the chorus of Indian voices calling for the abolition of the Indian Bureau, the federal organization that drew the anger of all tribes for its meddling in and control over Native peoples' affairs. Division and individual tribal issues that drew members to their home reservations and communities increased, and as a result the SAI was weakened.

Bonnin successfully pushed *The American Indian Magazine* to devote a special issue to the Sioux in 1917. For this issue she wrote "A Sioux Woman's Love For Her Grandchild" and an editorial in which she attacked the Indian Bureau as "unAmerican." Eventually, Bonnin became the publication's editor, writing about the importance of Indian self-determination and the need for Native people to hold on to their land. She served with the SAI in this capacity until 1920, when, opposed to the declining organization's new political direction under Thomas Sloan (Omaha), a lawyer who defended peyote usage, she resigned from her activities and membership.

As if to sum up one side of her activities, Bonnin gathered several of her writings for a new book, *American Indian Stories,* published by Hayworth Press in 1921 under the name Zitkala-Sa. Bonnin probably felt her early writings were still timely for their pro-Indian self-determination stance. Meanwhile, in 1924 the Indian Rights Association—an organization that Bonnin had supported for many years—published a small volume, *Oklahoma's Poor Rich Indians, an Orgy of Graft and Exploitation of the Five Civilized Tribes, Legalized Robbery,* which Bonnin wrote with Charles H. Fabens and Matthew K. Sniffen. This study reported on Indians being murdered and swindled out of the recently discovered oil-rich land on which they had been living since forced there from the southern states in the nineteenth century.

New vigor for Indian rights

Otherwise pushed to a less important position among her former pan-Indian associates, Bonnin fought with new determination for Indian rights, encouraged by the Indian Citizenship Act of 1924. She helped found the National Council of American Indians in 1926 and became its first president; her husband was elected secretary-treasurer. The National Council's main objective was to make "a constructive effort to better the Red Race and make its members better citizens of the United States." It became Bonnin's platform for calling upon Indians to support rights issues, to encourage racial consciousness and pride, and promote pan-Indianism.

Despite Bonnin's efforts, educated Indians during the period between the two world wars continued to be involved with tribal issues rather than national Indian concerns. As a pan-Indian organization, the NCAI thus declined for many years, and—partly because of Bonnin's charismatic self-reliance and leadership—potential Indian allies felt their participation was unnecessary. (After the National Council ended, a new reform organization, the National Congress of American Indians—which would have an identical acronym, or abbreviation—was established in 1944.) Yet the organization's lack of progress and the criticism confronting her from time to time did not lessen Bonnin's interest in Indian rights. She supported the ideas of John Collier (excepting his tolerance of peyote usage) before and during his celebrated career as Indian Commissioner under U.S. president Franklin D. Roosevelt's New Deal social welfare programs, because he respected the integrity of Native American cultural traditions.

Gertrude Bonnin continued lecturing on Indian reform and Indian rights until her health began to fail. The NCAI dissolved when she died on January 26, 1938, in Washington, D.C. Later that year the Indian Confederation of America, a New York City-based group, honored her memory at its annual powwow. Her reputation as an effective writer and activist at the forefront of the struggle to gain respect for Native Americans has gained wider appreciation thanks to the republication of her two books and various scholarly articles analyzing her writing. Whether under her "American name" or as Zitkala-Sa, Gertrude Bonnin remains one of America's outstanding human rights activists.

Further Reading

Atlantic Monthly, December, 1902, pp. 801-803.

Bonnin, Gertrude Simmons (as Zitkala-Sa), *American Indian Stories,* [1921] Lincoln: Bison Books, University of Nebraska Press, 1985.

Bonnin, Gertrude Simmons (as Zitkala-Sa), *Old Indian Legends,* [1902] Lincoln: Bison Books, University of Nebraska Press, 1985.

Fisher, Dexter, "Zitkala-Sa: The Evolution of a Writer," *American Indian Quarterly,* August 1979, pp. 229-238.

Ruoff, A. LaVonne Brown, *American Indian Literatures: An Introduction, Bibliographic Review, and Selected Bibliography,* New York: Modern Language Association, 1990.

Mary Bosomworth

Creek tribal leader
Born 1700
Died 1763

For better or worse, in the course of her life Mary Bosomworth played a vital role in colonial America, championing English interests and soothing conflicts.

Mary Bosomworth was an influential Creek who supported England against Spain in the struggle for power and land in colonial Georgia. The English considered her a valuable ally as they negotiated with the Creek. Her respected position among her people was useful to them, as were her skills as interpreter and diplomat. A charismatic and determined leader, Bosomworth at one time declared herself "empress" of her tribe. Her story is remarkable both for the view it provides of the rough and often corrupt life in colonial America, where diverse groups schemed for money, power, and land, and for the sheer drama of her bold nature, manipulating and overpowering the colonial authorities.

Although Bosomworth's motives may at times have been questionable, her never-say-die attitude always led to colorful events. In fact, late in her life, Bosomworth headed an army that marched on the colonial government of Savannah, a feat that won her land and a large sum of money.

Bosomworth was born to an English father and a Creek mother and was removed from tribal land in her youth. Taken to South Carolina, she was baptized into the Church of England and educated as a white Christian. Later, when she ventured back to Creek territory, she met a half-blood trader named John Musgrove, whom she married. In 1733, the British governor of the Georgia colony enlisted Bosomworth as a Creek interpreter. She used this unique position to gain influence in the tribe, while at the same time her kinship ties with Creek leaders gave her a special advantage with the English.

Becomes influential with English

By 1733, Bosomworth and John Musgrove had developed their plantation and trading post on the Savannah River into a splendidly prosperous enterprise. Bosomworth helped smooth over differences between the Yamacraw, an outlawed Creek faction, and the new colonists who sought to settle on lands promised to the Yamacraw. While resolving this dispute, she helped convince her fellow Creek to support the English against the Spanish, who were also angling for power in the region.

Soon the tribe signed a friendship and land cession treaty with the English Crown. In return, General James Oglethorpe,

"Mary Bosomworth inciting Indians to violence"

founder of the Georgia colony, agreed to safeguard Indian interests. The Musgroves increased their standing considerably as a result of this agreement. They had established themselves to Oglethorpe as an important influence among the southern tribes and they had also acquired a new market for their plantation's crops: the incoming white settlers. John Musgrove accompanied the Yamacraw chieftain Tomochichi and some of his people to England, where they were received by the king and queen, met the Archbishop of Canterbury, and discussed Indian trade with trustees of the government. As interpreter, Musgrove was paid handsomely in cash and land by the trustees; he soon became Georgia's richest man.

Trouble, however, was brewing at home. Musgrove's partner, a man named Watson, took advantage of his absence and helped himself to the profits of their deerskin trade. As a result, he made enemies of Bosomworth and the Creek. In a bout of drinking one day, Watson accused Bosomworth of being a witch. Not one to take such an insult quietly, she sued him for slander in the Georgia court and won. Watson, however, had a violent nature. Angered by her victory in court, he went after her with a gun. Bosomworth defended herself and then sued him for assault. Watson, who was later charged with the murder of a Yamacraw named Skee, eventually locked himself in the store with Mary's black slave Justice, who was killed in the ensuing confrontation. To protect Watson from the Yamacraw, Georgia's trustees declared him insane and confined him; he was ordered to pay Bosomworth for the death of Justice. Watson would later assemble a group of discon-tented settlers that evolved into Georgia's anti-Trustee party.

Remarried and continued support of the English

Musgrove's return and immediate appointment as a constable helped calm the situation. When he died in 1735, the widowed Mary retained his considerable wealth and her own unique stature among the Creeks. She married an indentured servant who worked on the property, Jacob Matthews, whose arrogance and abuse of alcohol—along with his involvement with the anti-Trustee radicals—recalled the behavior of Watson. Through Matthews's actions, the Musgrove fortune withered. Yet Bosomworth's influence with the Creeks was undimmed; she interpreted between Georgia officials and her important kinsmen, prolonging the peace Tomochichi and Oglethorpe had worked for. She also interpreted for the well-known Methodist missionary John Wesley in his attempts to bring Christianity to the Creek, though he eventually judged them too corrupt for salvation and headed back to England.

Eventually, war between Spain and England over the southern colonies seemed imminent. Oglethorpe convinced Bosomworth to set up a trading post as a kind of Creek center for strategic purposes, and planned to use her as a liaison with the tribe. Though the tribe didn't participate in what would be known as the Spanish Border War to nearly the extent that Oglethorpe had hoped, Bosomworth did her utmost to boost their involvement. But conflicting impulses among the tribal headsmen and the intrigues of the French, who for their own reasons wanted to disrupt the English-Creek alliance, diluted their contribution. Eventually, Oglethorpe had to withdraw in the midst of an English siege. The Creek were soon distracted by war with the Cherokee, a conflict that disrupted English plans and even threatened Oglethorpe's safety. Since he had been an ally of the Cherokee as well, Bosomworth now had to intervene to prevent the Creek from attacking him.

Jacob Matthews, meanwhile, was made a captain of Oglethorpe's army. He became embroiled in and lost a paternity suit at Savannah, and died in 1742. Mary's substantial losses were compounded by a raid by Yamasee Indians representing the Spanish; she lost her trading post and goods. Oglethorpe called upon her again to act as interpreter, and rewarded her with a diamond ring, two hundred English pounds, and guarantees of future payments. Soon thereafter she met Thomas Bosomworth, a soldier of fortune who had become a minister of the Church of England, it seems, so he could enjoy a comfortable church-supported dwelling in Savannah. According to historian David H. Corkran, the coming together of these two figures, "the half-blood widow with wealth and the ambitious English adventurer, boded ill for Georgia and was to become a major factor in Creek affairs for a decade and a half to come." They married in 1749.

Asserted "royal" claim to escape debt

Bosomworth, thanks in part to his marriage to Mary, got a large commission from the South Carolina colony as a Creek agent. In the meantime, her relations with Georgia had deteriorated, and as a result her kinsmen among the Creek were less inclined to support the English and more willing to discuss terms with the Spanish and French. The intervention of the British colonel Horton brought them back into English service, however, and Creek leaders were prevailed upon not to align with the other powers.

Mary suggested to the British that they send an agent to the Indians with presents—to fulfill a ritual obligation that the English had been neglecting—and promises of faithful offerings in the future. Thomas Bosomworth's brother, Abraham, a steadfast friend of the Creek, successfully undertook this errand and eased much anti-English feeling among the Creek. His service further elevated the standing of Mary and of Thomas. The English colonel Heron, in a letter to the Duke of Newcastle, insisted, "It will be impossible for me to establish a strict friendship with the Creek Indians without the friendship of Mrs. Bosomworth." He called Mary "a most useful person" who "may be of infinite service to the Crown of Great Britain."

The Bosomworths, of course, were not about to squander the opportunity to be rewarded for their services. They petitioned the English government for redress of grievances, demanding large amounts of money and land. Mary proclaimed herself "empress of the Creek Nation," encouraged by her husband. Because of her high standing among the Creek, she and Thomas insisted, they were entitled to a chunk of South Carolina and several islands off the Georgia coast. The colonial authorities in Savannah increasingly viewed them as arrogant schemers, especially since their debt had, by now, become enormous.

To enforce their claim, the Bosomworths notified Oglethorpe that the "empress" would be coming to claim what was rightfully hers. Dressed in ceremonial robes, she assembled an army of Creeks and marched on Savannah at the head of the procession with Thomas by her side. Met by the cavalry at the outskirts of town, they surrendered their weapons and over the next couple of days met in council with Georgia's authorities. The Creek managed to get their weapons back, however, and seemed about to massacre the English when the Bosomworths were seized and held captive. Somehow, through apologies and gifts, the conflict ended without violence.

The Bosomworths pursued their claim with the English government; eventually they were granted title to the island of St. Catherine and the sum received for the sale of the islands of Ossabo and Sapelo. This was a compromise measure designed to balance their claims with those of other Creek. Little is known of Bosomworth's last years, but she reportedly died in 1763. For better or worse, in the course of her life she played a vital role in colonial America, championing English interests and soothing conflicts, as well as amassing her own fortune.

Further Reading

Corkran, David H., *The Creek Frontier, 1540-1783,* Norman: University of Oklahoma Press, 1967.

Hodge, Frederick Webb, *Handbook of American Indians North of Mexico* part one, New York: Pageant Books, Inc., 1962.

Native North American Almanac, edited by Duane Champagne, Detroit, Gale, 1994.

Elias Boudinot

Cherokee editor, translator, author, orator, and religious and political figure
Born c. 1803, Cherokee Nation (now Georgia)
Died, June 22, 1839, near present-day Tahlequah, Oklahoma

When he returned to the Cherokee Nation in the summer of 1832, Elias Boudinot assessed the situation and the deteriorating fortunes of his tribe and began to change his position on removal.

At age 25, Elias Boudinot became the first editor of the bilingual (Cherokee and English) newspaper the *Cherokee Phoenix,* which began publication in the Cherokee Nation East (now Georgia) in 1828. His frustrated attempts to print a discussion of a controversial tribal issue led to his resignation from the paper. He then became prominent in the Treaty party and was a signer of the Treaty of New Echota in 1835. This treaty was not authorized by the Cherokee and had the effect of ceding, or giving up, tribal land, a capital offense to the Cherokee. The tragic consequence of the treaty was the Trail of Tears, during which over one-fifth of the tribe died en route to Indian Territory, in present-day Oklahoma.

In 1837 Boudinot moved west, where he joined in a publishing venture that produced the first book ever published in Oklahoma. When the main body of the Cherokee completed their journey in 1839, Boudinot was assassinated—along with his relatives Major Ridge and John Ridge—in retribution for his role in the treaty.

Elias Boudinot

Boudinot was born in the old Cherokee Nation (now part of the state of Georgia) around 1803 (some say 1805). His father was David Oowatie, and Stand Watie, the noted Confederate general, was his younger brother. Boudinot's Cherokee name was Galagina (pronounced Kill-ke-nah). He assumed the name of Elias Boudinot, who had been a prominent figure in the Revolutionary War and was his benefactor, at Boudinot's request.

Boudinot's education began at the school of the Moravian Mission at Spring Place (now in Murray County, Georgia). The Moravians—a Protestant sect dedicated to strict religious practice and simple living—had been active among the Cherokees since

1800. Around age 15, Boudinot traveled to the Foreign Mission School in Cornwall, Connecticut, and spent one night with his benefactor and namesake en route.

Marriage stirred controversy

After graduation, Boudinot announced his intention to marry a white woman from Cornwall. Two years earlier Boudinot's cousin **John Ridge** (see entry) had married a white woman, provoking a controversy in the community that prompted the local newspaper to call for the closing of the Cornwall Mission School. Knowing this, Boudinot asked Harriet Ruggles Gold to be his bride. Many Cornwall residents strongly opposed the marriage, and the bride's brother burned the two in effigy—burned figures or dummies that represented the couple—as Harriet went into temporary hiding for her own safety.

During that same demonstration, the church bells tolled a death knell, and members of the church choir, to which Harriet belonged, were asked to wear black mourning bands for their lost sister. Harriet's family also were reluctant to approve the marriage, and Harriet became seriously ill. As she grew steadily worse, her parents rethought their position and approved the union, trusting they were following God's will. Eventually, Harriet's health was restored and marriage plans proceeded.

Harriet was deeply religious and longed to do missionary work. Her love for Boudinot and for a life of religious work combined to help the couple weather the storm. Boudinot had taken classes at Andover Theological Seminary in Andover, Massachusetts, hoping to teach the Gospel of Christianity to his people. Love prevailed, and the couple were married in the home of her parents on March 28, 1826. However, as a result of the marriage, the Cornwall School was closed in autumn 1826. Harriet Gold Boudinot died ten years later at age 31, after bearing six children. In 1836, Boudinot married Delight Sargent, also a white woman; they remained childless.

Returned to Georgia and edited newspaper

With his course at Cornwall and his study at Andover Theological Seminary, Boudinot was one of the best-educated citizens of the Cherokee Nation. He went on a fund-raising speaking tour before teaching at a mission school in High Tower, Cherokee Nation, from 1826 to 1827. In 1828 he became editor of the *Cherokee Phoenix,* which used the Cherokee alphabet developed by the famed linguist **Sequoyah** (see entry). By 1833, Boudinot published a novel in Cherokee, *Poor Sarah; or, The Indian Woman.* This fictional account of an Indian girl's religious conversion is considered the first written work of American Indian fiction.

In 1827, Boudinot was named clerk of the Cherokee National Council (legislature). The major issue facing the council was increasing pressure from the U.S. government to relocate the Cherokee from their ancestral land in Georgia to Indian Territory (present-day Oklahoma). The Cherokee council, meeting in October 1829, decided to stand firm, opposed to the loss of their ancestral land. The council adopted a resolution (drafted by Major Ridge, Boudinot's uncle) that any tribal member who undertook "to cede any part of their tribal domain" would receive the death penalty.

The faction to which Boudinot, Ridge, and Watie belonged was apparently content with this until 1831, when the council named John Ross principal chief (over John Ridge) for an indefinite period. Ross and his majority believed that they could retain their land by using the U.S. court system and by eventually signing treaties with Georgia and/or the U.S. government to keep their lands.

In March 1832, Boudinot and John Ridge traveled to Boston and other northern cities to speak and raise support for the Cherokee cause. In the meantime, Georgia continued its efforts to enforce the Georgia Compact, which would move the Cherokees to the West. When he returned to the Cherokee Nation in the summer of 1832, Boudinot assessed the situation and the deteriorating fortunes of his tribe and began to change his position on removal. He resigned as editor of the *Phoenix* in September, under pressure from the tribal government. He wanted to use the newspaper as an instrument of discussion, but John Ross forbade the editor to print a word in favor of removal.

Reversed position on removal

At this time, Boudinot and his family began considering their own situation. They ultimately decided that a treaty with the U.S. government, ceding land in exchange for new land in the West, was their best hope. They formed the "Treaty party" and made a trip to Washington, D.C., in 1835 to negotiate unofficially on behalf of the Cherokees. On December 29, the Treaty of New Echota was signed by Boudinot, John Ridge, Major Ridge, Stand Watie, and 15 others, none of whom had authority to do so.

The treaty provided for surrender of Cherokee lands and removal of the people to

Indian Territory (now Oklahoma). The lawful government of the Cherokee Nation was outraged and sent petitions with signatures of more than 90 percent of the tribal members to the Senate, pleading against ratification. Nonetheless, the treaty passed on May 23, 1836, by one vote.

Boudinot and his family were able to choose their time for passage to the West, since they were part of a favored group who had signed the Treaty of New Echota. They traveled to Indian Territory in September 1837, along with John Ridge and his family. When they arrived, they joined Dr. Samuel Austin Worcester, a medical missionary, in Park Hill, near the capitol at Tahlequah.

Joined Worcester in publishing venture

Worcester, known as the "Cherokee Messenger" among the Cherokee, had worked with Boudinot since 1826 in the old Cherokee Nation. He established the new Worcester Mission in 1836. Worcester worked fervently among the Cherokee, learning the language with Boudinot as his interpreter. Together they wrote textbooks and translated several books of the Bible into Cherokee. Worcester was imprisoned in Georgia for helping the Cherokees and became famous through the U.S. Supreme Court case *Worcester* v. *Georgia,* decided in 1832, which established tribal sovereignty and protected Cherokees from Georgia laws. The decision also freed Worcester, although Georgia ignored it until Worcester was pardoned in early 1833.

After the pardon—which required him to leave Georgia—the missionary taught and preached among the Cherokee in Indian Territory, taking his printing press with him.

The most noteworthy result of Boudinot and Worcester's collaboration was the publication of the first book in what is now Oklahoma in August 1835. The title was *I Stutsi in Natsoku,* or *The Child's Book.* In 1836, the press was moved to the recently established community of Park Hill and Worcester's mission work continued. Boudinot had served as his interpreter and assistant for several years and together they issued more than 13 million printed pages.

Assassinated for role in treaty

The work continued until Boudinot's assassination on June 22, 1839, on the same day that his relatives John Ridge and Major Ridge were killed. Only Stand Watie escaped the plot. Boudinot was lured from the home he was building at Park Hill by three men who told him they wanted him to go with them to the home of Dr. Worcester for medicine. He was killed by the three as they approached the mission. No one was ever brought to justice for his murder (or for the deaths of the Ridges). It was assumed that the responsibility lay with Ross sympathizers, although not with John Ross himself.

Boudinot is buried in the Worcester Mission Cemetery at Old Park Hill, near Tahlequah, Oklahoma, the capital of the Cherokee Nation since 1839. The site is approximately 300 yards north of the spot where he died, and the cemetery is the only remaining part of the mission. At Boudinot's death, his wife, Delight, took all six children east to escape the violence in the Cherokee Nation. They were placed with relatives of Harriet Gold Boudinot. The best-known of the children was Elias Cornelius Boudinot, who studied engineering and then law, became active in politics, and was eventually elected to the Confederate Congress.

Further Reading

Boudinot, Elias, *Poor Sarah; or, The Indian Woman,* New Echota: Cherokee Nation East, United Brethren's Missionary Society, 1833.

Cherokee Cavaliers: Forty Years of Cherokee History as Told in the Correspondence of the Ridge-Watie-Boudinot Family, edited by Edward Everett Dale and Gaston Litton, Norman: University of Oklahoma Press, 1939.

Gabriel, Ralph Henry, *Elias Boudinot, Cherokee & His America,* Norman: University of Oklahoma Press, 1941.

Wilkins, Thurmond, *Cherokee Tragedy: The Story of the Ridge Family and of the Decimation of a People,* New York: Macmillan, 1970.

Joseph Brant

Mohawk tribal leader
Born 1742, near upper Ohio River
Died 1807, Grand River, Ontario

Joseph Brant adjusted from the wilderness of the Ohio frontier to the complexities of the white man's world with ease.

J oseph Brant was a Mohawk chief and officer of the British army who led Indian troops into battle during the Revolutionary War. He was born in 1742 in the forest along the upper Ohio River. His father, Tehowaghwengaraghkwin, was a Mohawk Wolf clan chief. His mother was either a full- or half-blood Indian. After his father's death, his mother married Nichaus Brant, a respected Mohawk whose family had used the English surname for several generations. Brant's family connection with Sir William Johnson, British superintendent of Indian affairs in the colony of New York, allowed him to move with ease between the world of an English gentleman and the fields and councils of Indian tribal life, respected by both groups. During and after the American Revolution he negotiated in both Canada and the United States for land rights for his people.

Transition from Indian to white society

Brant spent his childhood in the clan's long-established residence at Canajoharie near the Ohio River. This gave the young man access to both white and Indian cultures: the Indians in the town had been in contact with white settlers, yet life to the west along the Ohio River was still largely untouched by Europeans. This offered Brant freedom to learn hunting, fishing, swimming, trapping, and canoeing in preparation for his role as an adult hunter-warrior. When his half-sister Molly married Sir William Johnson—who was highly respected by the Iroquois—the English trader and ambassador took an interest in his young brother-in-law. At the age of 12, Brant was summoned to live with them at Fort Johnson in the Mohawk River Valley of upstate New York.

Brant adjusted from the wilderness of the Ohio frontier to the complexities of the white man's world with ease. At 13, he served with Johnson at the Battle of Lake George during the French and Indian Wars, in which England and France fought for

Joseph Brant

colonial land in America in the years 1689 to 1763. At 17, he was among Johnson's troops during the Niagara campaign of 1759. Two years later, Johnson sent Brant to Eleazar Wheelock's Indian Charity School in Lebanon, Connecticut, the forerunner of Dartmouth College. Again, Brant had no trouble adjusting to his new environment. While at Wheelock's school, Brant converted to Christianity and spent time translating parts of the Bible into Mohawk.

Recognized as a leader among both Indians and whites

Brant was 21 when he left school in 1763, after Molly sent word that he should return to Fort Johnson. Rumors of war were thick in the air; Pontiac, an Ottawa chief, was organizing bands to attack the British in the Great Lakes area. Brant led a company of Mohawk and Oneida volunteers, together with troops organized by Johnson and led by Andrew Montour, against Pontiac's followers. After the war, Brant did not return to school; instead, he became an advocate for the Mohawk in the land difficulties they faced. His services as an interpreter were especially valuable.

Sir William Johnson died in 1774 and his nephew was appointed as his replacement. Brant served the new superintendent of Indian affairs as secretary. Shortly afterward, he was commissioned a British colonel and led forces in raids planned to devastate the materials and food supplies to the American troops. Composed of members of the fragmented Iroquois League—the once-mighty confederacy of the Mohawk, Oneida, Onondaga, Cayuga, and Seneca tribes—as well as British soldiers and Tory compatriots (colonists who supported the British), Brant's company fought at Cherry Valley, Minisink, and the Battle of Oriskany, among others. At the end of the war he was rewarded with a land grant at Anaquaqua, along the Grand River in Ontario, Canada. He retired as a British officer on half pay. Many Mohawk and other Indians from the Iroquois League followed him to Anaquaqua. The area eventually became the Six Nations Reserve.

Brant had three wives and nine children during his lifetime. He married his first wife, Christine, at age 22. She was the daughter of an Oneida chief. They had two children, Issac and Christiana. Christine died eight years later, and Brant married her sister. Within a few years she also died, leaving him no children. His third wife, a half-blood

Indian, Catherine Croghan, bore him seven children and remained his faithful partner until his death on November 24, 1807, at Grand River. He was buried near the church he built, the first Episcopal church in Upper Canada, located at Brantford, Ontario.

Further Reading

Dockstader, Frederick J., *Great North American Indians,* New York: Van Nostrand Reinhold, 1977.

Kelsay, Isabel Thompson, *Joseph Brant, 1743-1807: Man of Two Worlds,* Syracuse, NY: Syracuse University Press, 1984.

Native North American Almanac, edited by Duane Champagne, Gale Research, 1994.

Van Every, Dale, *A Company of Heroes: The American Frontier, 1775-1783,* New York: William Morrow and Company, 1962.

Molly Brant

Mohawk tribal leader
Born 1736, Canajoharie, New York
Died 1796, Kingston, Ontario, Canada

Molly Brant could not have known the outcome of the wars she attempted to influence. She was behaving in accordance with the laws of her people, trying to carry on negotiations and an alliance with those she saw as the greatest allies to the Iroquois.

Historians consider Molly Brant the most influential Mohawk woman in the New World from 1759 to 1776. She was born in 1736 to Margaret and Peter, Canajoharie Mohawks registered as Protestant Christians in the Anglican chapel at Fort Hunter in what is today northeastern New York State. Some reports do not list the names of her parents, but simply say she was the daughter of a sachem (chieftain) and came from Canajoharie, a Mohawk village located in present-day upstate New York. Molly likely received her surname from her stepfather, a man named Brant, who was a close friend of William Johnson, an English official responsible for maintaining Indian relations in the colonies during the period before the American Revolution. Active and gregarious, Molly became the object of Johnson's attention when, in 1753, she accepted a British officer's challenge to participate in a horse riding competition between the English and the Mohawks. She later married Johnson in a Mohawk ceremony.

The power of women: Iroquois versus European societies

Great upheaval and cultural change took place among all the Iroquois tribes during the eighteenth century, especially during the second half of the century, when the colonial settlers sought independence. The Mohawks stood out among the Iroquois for their aggressive resistance to European occupation. With the loss of their land along the Mohawk River in east-central New York, there was immense pressure on the tribe to assimilate, or blend in culturally, to survive. European culture was most visibly different from Mohawk culture in terms of relations between the sexes, and this cut at the basic fabric and structure of Iroquois life. For this reason, Molly Brant's life with Johnson, a powerful British official presiding over the British Indian Department's northern district, became a living illustration of the processes of blending two cultures.

Before the arrival of the Europeans, the Mohawk were a matrilineal society, meaning that power descended through women. Relationships between the sexes were marked by a more equal distribution of power, and more balanced recognition of the contributions made by men and women to the needs of the community, than in European society. Primarily through their agricultural achievements and status as providers, Mohawk women were able to exert a greater degree of influence upon men's decisions than their European counterparts. In this way, assertion of male dominance was met with resistance by Mohawk women. By withholding food, making their opinions known at village meetings, and utilizing their appointed clan positions in choosing the village chief/sachem, women banded together to accomplish their goals in a way wholly unfamiliar to women in European culture.

Because British law did not recognize the Mohawk marriage of Johnson and Brant, she is said to have been the "common-law" wife of Johnson, and some sources call her his mistress. The wedding took place during the Seven Years War (1756-63)—a worldwide conflict among European powers. During this war the French and the English competed for Indian allies to support their claims for land in the New World, and Johnson may have married Brant to gain stronger political connections with the Indians. Certainly he needed Iroquois help in his war with France's army. He learned the Iroquoian dialects, adopted several Mohawk customs, but reportedly did not choose to live among Natives. Molly's influential

position among the Mohawk would have been vital to him.

Influenced the American Revolution

Brant had been well known and was politically active in her village before joining Johnson at either Fort Johnson or Johnson Hall, his residence located near Schenectady, on the border of Mohawk territory. From 1754 to 1755, she accompanied a delegation of elders to Philadelphia, Pennsylvania, to address Iroquois land conflicts. Relatively little is known about her life in the village during her early years. Her correspondence, written in a clear and legible script, indicates that she may have attended the English school at Canajoharie as a child.

Unlike the children of her predecessor as Johnson's partner, Catherine Weissenberg, who bore him three children, Brant's eight (some sources say nine) children received Johnson's surname. Weissenberg, a German indentured servant, was Johnson's housekeeper at Fort Johnson. Whereas Johnson regarded Weissenberg as beneath him in status, and her role in his household was minimal, Molly Brant accepted no such restrictions. She refused to do housework, leaving such chores to the servants and slaves, and in Johnson's absence is said to have controlled the affairs of the estate. There is some suggestion that in doing so, she also supervised the daily operations of the Indian Department, of which Johnson was superintendent.

Johnson Hall was elegant and considered plush by frontier standards, and Brant was highly admired among Johnson's peers as a model hostess. She was mentioned warmly in correspondence and was as generous with her own people living in the village as she was with European guests. Using Johnson's position and line of credit with merchants, she apparently made large purchases of blankets, clothing, and alcohol, which she gave away to various Iroquois people. Traditional Iroquois custom dictated that individual economic gain was to be put to the good of the community by distributing wealth during a ceremonial giveaway. The more one gave away, the more one rose in honor and prestige within the group. Brant participated in this practice with such purchases, in addition to distributing cash and providing meals. By so doing she gained increasing influence and thus became, in historian Gretchen Green's words, "the most influential Mohawk woman in the valley."

Remains an active Loyalist

After Johnson's death in 1774, Brant was turned away from his estate; she returned to Canajoharie, taking expensive clothing and various luxury items with her. There she lived primarily on credit, engaging in commerce with the villagers. Because conflicts were rising between the Loyalist, or pro-British, and patriot, or pro-revolution, colonials, Brant's influence among Indians was increasingly important to the British. Both sides attempted to rally the support of the Six Nations (Iroquois league), and patriots regarded Brant as a threat to their interests. She, unlike most Mohawk, felt strongly that the interests of her people would be best served by an alliance with the Crown. Despite her tremendous popularity and respect among her people, she was unable to sway significant numbers toward action, for most preferred not to take sides in the British-American conflict.

Brant herself took an active Loyalist stance, housing Loyalist refugees, providing weapons, and infiltrating intelligence activities where possible. During 1777 she reportedly engaged in spy activities, which were instrumental to the British in gaining military ground. As a result, American colonials and Oneida Iroquois patriots exacted revenge by driving her from her home. Angered, she fled in exile into Canada, where she fiercely resumed Loyalist activities as a liaison among the Iroquois while residing at the Niagara garrison.

Molly Brant was controversial because she was an advocate for both the British and the Iroquois, even when the interests of these groups seemed to be opposed. Brant spoke only her native tongue, styled her wardrobe after Mohawk tastes, and encouraged her offspring to do the same. She was an active dissident, remaining loyal to the preservation of her people, yet she was criticized for involving them in a dispute that ultimately cost them their lands and left them at the mercy of a hostile government. Molly Brant could not have known the outcome of the wars she attempted to influence. She was behaving in accordance with the laws of her people, trying to carry on negotiations and an alliance with those she saw as the greatest allies to the Iroquois.

The British supported her Loyalist endeavors, giving her provisions and doing what was necessary to foster her activism. As a political instrument among the Iroquois, she was unequaled. After the American Revolution, the British generously provided her with a pension, land in the area of her choosing, and an English home for her service to the Crown. In addition she received a substantial inheritance from

Johnson's estate. Retiring from political affairs, Brant finally settled in Kingston, Ontario, Canada, near three of her daughters. She died in 1796 of unknown causes.

Further Reading

Green, Gretchen, "Molly Brant, Catherine Brant, and Their Daughters: A Study in Colonial Acculturation," *Ontario History* 81, 1989, pp. 235-250.

Gundy, H. Pearson, "Molly Brant—Loyalist," *Ontario History* 14, 1953, pp. 97-108.

Native North American Almanac, edited by Duane Champagne, Detroit: Gale, 1994.

Mary Brave Bird

Lakota Sioux activist
Born 1953, Rosebud Reservation, South Dakota
Also known as Mary Crow Dog, Chitika Win
   ("Brave Woman")

The American Indian Movement "made medicine men radical activists, and made radical activists into sundancers and vision seekers.... It restored women's voices and brought them into the tribal councils."— Lakota Woman

Mary Brave Bird dictated her life story in the two books *Lakota Woman* and *Ohitika Woman* to Richard Erdoes, a photographer and illustrator who himself became involved in political activism through having taped and transcribed her story. In these two books, written 15 years apart, Brave Bird told how the American Indian Movement (AIM) gave

meaning to her life. *Lakota Woman,* written under the name Mary Crow Dog, portrays her life from her birth to 1977, and *Ohitika Woman* written under her current name of Mary Brave Bird, covers events up to 1992 and adds new details to the earlier history.

A difficult childhood

Mary Brave Bird's mother, Emily Brave Bird, had been raised in a tent in the village of He-Dog on the Rosebud Reservation in South Dakota, then taken to St. Francis Mission boarding school where she was converted to Catholicism. While she studied nursing in Pierre, South Dakota, her four children were raised by their grandparents. Robert Brave Bird trapped in the winter and farmed in the summer. He was a descendant of the legendary warrior Pakeska Maza ("Iron Shell"), who became chief of the Wablenicha ("Orphan Band") of the Brulé or Sicanju tribe of the Lakota Sioux.

Growing up on the Rosebud Reservation, Brave Bird faced poverty, racism, and brutality from an early age. Although she descended from a distinguished family, she was not taught a great deal about her heritage. Her mother would not teach her her native language because, she said, "speaking Indian would only hold you back, turn you the wrong way." She was sent to St. Francis Mission boarding school at the age of five, where she reported that nuns beat Indian students who practiced native customs or spoke their native languages. She later ran away from the school and began her teenage life drinking heavily and getting into fights.

While still a teenager, Brave Bird became involved in the protest activities of AIM, where she began to find new spirit and meaning in being Indian. In 1972, at the age of 16, she participated in the Trail of Broken Treaties march on Washington, D.C., after which protesters occupied the Bureau of Indian Affairs building. At that time, Brave Bird met Leonard Crow Dog, a Sioux medicine man who was active in AIM and taught her much about Indian traditions. They were married the following year.

Cankpe Opi ("Wounded Knee")

In February 1973 in Custer, South Dakota, Sarah Bad Heart Bull protested the release of the murderer of her son, Wesley Bad Heart Bull, and requested AIM's help at the Custer courthouse. When AIM protesters in Custer learned that the police had used violence on Bad Heart Bull's mother, they rioted. The riot was followed by a meeting attended by medicine men Frank Fools Crow, Wallace Black Elk, Henry Crow Dog, and Pete Catches, all there to consider how to protest this incident. At the time the Pine Ridge Reservation was calling for AIM to help protest the corrupt rule of Richard Wilson, the elected chairman of the reservation. Two elders suggested that they take a stand at Wounded Knee, where the U.S. cavalry had massacred hundreds of Sioux in 1890.

On February 27, under AIM leadership, a group of Native Americans, Brave Bird and Crow Dog among them, did take a stand at Wounded Knee. They dug trenches, put up cinderblock walls, and became warriors. The siege lasted 71 days. On March 12, surrounded by armored cars spewing bursts of gunfire, a declaration was drafted for the independent Oglala Nation proclaiming its sovereignty. Two Native Americans were

Mary Brave Bird at demonstration in 1970s; photo by Richard Erdoes

killed, and many were wounded. Leonard Crow Dog treated the injured survivors with medicinal herbs; he led sunrise prayers and brought back the Ghost Dance for which his ancestors had been slaughtered in 1890. For four days, and for the first time in 80 years, on sacred ground, they circled a cedar tree, dancing in the snow.

On April 11, Mary Brave Bird's baby was born. She named him after Pedro Bissonette, a man who was killed by tribal police for having founded the Oglala Sioux Civil Rights Organization (OSCRO). The terrorist reprisals by Wilson's "goons" (Guardians of

Mary Brave Bird, 1994; photo by Richard Erdoes

the Oglala Nation) resulted in the deaths of 250 people, many of them children, on the reservation. Among those murdered was Delphine, Leonard Crow Dog's sister, who was beaten to death.

Reclaiming Indian values

The American Indian Movement (AIM) played a crucial role in Brave Bird's life. Without the organization, she lived in poverty and despair, coping with alcoholism, domestic violence, joblessness, and hopelessness. Within the movement, she felt a sense of purpose. The alliance that AIM members made with the traditionalists restored for them their own ancient ways.

Meanwhile, the tribal elders were given back their traditional roles as communicators of their culture. Brave Bird, sober, working for the cause, was heroic. She learned from her work in the movement that pan-tribal (involving Native people from all tribal lines) unity can give spiritual power to even those who are treated as the dregs of society. She described the movement's ability to strengthen Native communities in her book *Lakota Woman,* which became a national best-seller, won a movie contract, and earned the American Book Award for best nonfiction.

Both *Lakota Woman* and *Ohitika Woman* retell the ancient myths and explain the meanings of many Native American ceremonies. As Brave Bird wrote, "AIM made medicine men radical activists, and made radical activists into sundancers and vision seekers.... It restored women's voices and brought them into the tribal councils." But while *Lakota Woman* is a breathless first-hand account of AIM's early demonstrations from the perspective of a teenager who had been involved in those heady events, *Ohitika Woman* presents them from the viewpoint of a mature woman, adding needed historical background.

Marriage to a shaman

Brave Bird's life did not necessarily become smpler with her new outlook, however. Even the large gap between their ages—Mary was 17 and Leonard was 31 when they married in 1973—was less of a problem than their cultural differences. Leonard had to teach Mary the ceremonies, the use of healing plants, and reconcile her to the role of a medicine man's wife. This involved feeding multitudes of uninvited guests at the feasts following every service. It also meant never getting enough rest; as tribal counselor, Leonard Crow Dog was always on call, traveling constantly, and taking his family along when he was summoned. Since he did not charge for healing, and gave everything away, there was never enough money to feed the family. Brave Bird raised seven children. In addition to Richard, Ina, and Bernadette from Leonard's first marriage, she had four more with him: Pedro, Anwah, June Bug, and Jennifer Louise.

On September 5, 1975, with helicopters whirring overhead, 180 agents broke into Crow Dog's home and took him away in handcuffs. After three trials, he was sentenced to 23 years in prison for his political activities. Brave Bird addressed rallies to raise funds, but it took contributions of $200,000 from friends, Amnesty International, and the World Council of Churches to get him out of prison. Famed activist attorney William Kunstler argued on his behalf. At Lewisburg Penitentiary Crow Dog's cell was so small that he could not stand upright in it, while authorities at Leavenworth tried to disorient him by keeping a neon light glaring 24 hours a day. Filmmakers Mike Cuesta and David Baxter made a documentary about his imprisonment, and as a result a number of celebrities rallied to his support. When he returned to Rosebud, the entire tribe welcomed him with honoring songs.

After many separations and reconciliations Brave Bird and Crow Dog divorced. Brave Bird married Rudi Olguin, a descendent of Zapotecs, Mexican Indians, on August 24, 1991, in Santa Fe, New Mexico. Together they had a daughter, Summer Rose.

In her books Brave Bird tells what it means to be a Sioux woman—caught between the forces of tradition and the feminist movement, often subject to sexual harassment and degradation. In *Ohitika Woman,* she speaks about her recurring problems with alcohol abuse, and the healing she has found in the Native American Church. Still, like many other feminists who are also Native Americans, she tends to place the economic, political, and legal struggles of Indian peoples before the pursuit of women's rights.

Further Reading

Crow Dog, Mary, and Richard Erdoes, *Lakota Woman,* New York: Grove Weidenfeld, 1990.

Brave Bird, Mary, and Richard Erdoes, *Ohitika Woman,* New York: Grove Press, 1993.

Ben Nighthorse Campbell

Northern Cheyenne politician, business executive, and athlete
Born April 13, 1933, Auburn, California

"It did seem a fiercely weird and capricious act, the sort of thing a ponytailed, Harley-riding, jewelry-designing Colorado Native American rancher-politician might do in a fit of pique."—Joe Klein, Newsweek

I n the mid-1990s Senator Ben Nighthorse Campbell was the only Native American serving in the United States legis-

Ben Nighthorse Campbell

lature. Before entering politics he was an athlete, educator, jewelry designer, and rancher. He was born in Auburn, California, in 1933 to Mary Vierra, a Portuguese immigrant, and Albert Campbell, who was part Apache, Pueblo, and Northern Cheyenne. Senator Campbell and his wife, the former Linda Price, have two grown children, Colin and Shanan.

Campbell dropped out of high school after his junior year, having earned a written observation from a teacher that he was "born 100 yrs. too late!" He later obtained a General Education Degree and an undergraduate degree from San Jose State in 1957. Because of his special interest in judo, a martial art, he also studied at Meiji University in Tokyo, Japan, in 1960. From 1951 to 1953 he served in the U.S. Air Force, including a period as a military policeman in Korea.

Campbell first moved to Colorado in 1969. He served two terms in the Colorado state legislature, from 1982 to 1986, before being elected to the U.S. Congress in 1987.

Campbell attributes much of his success outside of the political arena to the discipline he acquired as a determined judo participant, at a time when it was not a standard part of the American sports scene. During his association with the sport, he earned All-American status, a gold medal at the 1963 Pan-American games, and the titles of captain of the U.S. Olympic team in Tokyo in 1964 and coach of the U.S. International Team. The three-time U.S. champion is also the author of a book, *Championship Judo: Drill Training.*

Native American identity

Since the 1960s, Campbell's identity as a Native American has been a crucial part of his life. Before that his search for his "roots" was obstructed by limited records and the attitude of his father, who "insisted we keep our Indian background a secret," Campbell told Herman J. Viola, the author of his biography, *An American Warrior: Ben Nighthorse Campbell.* The scattered evidence suggests that Campbell's father's family was linked to several tribes, but at the age of ten he ran away to live with the Black Horse family on the Northern Cheyenne Reservation in Montana. The ancestors of the Black Horse family had been directly involved in the famous Battle of Little Bighorn in 1876, in which several bands of Sioux, united in their efforts to protect the sacred Black Hills from gold miners, massacred an army unit led by Lieutenant Colonel George Armstrong Custer in one of the worst defeats suffered by the U.S. Army forces in their battles against Indian nations. Campbell's great-grandmother, meanwhile, was one of the Indians attacked in the Sand Creek Massacre in Colorado in 1864, in which Colonel John Chivington led a force from Colorado in a brutal and unprovoked attack on a Southern Cheyenne and Arapaho camp, killing an estimated 500 men, women, and children. Campbell visited the Northern Cheyenne Reservation regularly starting in 1968 and was enrolled in 1980. He was later inducted into the Council of 44 Chiefs of the Northern Cheyenne Tribe.

Before entering politics, Campbell achieved success as a jewelry designer. His unique all-metal patterns represented an evolution in Native American design and resulted in numerous awards, as well as an income of about $150,000 per year. Real financial independence occurred after he was featured in a 1979 issue of *Arizona Highways*.

In addition to the creation of new designs, Campbell dedicated part of his time to the training of Indian students at Folsom Penitentiary in California and at Fort Lewis College in Colorado. Later, as a member of Congress he updated the 1936 Indian Arts and Crafts Act, which was established to prevent the manufacture and sale of counterfeit Indian arts and crafts. Although the initial intent of the act was clear, there had never been any prosecution for the sale of fake Indian art. The new law required that the artists be able to document their background. In Campbell's words, "If an artist is proud of advertising that he is a specific kind of Indian, then he should have no problem tracing his background, even if he is not enrolled."

Entered the political arena

Campbell's movement into Colorado politics was quite accidental. When an airplane flight was delayed because of bad weather conditions, Campbell decided to sit in on a local political meeting. As a result, he was drafted to be the Democratic candidate for the state legislature.

At the time, he had never been to the state capitol building and his political stance was not very well defined, although he considered himself a social Democrat and a fiscal conservative. Campbell was elected by a substantial margin. Although he was not responsible for any major legislation during his first year, he worked with the Colorado Historical Society in promoting an improved marker at the 1864 Sand Creek Massacre site, where some of his Cheyenne ancestors had lost their lives. His colleagues also voted him one of the ten best legislators in the state.

Goes to Washington

Although Campbell intended to retire from politics, he was attracted by a Democratic opening for the eighth-largest congressional district in the United States. He beat the incumbent by only a four percent margin. The last Native American congressperson had been Ben Reifel of South Dakota, who left office in 1970. During the first term Campbell's record earned the praise of Colorado newspapers. He was reelected with 78 percent of the vote, and a third term followed. As a member of the House he served on the committees on Agriculture, the Interior, and Insular Affairs, the last of which had a subcommittee on Indian affairs.

When Campbell was elected as one of Colorado's representatives to the national government, he was unavoidably cast in the role of lone Indian representative. In that role he was involved in four highly symbolic events. First, along with Senator Daniel K. Inouye of Hawaii, he promoted the Museum of the American Indian on the Mall in Washington, D.C. Second, he was the spokesperson for the 51 Native American delegates at the 1988 Democratic Convention. Third, in December 1991 he was responsible for legislation changing the name of the Custer National Battlefield Monument to the Little Bighorn National Battle Field Monument. Finally, on New Year's Day of 1992 he served as co-grand marshall of the Tournament of Roses parade with Cristobal Colon, a twentieth-generation descendant of Christopher Columbus. Campbell rode his horse Black Warbonnet in full regalia ahead of the vehicle carrying the foreign visitor.

The unexpected decision of Senator Tim Wirth not to seek reelection gave Campbell the opportunity to run for the U.S. Senate in 1992. He won by nearly a 10 percent margin. His five committee memberships include Energy and Natural Resources, Banking, Housing, and Urban Affairs, Democratic Policy, Veterans Affairs, and Indian Affairs. Upon his election, he issued a statement that included the following assurance: "I have always had a special sensitivity to Indian issues, and that will continue in the Senate." In January 1993 Campbell, joined by other Native American riders, was a significant part of the Inaugural Parade following the election of President Bill Clinton.

"A very *individual* individual"

In the winter of 1995 Campbell created a stir in Washington when he announced that he was leaving the Democrats for the Republican Party. He was opposed to the Clinton administration's land-use policies, and disagreed with the Democratic stands on balanced budgets, term limits, and capital-gains-tax reduction. Joe Klein commented about Campbell's defection in *Newsweek:* "It *did* seem a fiercely weird and capricious act, the sort of thing a ponytailed, Harley-riding, jewelry-designing Colorado Native American rancher-politician might do in a fit of pique." Klein suggested that Campbell represents a growing part of the population that is dissatisfied with both parties and may be striking out after something new in politics. He cited one of Campbell's colleagues, who described Campbell as "a very *individual* individual."

Further Reading

Brock, Tom, "Senator Ben Nighthorse Campbell: Interview," *Boulder Magazine,* summer 1994, pp. 6-10.

"Campbell Wins Senate Seat," *Medium Rare: A Publication of the Native American Journalists Association,* fall 1992, p. 1.

Klein, Joe, "How the West Was Lost: Why Ben Nighthorse Campbell's Defection Signals a Democratic Disaster," *Newsweek,* March 20, 1995, p. 31.

Viola, Herman J., *An American Warrior: Ben Nighthorse Campbell,* Orion Books, 1993.

Captain Jack

Modoc tribal leader
Born c. 1837, northern California
Died October 3, 1873, California

Captain Jack made a final plea for a reservation to be established for his people at Hot Creek in northern California. According to accounts of what followed, the inevitable failure of his plea made him decide in favor of violence.

Kintpuash, son of a Modoc chief, was commonly known as Captain Jack because he often wore a blue military jacket with brass buttons. A major figure in the Modoc War of 1872 to 1873—which arose out of the unsuitable conditions on the Klamath Reservation—Captain Jack led a band of about 50 Modoc warriors, women, and children who were resisting forced removal by U.S. troops from their former ancestral lands. They were able to hold off the army for nearly a year. He was captured and executed in 1873 for fatally shooting General Edward Canby during negotiations. His death marked the end of a story of discrimination and infighting.

Little is known about Captain Jack's life prior to the age of 25. He was born along the lower Lost River, near the California-Oregon border, in Wa'chamshwash village, around 1837. The Modocs lived relatively peacefully in the territory surrounding Clear Lake, Tule Lake, and the Lost River. By the 1850s, however, pressure for Indian land, aggravated by the 1848 California Gold Rush, led to conflicts. In the early 1850s, a wagon train of immigrants on their way to the West Coast was attacked by Indians. Because the horses from the train turned up in the possession of the Modocs, the tribe was blamed for the raid.

A reprisal party led by a miner, Jim Crosby, did not find the responsible parties, who were members of the Pit River tribe, and took out their frustrations on the Modocs instead. The Modocs, including Captain Jack's father, responded with violence. In 1856 the Modocs ambushed another wagon train at a place called Wagakanna, which the white survivors later labeled "Bloody Point." In response to the massacre, the well-known mountain man and Indian fighter Ben Wright organized a vigilante group specifically to stalk and kill Indians. In an attempt to preserve the peace, 45 of the Modoc leaders were invited to a conference. There they were ambushed by Wright and his men. Wright himself shot Captain Jack's father with a revolver.

Life at the Klamath Reservation

Captain Jack is said to have replaced his father as chief of the clan, but it was actually his uncle, Old Schonchin, who acted as chief when he insisted that the Modocs abide by the Treaty of 1864. This treaty established a reservation at Klamath Lake, across the California-Oregon boundary. All the Modoc, Klamath, and Pit River Indians were to be removed to this tract of land. The reservation, however, was located on former Klamath territory and included none of the Modocs' former hunting grounds. The Kla-

Captain Jack

math people soon took advantage of their superior status, gaining control of power and resources.

The treatment of the Modoc by the Klamath, together with the rules of the reservation, caused a rift among the Modoc. Captain Jack renounced the Treaty of 1864 and left the reservation in 1865. Some of the Modoc left with him, and the band returned to their hunting area along the Lost River. Various groups of Indian agents and military officers visited Captain Jack, trying unsuccessfully to persuade him to return to the reservation. In December 1869, a delegation organized by Alfred B. Meacham, the newly appointed Indian superintendent, finally convinced him. Captain Jack took with him to this meeting, in addition to soldiers, Captain O. C. Knapp and Ivan Applegate, who

served as agents for the reservation. Also included were Old Schonchin, and Frank Riddle and his Modoc wife, Tobey (later known as Winema), to serve as interpreters.

The Klamath and Modoc Indians lived peacefully together on the reservation for several weeks of the new year, but conflicts soon arose again. The agent at the reservation, Knapp, refused to become involved, telling the Modocs to work out the problems themselves. In April 1870, Captain Jack called a meeting of all Modocs. They made plans to leave the reservation and, at the end of April, Captain Jack and 371 Modocs returned to Lost River. The rest of the tribe, led by Schonchin, remained on the reservation, although they moved away from the Klamath and settled in Yainax.

Establishment at Lost River

The Modoc presence in northern California caused unrest within the white population. Settlers in the area around the Tule Lake basin began to demand the removal of the Modoc. In 1870, Captain Jack made a formal request for a Modoc reservation on the Lost River. The Indian agent Meacham recommended that the request be granted, but the settlers were enraged. In response, General Edward Canby, a distinguished Civil War veteran with experience in Indian battles, was dispatched to the area. He was placed in charge of a small troop and instructed to keep Captain Jack under control.

The settlers were growing impatient with Meacham's lack of action, but neither he nor Canby would make a move until a decision was reached about a reservation site. Finally, in 1872 the Interior Department replaced Meacham as Indian superintendent with T.

B. Odeneal, who, historians agree, knew little about the events and people behind the conflict.

The final act of the drama began when Jack's niece fell ill. Curly Headed Doctor, the group's shaman or tribal doctor, was absent from the encampment at the time. The nearest healer was the shaman from Klamath. He was sent for and took his payment in advance, but the girl died just the same. Grieved by the unnecessary death and in accordance with tribal custom, Captain Jack killed the shaman for his inefficiency.

The Klamath informed the Indian agent of the killing, and a warrant was issued for Captain Jack's arrest. After a series of unsuccessful conferences, Odeneal made a recommendation to the commissioner of Indian affairs on June 17. His solution was to arrest Captain Jack and hold him in custody until he accepted Schonchin's leadership and returned to the reservation at Yainax. It was agreed to take action in September so additional forces could be dispatched if Captain Jack's band resisted.

Captain Jack may have suspected the military's true intentions. In September 1872, he resisted all their attempts to meet with him. The order was finally given, at the end of November, to arrest him, Black Jim, and Scarfaced Charley by the next morning, forcibly if necessary. Troops left Fort Klamath for Captain Jack's stronghold, beginning the first battle of the Modoc War. Captain Jack and 50 of his warriors fought the troops while around 175 women and children fled across the lake to the Lava Beds. The volcanic rock formations absorbed the bullets and offered cover. Few Indians were killed or wounded, compared to casualties on the American side. The fighting Modocs held out against superior numbers, including approximately 400 reinforcements who arrived in January 1873.

At the end of January, northern California was hit by blizzard. The snow immobilized supply trains as well as the advance of additional troops. Captain Jack used the snowstorm as cover in sending a messenger to the military camp. He wanted to speak with John Fairchild, a rancher who was well liked and trusted by both settlers and Indians, about a settlement. Word was sent that Fairchild would visit when weather permitted. Captain Jack may have wanted peace, but his advisers wanted land. They convinced him to continue with the war, holding out with the weather, which was working to their advantage in demoralizing the opposing troops.

Though Fairchild made several trips to and from the stronghold, no agreements were reached. Fighting continued on and off until March, when Captain Jack agreed to meet with the whites in council. By this time Lost River had officially been rejected as a reservation site. Entering the negotiations assuming that the other side wanted a compromise, Captain Jack suggested two other sites as possible reservations for the Modocs. General Canby promptly refused. It soon became clear that the Modocs would be offered nothing except terms for surrender.

Planning "final" negotiations

At this point Captain Jack called a council among his own people in the Lava Beds. Schonchin John and Black Jim, two tribesmen who were wanted by the authorities for killing soldiers, challenged Jack's leadership. They insisted he prove his commitment to the Modoc cause by killing the white representatives, placing him in a difficult position. For himself he wanted peace, but as a leader he was obliged to fulfill his people's need for land of their own. Captain Jack spent the following two days alone in a cave, struggling with this decision. A mutual friend warned Winema (Tobey Riddle) that the negotiators would be murdered. When she, in turn, tried to warn Canby and the other representatives, they did not believe her.

The council met again on April 11, 1873. Captain Jack, Schonchin John, Boston Charley, Bogus Charley, Black Jim, and Hooker Jim met with Captain Meacham and General Canby, and the Reverend Mr. Thomas. Frank Riddle and his wife, Winema, served as interpreters. Captain Jack made a final plea for a reservation to be established for his people at Hot Creek in northern California. According to accounts of what followed, the inevitable failure of his plea made him decide in favor of violence. He shouted the Modoc phrase *Ut-wih-kutt*" ("Let's do it") and killed General Canby with a revolver he had hidden.

Captain Jack knew the fate of the Modocs was sealed. Whether judged by their fellow Indians or by a jury of white men, they had committed an unforgivable act by striking down an unarmed man during negotiations. Jack later said that after killing Canby, he returned to the Lava Beds thinking he would die in the fighting that followed. The Modoc representatives fled back to the Lava Beds and fighting resumed on April 14.

Capture and trial

By May the Modoc resistance had begun to crumble. Quarrels among the Indian lead-ers caused the group to fragment and surrender piecemeal. Hooker Jim even offered to turn Captain Jack over to the U.S. soldiers in return for his life and liberty. Captain Jack turned in his gun in late May, accompanied by Schonchin John, Black Jim, and Boston Charley. His trial began on July 5 at Fort Klamath. Steamboat Frank, Hooker Jim, and Bogus Charley—who had convinced Captain Jack to kill the negotiators—were also present at the trial but not in custody. The four men were hung on October 3, 1873. Captain Jack had been asked to name his successor, but refused. The entire Modoc band from Lost River was forced to witness the execution. All the soldiers from Fort Klamath were also required to attend.

After the bodies were buried, Captain Jack's was exhumed and taken by freight train to Yreka. Some reports claim his body was embalmed and then sent to Washington, D.C. Others suggest it was decapitated and his head then used in carnival side shows. The heads of both Captain Jack and Old Schonchin, however, wound up at the Smithsonian Institution. In the 1970s it was discovered that his skull was part of the museum's physical anthropology collection, and the anger aroused by this spurred legislation to return Native American remains to their tribes of origin.

After Captain Jack's death, it was clear that the Modocs had gained no ground for their efforts. The cost of the Modoc War was enormous compared to its results. The tribe requested a reserve of land with a value of approximately $20,000, according to most sources. Meanwhile the government spent only $500,000 and lost fewer than a hundred men, and gained control of a huge parcel of land as a result. The remaining Modocs were escorted to a reservation on Shawnee land in the Indian Territory. They arrived at their destination, Seneca Springs on the Quapaw Agency, almost one year after the war began.

Further Reading

Britt, Albert, *Great Indian Chiefs,* Books for Libraries Press, 1938.

Dockstader, Frederick J., *Great North American Indians,* New York: Van Nostrand Reinhold, 1991.

Murray, Keith A., *The Modocs and Their War,* Norman: University of Oklahoma Press, 1959.

Native North American Almanac, edited by Duane Champagne, Detroit: Gale, 1994.

Harold Cardinal

Cree tribal leader
Born January 27, 1945, Cree Reserve, Alberta, Canada

Harold Cardinal's activism helped Natives resist the Canadian government's termination policies, which attempted to phase out treaty obligations.

Harold Cardinal, a charismatic Cree tribal leader and author, presided over the Indian Association of Alberta, Canada, as a young man in the 1970s. His 1969 book, *The Unjust Society: The Tragedy of Canada's Indians,* had a powerful effect on public opinion about the rights of indigenous people. As a politician and a writer, Cardinal has effectively fought against the Canadian government's attempts to take away the rights to land and self-government granted by treaty to Canada's First Nations.

Early background

Cardinal was born on January 27, 1945, one of 18 children. He grew up on the Cree Reserve on Sucker Creek in Alberta, Canada. In 1965, he went east to Ontario to enroll at Saint Patrick's College, where he studied sociology for two years. In 1967, he left the academic world for politics, becoming associate secretary for Indian affairs for the Canadian Union of Students. By 1968, he had been elected president of the Canadian Indian Youth Council.

Cardinal proved himself to be such a dynamic leader that by the time he was 23 he had been elected president of the Indian Association of Alberta; he was the youngest president ever elected. Under his administration, many programs to affirm Indian culture were initiated. He would serve nine terms in office. He became a board member of the National Indian Brotherhood in 1968.

In 1970, he helped to draft *Citizens Plus,* which became known as "The Red Paper." It was the result of many months of consultation by Cardinal and his staff with the 42 bands of Indians in Alberta. Cardinal's *Citizens Plus* presented to the Canadian government the official position of these western reserves.

In 1969, Cardinal published *The Unjust Society: The Tragedy of Canada's Indians* in response to a policy proposed by the Canadian government in 1966, which Cardinal called "a thinly disguised program of exter-

Harold Cardinal

granted to Indians in treaties. The White Paper dismissed aboriginal land claims, saying that they were too "general and undefined" to be upheld. Cardinal opposed the claim that Indian organizations weren't developed enough to manage their own affairs and made powerful arguments for self-determination. *Unjust Society* quickly became a Canadian best-seller.

The Cree, for whom Cardinal spoke, are the most populous indigenous (native) group in Canada, extending from Alberta in the west to Quebec in the east and having more than 60,000 registered members, and countless others who have not publicly identified themselves. Divided into three major groups according to their territory are the Plains Cree, the Woods Cree, and the Swampy Cree. They all desire self-government and economic development. Cardinal discussed these ideas in his 1977 book *The Rebirth of Canada's Indians*.

Life in public service

In 1977, Cardinal left provincial Native politics to become a regional director general, an official Canadian government position. He was the first Indian to receive such an appointment in Alberta and helped bring about a number of innovative reforms during his seven-month term. At that time he wrote his book *The Rebirth of Canada's Indians*. Then, for several years, he served as consultant to Indian bands in northern Alberta. In 1982, he was elected the chief of the Sucker Creek band; in 1983, the Assembly of First Nations appointed him vice chief for the prairie region. In 1992 Cardinal entered the University of Saskatchewan to study law.

mination through assimilation"—in other words, an attempt to wipe out Indian culture by forcing Natives to blend into white culture. *Unjust Society* specifically denounced the *Statement of the Government of Canada on Indian Policy* (the White Paper), the Canadian government's 1969 policy statement that proposed legislation to end all legal and constitutional distinctions relating to Indians, thus ending many of the rights

Cardinal's activism helped Natives resist the Canadian government's termination policies, which attempted to phase out treaty obligations. Had Indians on reserves become subject to provincial laws and taxes, their already depressed economic circumstances would have become much worse. Emboldened by new assertiveness, Canadian Indians began asking for settlement of land claims for territories that had never been formally ceded. These demands led to more government money and better negotiating terms for indigenous peoples. Cardinal's work was instrumental in finally giving the Cree a public voice.

Further Reading

Cardinal, Harold, *The Unjust Society: The Tragedy of Canada's Indians,* Alberta: New Press Publishers, 1969.

Cardinal, Harold, *The Rebirth of Canada's Indians,* Toronto: New Press Publishers, 1977.

Josephy, Alvin, Jr., *The Indian Heritage of America,* Boston: Houghton Mifflin, 1991.

Mawhiney, Anne-Marie, *Towards Aboriginal Self-Government,* New York: Garland Publishing, 1994.

Surtees, Robert J., "Canadian Indian Policies," in *Handbook of North American Indians,* Volume 4, Washington, DC: Smithsonian Institution, 1988.

Symington, Fraser, *The Canadian Indian,* [Toronto], 1969.

Tantoo Cardinal

Métis actress
Born 1950, Anzac, Alberta

"So I come from two worlds in a sense. But I feel a responsibility to the Indian world."

One of North America's most widely recognized Native actresses, Tantoo Cardinal has appeared in numerous plays, television programs, and films, including the American movie *Dances with Wolves* and the Canadian picture *Black Robe.* She has received several awards for her acting and others for her activity within the Native community. According to Cardinal, "With acting I have found a way to do my own part to tell my people's story."

Cardinal was born in 1950 in Anzac, Alberta, a rural town 400 kilometers (about 250 miles) north of Edmonton and 40 kilometers south of Fort McMurray. She was the youngest child of a Cree woman and a white man, making Cardinal a Métis—a French term meaning one of mixed blood. Her father abandoned the family six weeks after Tantoo was born, just before his wedding date with her mother. When Cardinal was six months old, she and her siblings were sent to live with her maternal Cree grandmother, who had also named her; Tantoo was taken from the name of a mosquito repellent. It was her grandmother who taught Cardinal the Cree language and way of life. Regarding her upbringing, Cardinal explained, "I am an Indian woman and I was raised by my Cree grandmother; and then

Tantoo Cardinal

I'm a half breed woman, as I was also influenced in the early years by my English grandfather. So I come from two worlds in a sense. But I feel a responsibility to the Indian world."

Begins acting career with no training

In 1966 Cardinal attended high school in Edmonton, Alberta, and boarded with a Mennonite (a Protestant sect whose faith is based strictly on the Bible) couple and their son, Fred Martin, who was then a university student and a Native rights activist. Shortly after her high school graduation in 1968, Cardinal and Martin were married. While still in high school, she had joined United Native Youth, and in 1971, she became pres-

ident of the group. That same year, without any formal theatrical education or training, she began her professional acting career with a small role in a Canadian Broadcasting Company (CBC) dramatized documentary entitled *Father Lacombe,* a film about a nineteenth-century Alberta priest. Recalling the incident, Cardinal asserted, "Right away I knew this is the way to get ideas into people's hearts and minds." In 1973 she and Martin had a son, Cheyenne. They were divorced in 1976.

Cardinal became increasingly active in theater; in 1979 she earned a starring role in her first feature film, *Marie-Anne.* This led to her 1982 title role in the Saskatoon, Saskatchewan, production of the play *Jessica,* a psychological drama about a Canadian woman of mixed blood, written by the actress-playwright Linda Griffith. In 1986 Cardinal again played the role of Jessica in a Toronto production; the drama won the city's best new play award and was selected by the Quebec International Theater Festival as the top play of the season. Reviewers raved over Cardinal's performance, admiring her natural instinct and realism. As Griffith said of the actress in an interview in *Maclean's* magazine, "There's a relentless vigilance to her. And she has this incredible sense of grounding."

In the critically acclaimed 1986 CBC movie *Loyalties,* directed and coproduced by Edmonton's Anne Wheeler, Cardinal played the role of Roseanne, a single woman whose daughter is raped by a doctor. For her stirring performance, Cardinal was nominated for the prestigious Canadian film award, the Genie, and won the American Indian Film Festival's best actress award.

During that time, Cardinal met the actor Beaver Richards, an American Indian from South Dakota who also had a role in the film. In 1985 the couple had a son, Clifford. Only two weeks after the birth of Clifford, Cardinal landed the leading role in *The Young Poundmaker,* a play by Native writer Ernie Carefoot and performed in Saskatoon.

Dances with Wolves

In 1988 Cardinal married an American, actor John Lawlor, and moved to Los Angeles with their new-born daughter Riel, named after **Louis Riel** (see entry), the famous nineteenth-century Métis leader. Two years later, Cardinal had her first supporting role in a major U.S. film. She played Black Shawl, the headstrong wife of Kicking Bird (the Lakota medicine man played by **Graham Greene**), in the Academy Award-winning movie *Dances with Wolves,* directed by Kevin Costner. Later that year, Cardinal won a Sterling Award for her portrayal of Kookom in the theater production *All My Relations.*

In 1991 Cardinal hosted *As Long as the Rivers Flow,* a public television series of five one-hour programs centering on the Canadian First People's movement for self-government. Also in 1991, she played the supporting role of an Algonquian woman in the award-winning Canadian film *Black Robe.* Directed by Bruce Beresford, the film tells the story of a French missionary's quest to convert Native people to Christianity.

In addition to her film work, Cardinal has made guest appearances in numerous television shows; she played the role of a Native band chief in the 1992 CBC television series *Street Legal* and also appeared on *Gunsmoke, The Lightening Incident, The Campbells,* and *Wonderworks.* In 1993 she won a First Americans in the Arts Totem Award for her portrayal of the character Katerina in *Widows.* Cardinal worked with the actor Lou Diamond Phillips in the movie *Sioux City* and played the title role in writer-director Sam Shepard's *Silent Tongue,* along with River Phoenix, Alan Bates, and Richard Harris. Cardinal received the San Francisco American Indian Film Festival's best actress award in 1993 for her performance as Bangor in *Where the Rivers Flow North.* She reached a huge audience in 1993 with her leading role in *Legends of the Fall,* costarring Anthony Hopkins, Brad Pitt, and Aidan Quinn.

Cardinal is very particular about the types of roles she plays. She is especially concerned with realism and has convinced several directors to change the content of their projects to portray Native Americans more accurately. For her contributions to the Native American artistic community, Cardinal was awarded the Eagle Spirit Award in 1990.

Further Reading

Biography of Tantoo Cardinal, Toronto: The Talent Group, 1994.

Maclean's, October 20, 1986, pp. 63-64; December 30, 1991, p. 42.

Native North American Almanac, edited by Duane Champagne, Detroit: Gale, 1994.

Cochise

Chiricahua Apache tribal leader
Born 1812 or 1823, Arizona Territory
Died June 7 or 8, c. 1874

While their forces only represented 500, Cochise and his father-in-law were briefly able to hold 3,000 troops at bay.

A chief and a brilliant military strategist, Cochise was perhaps the most influential Apache in the battle to retain Native land. He is remembered as a fierce and cunning enemy of both the U.S. and Mexican governments. Not much is known about Cochise's personal life and history. Historians disagree about the exact date and place of his birth and death. But the history of the Apaches is the story of more than 300 years of resisting Spain's northward expansion, and history will always know Cochise for his place within that resistance.

Cochise's name means "hardwood." He was a member of the Chiricahua, one of many factions of the Apache tribe. It is assumed that Cochise—like other youths of his tribe—grew up affected by the constant traditional tribal fighting between groups in his region and those in northern Mexico. It is likely that there was a bounty on his head among other groups, making it extremely dangerous for him to be caught by traditional enemies of his tribe. Hostilities among the Chiricahua Apaches and Native Mexican groups reportedly took the life of his father.

Cochise was relatively unknown to outsiders as a tribal leader until 1861, when he was brought to the attention of U.S. military personnel. In February of that year, a report came into the Arizona garrison at Fort Buchanan from a rancher. The rancher complained of an Apache raid, reporting not only cattle theft but also the abduction of his son. The child became known as Mickey Free, who later joined the army and became a scout.

George Bascom, a garrison lieutenant, organized a posse of 50 men in response to the rancher's complaint, leading them to Apache Pass, located along the heart of Chiricahua Apache country. The Southern Overland (Butterfield) Trail brought them to their final destination, a mail station from which Bascom could send word to Cochise—through a scout—requesting a meeting. As the story goes, Cochise agreed and appeared with his family members (including his youngest son Naiche) and a truce flag showing his peaceful intent. The lieutenant accused Cochise of the raid and placed him under arrest.

In February 1861 Bascom and Cochise first met in Bascom's tent. Bascom had just arrived from West Point Academy and was generally considered young and inexperienced. He seemed to believe firmly that Cochise had led his followers to abduct the child. Cochise, as spokesperson for his group, claimed complete innocence of the abduction. When Bascom either arrested or threatened Cochise with arrest if he did not immediately produce the boy, Cochise and his group were forced to flee and Cochise cut his way out of the tent. One member of Cochise's group was killed in the attempted escape, the other four members were taken prisoner, and Cochise, who was wounded, was the only one who

Cochise's Wrath, a painting by William Sampson

escaped. The Apache Wars are considered to have begun with this incident, known historically as the Bascom Affair.

Upon returning to his camp, Cochise garnered active support in his attempts to avenge the capture of his companions. Among those who joined him was his father-in-law Mangas Coloradas, from whom he received early leadership training, and with whom he was very close. In addition, his followers included members of the White Mountain (Coyotero) Apache tribe.

The Civil and Apache Wars

During this time, events in the eastern United States were leading up to the Civil War. Cochise had no way of understanding what factors outside of his immediate world would affect his situation. He spoke no English, and the officials he met probably had no facility with his dialect. Communication depended upon the skills and integrity of an interpreter.

Warfare was heavy in the Southwest as frontiersmen advanced west. Since the

Spanish had settled there with cattle, sheep, and horse, the Navajo had partially based their economy on raiding (stealing the stock from the Spanish). The Apaches had followed the Navajo in raiding, and it came to be a crucial means of the group's survival. Some sources blame Apache raids for the destruction that rocked Arizona and pushed Mexicans and Anglo-Americans from the state. Apache raids were also held responsible for the disruption of communications between the East and West Coasts.

Conflicting interests kept the region in turmoil, but many people considered the Apaches the source of much of the conflict. After the Bascom Affair, the government decided to send troops to the area to ease tensions. During the early years of the American Civil War, however, there was a shortage of men available for military duty. Western recruits were being sent to do battle in the East. As an alternative, General James H. Carleton arrived, leading 3,000 volunteers from California into the area. In response, Cochise and his father-in-law, a highly respected leader in his own right, devised a trap for the new soldiers. While their forces only represented 500, they were able to hold Carleton and his troops at bay with temporary fortifications known as breastworks until Carleton introduced short cannons (howitzers) onto the battlefield at Apache Pass. With Mangas wounded, Cochise retreated.

Father-in-law lost in battle

One year after Carleton descended upon Cochise and his followers with 3,000 volunteer troops, his soldiers captured and killed Mangas Coloradas. Cochise and his follow-

ers, numbering less than 200, were driven into the Dragoon Mountains. For a decade they kept the U.S. Army at bay by utilizing hit-and-run tactics to raid and kill whites. In an attempt to bring an end to the Apache Wars, General George Cook was sent there in June 1871. Experienced at hunting Native renegades, Cook instituted the use of Apache warriors as scouts to find Cochise. It isn't clear whether Cook tracked Cochise down and negotiated peace, or if Cochise eluded him. Sources do agree that Cochise turned down an offer to be relocated with his people onto a reservation located in Fort Tularosa, New Mexico.

A mail carrier by the name of Thomas J. Jeffords had lost 14 of his employees to Cochise and his warriors. Jeffords spoke a little Apache, and decided to go and talk to Cochise regarding the matter. Risking his life, he entered Cochise's camp alone and offered his firearms in exchange for talks. Cochise was so taken by Jeffords's bravery that he made him welcome. The result of this meeting was that Jeffords and Cochise developed a working relationship; Jeffords' carriers then passed through Cochise's territory unharmed.

With Jeffords acting as scout, General Oliver Howard was successful in arranging a negotiation meeting with Cochise during the autumn of 1872. Howard had been sent by President Ulysses S. Grant to make another attempt at putting an end to the Apache Wars. In exchange for Howard's promise to give Cochise and his people reservation land along Apache Pass (Chiricahua Mountains), Cochise agreed to stop killing whites. Cochise's one condition to the settlement was that Jeffords be the liaison between his people and the U.S. government; Jeffords reluctantly agreed. During the ensuing four years, the agreement was kept intact, but came apart after Cochise's death in 1874. Neither the cause of the great warrior's death nor the location of his burial mound has been found.

As for the settlement agreement, some sources say that at the succession of Cochise's sons, the eldest, Taza, attempted to maintain it, but that Naiche, the youngest, disregarded the pact after Taza's death. All agree that Jeffords was held responsible for the breach and fired from his post. The reservation was dissolved and its members either fled or were relocated to the San Carlos Agency.

Further Reading

American West, September/October 1983.

Biographical Dictionary of Indians of the Americas, American Indian Publishers, 1983, pp. 105-106.

Champagne, Duane, editor, *Native North American Almanac,* Detroit: Gale, 1994.

Prairie Schooner, fall 1993, p. 134.

Roberts, David, *Once They Moved Like the Wind: Cochise, Geronimo, and the Apache Wars,* New York: Simon & Schuster, 1993.

Sweeney, Edwin R., *Cochise: Chiricahua Apache Chief,* Norman: University of Oklahoma Press, 1991.

Crazy Horse

Oglala Brulé Sioux military and tribal leader
Born c. 1842, near present-day Rapid City,
        South Dakota
Died September 5, 1877, Fort Robinson,
        Nebraska
Also known as Horse Stands in Sight, Curly

Crazy Horse led the attack at the Battle of Little Bighorn, remarking that it was "a good day to die."

Crazy Horse is remembered in history for his defiant and skilled military leadership and also as a potent symbol of Indian resistance in the twentieth century. A fierce and yet mystical leader with remarkable courage in battle and brilliant wartime strategics, Crazy Horse is probably best known as one of the leaders of the Battle of Little Bighorn, at which George Armstrong Custer and his troops were killed by Cheyenne and Sioux warriors who were trying to protect the sacred Black Hills from gold miners.

Crazy Horse was probably born on Rapid Creek, just east of what is now the community of Rapid City, South Dakota, at the edge of the Black Hills. His father was an Oglala Sioux medicine man and his mother, Rattle Blanket, was a Brulé Sioux. He had brown eyes, light skin, and yellow-brown hair that earned him his early name, Curly. His mother committed suicide when he was young and Crazy Horse's father later married two sisters of the Brulé Sioux warrior and leader, Spotted Tail, who was probably his uncle.

Crazy Horse's early years were taken up with the quest for food for his people and demonstrating his bravery in battle with such tribal enemies as the Pawnee, Arapaho, Crow, and Shoshone. His reputation was established long before whites had heard of him. In his teens he was known as Horse Stands in Sight. When he was about seventeen years old his father, a holy man, bestowed his own name, Crazy Horse, upon him after watching his son's exploits in battle against another tribe. While still a young man, Crazy Horse had a vivid dream of a rider on horseback in a storm, which his father interpreted as a sign of future greatness in battle.

One of the major influences on Crazy Horse was a vision quest that he underwent in 1855. A vision quest—undertaken by an adolescent as a rite of passage to adulthood—is a solitary journey into the wilderness. By waiting in isolation for a period of days without food or water, the youngster is expected to learn something of his identity and destiny and possibly to be visited by his spirit helper, a supernatural entity that will guide him.

Crazy Horse faithfully followed what he learned during his vision quest until his death 22 years later. His vision told him to avoid self-decoration and to act rather than speak. He was assured of invincibility in battle and was warned that his death would come only with the restraint of one of his own people. His lifestyle, as a result of such prophesies, caused both respect and suspicion among his contemporaries. He did not join council meetings, singing or dancing, and he wore only a single red hawk feather in battle. This aloofness, along with his skill in battle, led whites moving into the land of the Lakota to fear his power.

Crazy Horse was sometimes unpopular with his own people for other reasons. He was infatuated with Black Buffalo Woman, the niece of the Oglala tribal leader **Red Cloud** (see entry). She was married to No Water and they had three children, yet Crazy Horse persuaded her to leave with him. Shortly afterwards No Water borrowed a gun, entered their lodge, and shot Crazy Horse in the face. He recovered, but he lost the role of shirt wearer, or special protector of his people. Crazy Horse later married Black Shawl in 1871 and they had a daughter, They Are Afraid of Her, who died at the age of two.

Crazy Horse chooses military response

The migration to the West, spurred in part by the Gold Rush of 1849, created a period of over 30 years of conflict. The military assumed the task of keeping the passageways clear and safe for settlers. In 1855 General W. S. Harney was sent with 600 troops to eliminate the Native threat to westward expansion. Over one hundred Indians were killed in the Battle of Blue Water in September of that year. Crazy Horse saved the life of Yellow Woman, the daughter of a Cheyenne medicine man. By 1857 he had seen three villages destroyed by soldiers, and so did not believe the promises white people made. He considered diplomacy little more than a clever form of trickery, and his mistrust of whites deepened.

In 1857 Crazy Horse attended a great council near the sacred Bear Butte at the eastern edge of the Black Hills. It was an unusual gathering of all the great camps of the Teton Sioux—the Oglala, Brulé, Min-

The death of Crazy Horse; drawing by Amos Bad Heart Bull

neconjou, No Bows, Blackfeet, Two Kettles, and Hunkpapa. These tribes feared that their sacred lands, lands presided over by the spirits of their ancestors and crucial to their cultural and religious lives, would be seized by encroaching white settlers. **Sitting Bull** (see entry), the great military, spiritual, and political leader of the Hunkpapa Sioux, and Spotted Tail were among those in attendance, as was Hump, whose life Crazy Horse saved only three years later.

Following the Civil War, President Ulysses S. Grant attempted to establish a "peace" policy. A treaty was signed by some of the Sioux leaders assuring safe passage through the Powder River country, and several forts were built along the Bozeman Trail. But there was strong resistance. Crazy Horse stood with those who refused to grant safe passage to the military and rejected the continuing flood of settlers. In 1865 he participated in a Sioux-Cheyenne attack on the Julesburg stockade in Colorado Territory in retaliation for the assault on the Sand Creek encampment led by former minister John M. Chivington, in which 500 peaceful

Cheyenne were massacred in an unprovoked militia attack.

Other fights with whites were to follow. Captain William J. Fetterman boasted that he could march through the Lakota nation with only 80 men. In December 1866 he led that number on a mission to protect wood gatherers heading for Fort Kearny. Crazy Horse skillfully led a decoy force that trapped the soldiers. All of Fetterman's men were killed, while only 12 Indians lost their lives; the bodies of the slain warriors were removed before other army forces arrived. Another important battle, the Wagon Box fight, occurred near the same fort in August 1867.

Little Bighorn and the end of resistance

The Fort Laramie Treaty of 1868 ended the war between the United States and the Sioux nation. This accord favored the Indians somewhat, since U.S. forces had been unable to defeat them militarily. The treaty therefore promised to safeguard the tribes' "absolute and undisturbed use and occupation" of reservations, to force out white settlers, and to punish any whites who injured Indians. Forts were abandoned along the Bozeman Trail, and Red Cloud and Spotted Tail agreed to move to their respective areas. But Crazy Horse, refusing to honor the treaty, took the position of war chief of the Oglala.

It only took the government six years to violate the treaty. The discovery of gold in the Black Hills in 1874 made the agreement pointless as hordes of prospectors flooded into the region. Partly to keep these miners and settlers safe, the military attempted to place all Native Americans on reservations by January 31, 1876.

The various tribes soon realized that a unified military effort was needed to preserve their traditional freedoms. The Cheyenne and Sioux gathered in a great encampment in the Rosebud area of Montana and then moved to the Little Bighorn. The unified forces showed courage in the June 17, 1876, conflict with the troops of General George Crook but the Little Bighorn battle of June 25 was the major event of the campaign. On a ridge above the river, General George Custer's isolated force of 225 men confronted a group of warriors that exceeded the total number of cavalry in the entire area. Crazy Horse led the attack across the river, remarking that it was "a good day to die." In fact, only about 20 of his followers lost their lives, while Custer and all of his troops were killed.

Although Little Bighorn remains a symbolically important event celebrated even today in the Native American community, the victory was short-lived. Escalating conflict with the military, as well as the pressures of hunger and conflict between the tribes led to the end of the resistance. The advantage the warriors held was lost when the different groups were forced to separate because of a shortage of food for men and horses.

Living conditions among the tribes were made worse because of unnatural patterns of migration, influenced by the army's presence, and the fact that trade with whites was largely restricted after 1864. Hopes were further crushed by a harsh winter, combined with the word that the sacred Black Hills had been sold. Crazy Horse continued to raid mining camps in the Black Hills, killing as many of the invading miners as he could find. But when his village was attacked by soldiers under the command of Colonel Nelson A. Miles on January 8, 1877, it was the final military upheaval. Although Crazy Horse and his warriors fought off Miles and his troops, their camp and supplies were ruined. By spring the great warrior and his 1,000 followers faced starvation.

Crazy Horse reluctantly led his followers (only 217 of them men) to Fort Robinson, in northern Nebraska, in early May 1877. He had been promised a reservation at one of two preferred locations in Wyoming, but the group's horses and weapons were taken away and they were forced to remain within three miles of the fort. During this period Crazy Horse married a third woman, Nellie Larrabee, the 18-year-old mixed child of a local French trader.

Death of the Sioux leader

The army did not know what to do about Crazy Horse and his followers and failed to understand their status in relation to the nearby camps of Red Cloud and Spotted Tail. Some suggested sending Crazy Horse to Washington, D.C., as a representative of his people. However, according to General Jesse Lee, a temporary agent in the area designated for Spotted Tail and his followers, Crazy Horse replied that he "was not hunting of any Great Father. *HIS* father was with him, and there was no Great Father between him and the Great Spirit." After only four months General Crook issued an order for the arrest of Crazy Horse, who showed reluctance to cooperate with the U.S. military by serving as a scout or combatant against the Nez Percé. A distorted interpretation of Crazy Horse's words left the impression that he would continue to fight with the whites. There was also a rumor that he would run

Crazy Horse Monument

away to Canada and join the Hunkpapa leader Sitting Bull, who had helped plan the victory at Little Bighorn.

As a result, Crazy Horse was returned to Fort Robinson on September 5, 1877, expecting to meet with the local commander. There is evidence that a special train was scheduled to send him to exile in Florida a few hours after his return to the fort. The exact events after his arrival are not clear, though several witnesses give distinct accounts. Crazy Horse, apparently fearing that he would be imprisoned in a guardhouse near the fort headquarters, broke away and pulled a concealed knife. In the ensuing struggle he was stabbed, probably by a private's bayonet. He died from that wound several hours later.

Touch the Clouds and Crazy Horse's father were with him at the time of his death and his body was taken to an unspecified location for burial, perhaps near Wounded Knee. Within a few weeks the remaining Sioux were sent to reservations in the area that would become South Dakota. Participants in subduing the great leader were awarded "Crazy Horse medals."

Historical and contemporary image

Judgements about Crazy Horse's historical role and importance varied widely among white writers of the time. Some called him the greatest Indian leader of his time, while others doubted he would even be remembered by history. As to more literal questions about his image, many people—including family members—insisted that no picture was ever taken of Crazy Horse. Other sources, however, refer to pictures taken of the leader on horseback. Ironically, a huge monument now under construction in the Black Hills of South Dakota could make his image as familiar as those of the four Presidents featured on Mt. Rushmore only a few miles away. The Crazy Horse monument is the result of a determined effort by skilled artist Korczak Ziolkowski, who worked briefly on the Mount Rushmore project in the 1940s.

In 1948 Ziolkowski selected the massive granite Thunderhead Mountain in South Dakota as the site for a monumental sculpture of Crazy Horse. The sculptor carved a figure on horseback pointing forward, representing the spirit of the Sioux leader. With the support of numerous Native American spokespeople, Ziolkowski proceeded with his project without state or federal assistance, believing the project should be an independent effort. He also envisioned a nearby university, medical center, and airport.

Although the 1977 completion date was abandoned, work continued on the project after the artist's death in 1982. Under the guidance of his widow, Ruth, the outline of the monument became more apparent. In the mid-1990s the features of the nine-story high face were clearly identifiable and work on the total outline proceeded. Mrs. Ziolkowski predicted "a 'sudden' visual impact (from the observation area) in the not too distant future." The final carved granite structure will be 563 feet high and 641 feet long. Over 1.2 million people visited the site in 1990. A thirteen-cent postage stamp honoring Crazy Horse, using an image provided by the creator of the monument, was issued in 1982.

Further Reading

Brown, Vinson, *Crazy Horse, Hoka Hey (It Is a Good Time to Die!),* Happy Camp, CA: Naturegraph Publishers, 1987.

Clark, Robert A., *The Killing of Chief Crazy Horse,* Lincoln: University of Nebraska Press, 1988.

Dugan, Bill, *Crazy Horse,* New York: HarperCollins, 1992.

Fort Robinson Illustrated (special issue), *Nebraskaland Magazine,* 64:1, January-February 1986.

Mary Crow Dog

See **Brave Bird, Mary**

Charles Curtis

Kansa/Kaw-Osage attorney, legislator, and politician
Born January 25, 1860, present-day Topeka, Kansas
Died February 8, 1936, Washington, D.C.

Curtis's role in the 1898 act bearing his name may have been no more than to negotiate a compromised bill in an effort to make the allotment process somewhat easier for the five tribes. Nevertheless, Curtis is remembered as the author of the legislation that destroyed tribal sovereignty in the Indian Territory.

Charles Brent Curtis was born on January 25, 1860, on Kansa/Kaw land that would later become part of north Topeka, Kansas. He was the eldest of the two children born to Orren Armes Curtis and Ellen Pappan Curtis. Curtis's father descended from English ancestors who originally arrived in America in the early 1600s. Born in Eugene, Indiana, in 1829, Orren Curtis appears to have been married several times prior to marrying Ellen Pappan, the mixed-blood daughter of his employer, in 1859. Ellen Pappan Curtis's mother, Julie Gonville Pappan, was of Kansa/Kaw, Osage, and very remote Potawatomi ancestry. She had married three times; her last husband, Louis Pappan, was of French ancestry. Julie Pappan's mother (Curtis's great-grandmother), Wyhesee, was a full-blood Kansa/Osage Indian. She was the daughter of the Kansa chief Nomparawarah ("White Plume") and the granddaughter of the Osage chief Pawhuska. White Plume is remembered by many because his portrait was painted by the well-known portrait painter Charles Bird King in the 1820s. Wyhesee married Louis Gonville who appears to have been of French Canadian and one-quarter Potawatomi ancestry.

Although Charles Curtis was later described as being of one-half, one-quarter, or one-eighth Indian ancestry, none of these appears to be correct. Technically, based on his somewhat confused and contradictory genealogy, Curtis could claim a little over one-eighth Indian ancestry, and was predominantly of English and French extraction. Whatever the case, he identified himself as an American Indian, although he was not sentimental about his ancestry and was not above using his Indian roots in whatever manner was most politically useful during his career.

Curtis's mother died of cholera in April 1864. The young boy had been raised among his numerous Kansa relatives on their Indian allotments along the north shore of the Kansas River. After his mother's death he lived with his maternal grandmother, Julie Gonville Pappan, on the Kansa reservation near Council Grove, some 60 miles west of Topeka. But because of southern Cheyenne and Arapaho raids and conflicts with the residents of the Kansa reservation that occurred between 1866 and 1868, Curtis was sent back to the relative peace of north Topeka in 1868. On his return to Topeka, he came under the dominant control and influence of his white grandmother, Permelia Curtis, who was to oversee his education and employment. She also laid the groundwork for Curtis's lifelong allegiance to the Republican party.

Charles Curtis

After completing three years at Topeka High School, Curtis studied law in 1879 with a local attorney and was admitted to the bar in 1881 at the age of 21. Almost immediately, he involved himself with local political affairs, an interest that was to occupy the rest of his life. In 1885 he was elected the county attorney for Shawnee County, Kansas. Curtis was elected to the United States House of Representatives as a Republican from the Fourth District in 1892 and remained in the House until January 1907, completing 14 years of service there.

Allotment and the Curtis Act

In the late nineteenth century, Curtis became involved in legislation which resulted in the General Allotment Act. Passed in 1887, the act divided reservation lands—which were traditionally held in common by all members of a tribe—into small parcels that were "allotted" to individual Native Americans to be privately owned. The surplus land that had once been part of the reservation but was not allotted to individual tribe members went to U.S. settlers. Allotment was disastrous for many tribes for several reasons. Notably, it entailed the loss of large amounts of land to settlers. In addition, private ownership of land disrupted tribal economic and cultural traditions. Often the allotted parcels of land were small, awkwardly located, or lacked adequate water, making farming difficult or impossible. Without other means of income, some individuals sold their allotted parcels simply to pay for food and other necessities. Also, treaties had promised Indian nations the right to self-government on reservation lands. Allotment fragmented the reservation communities, making self-rule nearly impossible.

Many people at that time believed that allotment was inevitable, and Curtis, an avowed assimilationist, was among them. Assimilationists believe that people whose cultural background differs from that of the dominant culture should change their habits and values in order to become more like the population around them. The policy of allotment was based on the expectation that, as private landowners, Indians would leave behind their traditional, communal ways of life, and become "ordinary" individuals within American society. Curtis, who held a 40-acre Kansa allotment jointly with his sister throughout his life, felt that the progress of the American Indian was being hindered by the continuation of communal ownership of lands, herds, and other tribal resources.

On June 28, 1898, the Curtis Act was passed. It applied the General Allotment Act of 1887 to the land belonging by treaty to the "Five Civilized Tribes" (the Cherokee, Choctaw, Creek, Chickasaw, and Seminole) of Oklahoma. Curtis's role in the act bearing his name may have been no more than to negotiate a compromised bill in an effort to make the allotment process somewhat easier for the five tribes. Nevertheless, Curtis is remembered as the author of the legislation that destroyed tribal sovereignty (self-rule) in the Indian Territory (later Oklahoma).

Politics and beliefs

In 1907 Curtis was designated by the Kansas State Legislature to fill an unexpired term in the United States Senate. In the same year he was elected to the Senate, but he lost a reelection campaign in 1912. In 1914, Curtis was reelected to the Senate and continued in that senatorial position until 1926, serving a total of 20 years in the Senate. During his years in the Senate, Charles Curtis's name was prominent on a number of bills; however, he was recognized more for his politicking (discussing party lines) on the Senate floor. He was a conservative Republican and party regular who was designated party whip (the member whose job is to enforce party discipline and ensure attendance of party members at important sessions) in 1915. Curtis replaced Henry Cabot Lodge as majority leader in 1924. That year also marked the death of his wife.

Curtis was philosophically and politically antagonistic to some forms of traditional American Indian tribal government. In his capacity as chairperson of the Senate Indian Affairs Committee in 1921, Curtis supported the bill of Secretary of the Interior John Barton Payne to minimize the sovereignty of the Pueblo tribal governments by clarifying how federal jurisdiction (the power and authority to enforce the law) was to be exercised over the Pueblos. With the end of the sixty-sixth Congress, the Payne Bill was not acted upon, although the complex issues involving American Indian sovereignty and land title were to be repeatedly addressed in future congresses.

According to writer William E. Unrau, Charles Curtis's political philosophy can be summarized as follows: "Curtis supported the gold standard, high tariffs, prohibition, restrictive immigration, deportation of aliens, and generous veterans benefits; opposed the League of Nations; and took the view that depressions were natural occurrences that inevitably would be followed by periods of prosperity ... championed female suffrage [and] government assistance to farmers," especially Kansans.

Becomes vice president

In 1928, at the Republican national convention, Curtis initially opposed Herbert Hoover's presidential nomination as the Republican candidate. His objections were resolved by fellow delegates, and Curtis was designated as the vice-presidential candidate. The Republican victory in the 1928 national elections was achieved only after a fierce struggle.

Curtis was inaugurated as the thirty-first vice president of the United States in March 1929, the first American Indian to have attained this office. During his time in office, Curtis spoke for American Indians whenever the occasion arose. He has generally been viewed by political analysts as having served a rather uninspired term as vice president. Some have disagreed, however, pointing out the effective role he played in complex behind-the-scenes policy negotiations. Although he attempted to avoid controversy where possible, Curtis was credited as a major player in negotia-

tions with American Indians. He was renominated with Hoover in 1932, but they were defeated. Curtis then retired from active politics and returned to the practice of law in Washington, D.C.

Curtis married Anna E. Baird of Topeka in 1884. The Curtises had one son and two daughters. Curtis died of a heart attack on February 8, 1936, in the Washington, D.C., home of his half-sister, Dolly Curtis Gann, who had served as his official hostess during his years as vice president. His remains were returned to Topeka, where he had started out his life.

Further Reading

"Charles Curtis: The Politics of Allotment," in *Indian Lives: Essays on Nineteen Twentieth Century Native American Leaders,* edited by L. G. Moses and Raymond Wilson, Albuquerque: University of New Mexico Press, 1985, pp. 113-138.

Kelly, Lawrence C., *The Assault on Assimilation: John Collier and the Origins of Indian Policy Reform,* Albuquerque: University of New Mexico Press, 1983.

Mixed-bloods and Tribal Dissolution: Charles Curtis and the Quest for Indian Identity, Lawrence: University of Kansas Press, 1989.

Unrau, William E., "The Mixed-Blood Connection: Charles Curtis and Kaw Detribalization," in *Kansas and the West: Bicentennial Essays in Honor of Nyle H. Miller,* edited by Forrest R. Blackburn, Topeka: Kansas State Historical Society, 1976, pp. 151-161.

Datsolalee

Washo basket weaver
Born 1835, near Carson City, Nevada
Died 1925
Also known as Dabuda ("Wide Hips"),
    and Louisa Keyser

One of Datsolalee's most famous baskets,
called "Myriads of Stars Shine over the
Graves of Our Ancestors," contains 56,590
stitches.

One of the most famous weavers in the world, Datsolalee was a major influence on the evolution of Washo fancy basketry and is recognized as the greatest basket weaver and designer among the Washo people. Born in Nevada's Carson Valley of unknown parentage, she learned the skills of traditional Washo basketry, perfecting the intricate design that used up to 36 stitches to the inch.

Datsolalee was married twice, first to a Washo man named Assu, by whom she had two children, then—after Assu's death—to Charley Keyser in 1888. When she married Keyser, Datsolalee took the name Louisa. However, it was the friendship and patronage of Dr. S. L. Lee of Carson City in the 1860s that earned her the nickname Datsolalee, which stuck for the remainder of her life.

In 1851 the Washo tribe got into a dispute with the Northern Paiutes, a tribe that had relocated to Carson Valley when white settlers forced them from their own homeland during the California Gold Rush. The Paiutes attacked and defeated the Washo.

After achieving victory, they imposed two penalties: the Washo could own no horses, and, more importantly for Datsolalee and her tribe, they could weave no baskets. The Paiutes wanted to eliminate their competition in order to sell their own basketry. This was disastrous for the Washo people, who had very little to offer for trade or sale without their basketry.

Datsolalee defies basket prohibition

By 1895 the Washo people were living in utter poverty. In a defiant move, Datsolalee took some glass bottles she had covered with weaving to a clothing store in Carson City. This shop, the Emporium Company, eventually became the major outlet for Datsolalee's weavings and those of the Washo people. It was owned by Abram Cohn and his wife, Amy (and later his second wife, Margaret), who had regretted the loss of Washo basketry through the years of Paiute rule. They were surprised to find that the Washo women had continued to weave despite the ban, which by now had gone on for more than half a century. Both recognized the high quality of Datsolalee's work and bought all of her baskets, asking her to create more and promising to buy all of them.

After that, the Cohns handled all of Datsolalee's work, as well as baskets from other Washo weavers. Although Abram Cohn took credit for discovering Datsolalee, apparently Amy Cohn was the first to become interested in Washo basketry and in Datsolalee herself. Amy kept very detailed records of Datsolalee's work, created a catalogue of her basketry, issued certificates to assure buyers each one was authentic, published pamphlets about the baskets, and took promotional photographs of them.

Datsolalee's baskets combined creative and unusual design work with a rare technical skill. She wove her baskets with tiny, detailed stitches, pulled tightly into a coil. In addition, the geometrical designs in Datsolalee's baskets contained illustrations of Washo life and history. It is believed that Datsolalee interwove designs that were part of her dreams and visions. All of her baskets are distinguished by small, repeated designs—often lines or triangles—woven with exact spacing. Her designs can be found on three major types of baskets: the cone-shaped *singam;* the *mokeewit,* a burden basket; and the *degikup,* a spherical ceremonial basket and Datsolalee's preferred style. Her tools were her teeth, her fingers, a piece of sharp stone or glass, and a pointed instrument such as a bone or iron awl.

After Datsolalee broke the ban, most Washo weavers first sold their work through the Emporium, but eventually they found their own buyers or sold directly to tourists at Lake Tahoe. Datsolalee, too, found another patron for her work. Every summer, the Cohns took their inventory of baskets to their branch shop in Tahoe City, and Datsolalee attracted attention by weaving her baskets outside this store. Here she met William F. Breitholle, who worked as a wine steward at a resort hotel at Lake Tahoe from 1907 to 1916. Because the Cohns gave her Sundays off from weaving, Datsolalee would visit the Breitholles for breakfast and eventually developed a close relationship with them.

William's son, Buddy, who currently owns 17 pieces of a private collection of Datsolalee's work, has said that the baskets were given to his parents without the Cohns' knowledge and are not recorded in the Cohn ledger. Amy Cohn may not have known that Datsolalee was weaving on Sundays for Breitholle, or she may have felt she had no right to the baskets Datsolalee was making in her spare time.

The Cohn ledger lists approximately 120 of Datsolalee's pieces, but it is estimated that she wove nearly 300 in her lifetime, including about 40 exceptionally large ones. Between 1904 and 1919, Datsolalee worked primarily on these large pieces, some of which took a year to complete. One of her most famous baskets, called "Myriads of Stars Shine over the Graves of Our Ancestors," contains 56,590 stitches.

Though nearly blind in the last years of her life, Datsolalee worked until her death in Carson City at the age of 90. She experimented with design, technique, and color and introduced a number of new approaches into Washo basketry. Five years after her death, one of Datsolalee's baskets sold for $10,000. In the 1990s, her baskets were considered collectors' items and sold for close to $250,000.

Further Reading

Cohodas, Marvin, "The Breitholle Collection of Washo Basketry," *American Indian Art,* 9, autumn 1984.

Cohodas, Marvin, "Dat So La Lee's Basketry Design," *American Indian Art,* 1, autumn 1976.

Dockstader, Frederick J., *Great North American Indians,* New York: Van Nostrand Reinhold, 1977.

Ramo, Joshua Cooper, "A Tisket, A Tasket ... Trends: Indian Baskets Are Hot Collectibles," *Newsweek,* December 13, 1993, p. 79.

Frank Day

Maidu painter and tribal historian
Born 1902, Berry Creek, California
Died 1976
Also known as Lydam Lilly
("Fading Morning Star")

Interestingly, the pictures meant to serve as memorials to Frank Day's own community speak powerfully to outsiders.

Frank Day did not begin painting until late in his life. He began showing his work at exhibitions in the 1960s; within a decade, he had become California's most honored Native American artist. The spiritual energy of his pictures sparked interest in the Maidu culture. A group of young Maidu interested in the tribe's traditions began meeting with him on weekends to hear stories of the past and to listen to his songs, which he translated so that they could interpret them. He also choreographed (planned the dance steps of) the traditional movements of the ancient Maidu dances, which celebrated the animals, the birds, and the earth. His efforts led to the formation of a performance group, the Maidu Dancers and Traditionalists, who performed a repertoire of 14 ceremonials they had learned from Day.

Day's father, Twoboe, was 60 years old his son was born in 1902 at Berry Creek, in Butte County, California. Twoboe shared the ways of the Maidu elders with his son, telling him stories of the sacred and historically important places. Each tree, spring, boulder, and canyon had a name, and Twoboe taught these names to his son. Maidu children were instructed to memorize their tribal boundaries, which were defined by these natural landmarks.

The Maidu lived in the mountain meadows of northwestern California about 4,000 feet above sea level, surrounded by groves of oak trees, with fish and waterfowl in the sloughs (swamps) and marshes. At the center of each Maidu village was an earth-covered dance house that was partly underground. According to legend, Wonommi, the Creator, told the Maidu to keep the sacred dance house, the sacred rattle, and the dances and to worship at night. Boys were initiated into the Kuksu cult, a small group of the tribe, to maintain the stability and order of the world, which depended on their continuing the dances.

An emotional encounter

One of Day's most mysterious and moving paintings recorded an event 60 years after its occurrence. One day in July 1911, when Day was nine, he had been walking with his father near the place where the forks of the Feather River join. There he saw **Ishi** (see entry), a Yaki tribesman, kneeling over a companion who had been shot in the stomach. Ishi had rigged an ingenious device to pull the bullet out of his wounded friend, with whom he had left his homeland in Mill Creek Canyon. Unable to resuscitate him, Ishi had staggered alone and miserable to Oroville two days later. The sheriff of Oroville had called Twoboe to the jail to try to communicate with Ishi, who lay dazed and starving in his cell. Twoboe could not comprehend Yaki, and Ishi was unable to understand Maidu, but the two men recognized each other because of their meeting on the trail. Day's picture captures the emotional power of that encounter.

A 12-year pilgrimage

When Twoboe died in 1922, his mourning son began a long period of wandering. For a dozen years, he sought out other tribes and walked to faraway places. He took odd jobs to survive, traveling to places as distant as Oklahoma. According to Maidu religious belief, the soul of the dead blows about like the wind, retracing each step it has taken in life, before it is released to the other world. Since the spirit stayed with the living until it was ready for departure, mourning was intense and lengthy, particularly for a father. Day depicted this in his paintings *Mourning at Mineral Springs* and *Spiritual Burial.*

Upon Day's return to California in 1934, anthropologists (scholars who study human societies, religions, and customs) sought him for his knowledge of the old ways. The archaeologist (a scholar who studies the physical remains of past humans and their activities) Donald P. Jewell encouraged him to paint his recollections as well as to sing them. Herb and Peggy Puffer of Pacific Western Traders in Folsom also urged Day to paint and then tape-recorded what he said about his pictures. Exhibits were mounted in Sacramento, California, at American River College in 1963, in San Francisco in 1967, at California State University in 1974, at the Governor's Office in Sacramento in 1975, and at the Crocker Art Museum in 1976.

After Day's death, an important show of his works was held at the Museum of the Plains Indian at Browning, Montana, in 1978. That same year, a retrospective (review) of his work was held at the Gorman museum on the Davis campus of the University of California. The Heard Museum in Phoenix, Arizona, paired his work with that of his fellow Maiduan, Harry Fonseca, who had begun a series of 25 drawings of the ceremonies and dances of the Chico Maidu. The show was called "Two Views of California: Day and Fonseca."

Fulfills the role of tribal historian

Because they tell such fascinating stories, Day's paintings—said to number about 200—have been eagerly collected. Interestingly, the pictures meant to serve as memorials to his own community speak powerfully to outsiders. Intended as records of his people's customs and legends, as historical recollections of events significant to his own tribe, they reached a more universal audience.

But he also brought back forgotten traditions to his own people. Day passed on what he knew about tribal custom to a group of young Indians who spent their spare time soaking up everything he had to teach. The group—founded at the Pacific Western Traders store in Folsom—became the Maidu Dancers and Traditionalists. Soon the young Indians' families were drawn into the process, beginning again to practice customs that had been neglected for decades. New materials were needed for ceremonies and were specially prepared by a medicine woman so they could be handled only by the dancers.

Day's painting *Toto at Bloomer Hill* shows a leaping man in an antler headdress and feather necklace, his waist cinched with a deer-claw belt. The Toto was danced at the winter solstice (the shortest day of the year), in buckskin skirts decorated with furs. As the participants fashioned their ceremonial clothing under Day's instructions, they relearned their traditions. They made musical instruments as Wonommi had told them to do. These included rattles, moth cocoons filled with seeds and tied into clusters to make a swishing sound, whistles made from birds' bones, and foot drums made from a hollowed log.

The Lowie Museum of Anthropology at Berkeley, California, has some phonograph recordings of Maidu music, which scholars have only recently begun to study. Had it not been for the inspiration of Day, these songs—and the rituals they accompany—would have been lost. Each of the Maidu instruments was once alive, and as the dancers restore motion to the bird's wing bones and other music-making inventions, they bring them back to life. Frank Day's own powers of restoring the spirit can be appreciated in this ongoing tradition as well as in the powerful stories he brought to life in his paintings.

Further Reading

"Chico Maidu Dancers," *News from Native California,* summer 1992; pp. 38-41.

Dixon, Roland B., "The Northern Maidu," *Bulletin of the American Museum of Natural History,* 17:3, 1905, pp. 119-346.

The Maidu Indian Myths and Stories of Hanc'ibyjim, edited and translated by William Shipley, Berkeley, CA: Heyday Books, 1991.

Simpson, Richard, *Ooti: A Maidu Legacy,* Millbrae, CA: Celestial Arts, 1977.

Ada E. Deer

Menominee social worker, activist, educator, and government official
Born August 7, 1935, Keshena, Menominee Reservation, Wisconsin

"I want to emphasize [that] my administration will be based on the Indian values of caring, sharing, and respect.... These values have been missing too long in the halls of government."

An advocate of social justice, Ada E. Deer was the first woman to head the U.S. Bureau of Indian Affairs (BIA). As assistant secretary for Indian affairs in the Interior Department, she was "turning the BIA upside down and shaking it," as she told hundreds of Navajos in Arizona a month after taking office in late July 1993. For Deer, an activist for the rights of American Indians, youth, and women, turning things upside down is nothing new. As a social worker, community and political leader, and defender of the Menominee people's fight for recognition, she has worked tirelessly in the service of human rights. As she told members of the Alaska Federation of Natives in August 1993, "I want to emphasize [that] my administration will be based on the Indian values of caring, sharing, and respect.... These values have been missing too long in the halls of government."

Deer was born in Keshena on the Menominee Indian Reservation in northeastern Wisconsin in 1935. She is the eldest

Ada E. Deer

Excels as student and public servant

Deer's career began with a solid education in Shawano and Milwaukee public schools. An outstanding student, Deer graduated in the top ten of her high school class before attending the University of Wisconsin-Madison on a tribal scholarship. She was one of two Native Americans of 19,000 students and became the first Menominee to graduate from the university. She received a bachelor's degree in social work in 1957; in 1961, she became the first Native American to receive a master's degree in social work from Columbia University.

While she was a graduate student and over the next ten years, Deer held several professional positions. She was employed as a social worker in New York City and in Minneapolis Public Schools and also worked with the Peace Corps in Puerto Rico. It was between the years of 1964 and 1967 that Deer had her first job with the BIA in Minnesota, as community service coordinator. From 1967 to 1968, she served as coordinator of Indian affairs in the University of Minnesota's Training Center for Community Programs.

During the same time frame, Deer served on the Joint Commission on Mental Health of Children, Inc., and in 1969 she became a member of the national board of Girl Scouts of the U.S.A., a post she held until 1975. During the summer of 1971, Deer studied at the American Indian Law Program at the University of New Mexico and then briefly attended the University of Wisconsin Law School. She left after one semester to work on an urgent tribal matter that was to become her major focus over the next several years.

of five children (her siblings are Joseph Deer, Jr., Robert Deer, Ferial Skye, and Connie Deer); four other children died in infancy. Her mother, Constance Stockton (Wood) Deer, is an Anglo American from Philadelphia, Pennsylvania, and a former BIA nurse. Her father, Joseph Deer, a nearly full-blood Menominee, was an employee of the Menominee Indian Mills.

For the first 18 years of Deer's life, her family lived in a log cabin near the Wolf River with no running water or electricity. Deer told the Senate Committee on Indian Affairs at the hearing to confirm her as head of the BIA, "while all the statistics said we were poor, I never felt poor in spirit. My mother ... was the single greatest influence on my life. She instilled in me rich values which have shaped my lifetime commitment to service."

Fights to regain Menominee tribe recognition

In 1954, the U.S. Congress passed the Menominee Termination Act, which was part of a larger effort to force the group to assimilate, or blend in, to mainstream U.S. society. Fully carried out by 1961, it meant the loss of federal recognition of the Menominee Tribe. Along with this loss of recognition came the closing of membership rolls, an end to benefits such as health and educational services, and the imposing of state jurisdiction, or legal authority, on the Menominee. The Menominee were taxed and had to sell off ancestral lands to pay the bills. As Deer testified in her confirmation hearing, the Menominee "literally went from being prosperous to being Wisconsin's newest, smallest and poorest county."

Deer left law school and returned to what was now Menominee County. She committed herself to bringing together tribal leaders to regain control of tribal interests from a group of Menominee elites—small, powerful groups—and to attempt to reverse termination. There, in 1970, Deer and many others created a new political organization known as Determination of Rights and Unity for Menominee Shareholders (DRUMS). With assistance from the Native American Rights Fund and local legal aid organizations, Deer and other leaders of DRUMS fought to regain federal recognition of the Menominee. Their tactics included the 220-mile "march for justice" from Menominee County to the capital in Madison.

As a vital part of the effort to restore their rights, in 1972 and 1973 Deer served as vice president and lobbyist in Washington, D.C., for the National Committee to Save the Menominee People and Forest, Inc. The efforts of Deer and the members of DRUMS attracted national attention to the issue of termination and finally resulted in the introduction of a bill in Congress to reverse this policy for the Menominee. On December 22, 1973, President Nixon signed the Menominee Restoration Act into law.

From 1974 to 1976, Deer chaired the Menominee Tribe and headed the Menominee Restoration Committee. After its work was completed, she resigned. In 1977, she became a senior lecturer in the School of Social Work and in the American Indian Studies Program at the University of Wisconsin at Madison, where she taught until 1993. Deer also entered into political activity more fully at this time, serving as legislative liaison (go-between) to the Native American Rights Fund from 1979 to 1981.

In 1982, Deer was a candidate for the position of Wisconsin's secretary of state. Two years later she served as delegate-at-large at the Democratic National Convention and vice-chair of the national Mondale-Ferraro presidential campaign. In 1992, Deer almost became the first Native American woman in Congress, after she made a strong showing in the Second Congressional District of Wisconsin. However, she lost in the general election to the Republican candidate, Scot Klug. May 1993, however, brought a nomination by President Bill Clinton from a field of four candidates (including the Navajo tribal chairman, **Peterson Zah**) to head the BIA. Congress, with overwhelming support from its members and from tribal leaders, confirmed her nomination in July of that year.

Turning the BIA around

In the BIA, Deer inherited an agency infamous for its bureaucracy and historically poor relations with tribes. Deer has had to contend with, among many other issues, budget reductions for her agency; conflicts between tribes and localities over land management, water resources, and mineral rights; tribal recognition; education; and religious freedom. Deer is a strong supporter of Indian self-determination; this coincides with the BIA's planned reorganization, which will shift more power to tribes.

Her approach in office has been to visit individual tribes and to bring them together with businesses, organizations, and government entities to find ways to work cooperatively. The goal of such meetings is to help tribes gain economic self-sufficiency. "I want to help the BIA be a full partner in the effort to fulfill the Indian agenda developed in Indian country," said Deer during her confirmation hearing. "The best way we can do this is for the tribes to decide what needs to be done and for the tribes to do it on their own terms, with our enthusiastic support."

Deer's personal motto is "One person can make a difference." Because she has made a difference in many spheres of activity, she has received numerous awards. Deer was one of the Outstanding Young Women of America in 1966. And in 1974, she received the White Buffalo Council Achievement Award, along with honorary doctorates from the University of Wisconsin in Madison and Northland College, in Ashland, Wisconsin. Other honors include the Woman of the Year Award from Girl Scouts of America (1982), the Wonder Woman Award (1982), the Indian Council Fire Achievement Award (1984), and the National Distinguished Achievement Award from the American Indian Resources Institute (1991).

Further Reading

Deer, Ada, "The Power Came from the People," in *I Am the Fire of Time: The Voices of Native American Women,* edited by Jane B. Katz, New York: Dutton, 1977.

Deer, Ada, and R. E. Simon, Jr., *Speaking Out,* Chicago: Children's Press Open Door Books, 1970.

Native American Women, edited by Gretchen M. Bataille, New York: Garland Publishing, 1993, pp. 76-78.

Peroff, Nicholas C., *Menominee Drums: Tribal Termination and Restoration, 1954-1974,* Norman: University of Oklahoma Press, 1982.

Richardson, Jeff, "Ada Deer: Native Values for BIA Management," *Tundra Times,* September 8, 1993, p. 1.

Deganawida

Huron prophet, leader, and statesman
Born c. 1550, near Kingston, Ontario, Canada
Died c. 1600

Deganawida is credited with the development of the advanced political system of the Iroquois League, which was primarily democratic and also gave women a major role.

Deganawida is best known as the great leader who, with **Hiawatha** (see entry) founded the Iroquois League or Confederacy, an alliance, established in about 1570, of five Iroquois tribes: the

Mohawks, Oneidas, Onondagas, Cayugas, and Senecas. Although the story of Deganawida's life is based mostly on legend, all accounts of the league's formation credit his efforts. In addition to pursuing his goal of unifying Iroquois tribes, Deganawida played a vital role in defining and establishing the structure and code of the Iroquois League.

It is believed that Deganawida was born around the 1550s in the present-day Kingston, Ontario, area and was one of seven brothers born to Huron parents. According to legend, his birth was marked by a vision his mother had that her newborn son would be indirectly responsible for the destruction of the Hurons. Hoping to protect the tribe, she, along with Deganawida's grandmother, tried three times to drown him in a river. Each morning after the attempts, Deganawida was found unharmed in his mother's arms. After the third unsuccessful attempt, Deganawida's mother resigned herself to her son's existence.

Creates the League of the Iroquois

When Deganawida was grown, he journeyed south to carry out his mission of peace among the Iroquois. He met Hiawatha (not the Hiawatha of the American poet Henry Wadsworth Longfellow's epic), a Mohawk, who joined him in his efforts to create an alliance of the Oneidas, Cayugas, Onondagas, Senecas, and Mohawks. The confederacy was Deganawida's vision, but because he had a speech disability, Hiawatha served as his spokesman. Deganawida's message to the Iroquois was that all men are brothers. Therefore, they should cease their practices of killing, scalping, and cannibalism. To-

gether, Deganawida and Hiawatha convinced the five tribes to make peace and join in an alliance of friendship, rather than continuing to destroy each other. As a part of their efforts, they planted together the Great Tree of Peace at the Onondaga Nation. This planting symbolically resolved blood feuds that divided the five groups, and instituted peace, unity, and clear thinking among the people. Deganawida passed on the Great Law, which is the constitution of the Iroquois Confederacy.

The powerful Onondaga chief Thadodaho (also known as Atotarho or Adario), who had at first been strongly opposed to the union of the five tribes, marked the beginning of the alliance when he made the decision to join. Deganawida also tried, without success, to encourage the Erie and other tribes to join. Because of their refusal, they eventually were dispersed, or scattered to live in other areas, by the Iroquois in the 1650s. Sometime after Deganawida's death, his mother's earlier vision was confirmed when the Huron nation was destroyed by the Iroquois Confederacy.

The alliance of the five tribes was referred to as the League of the Iroquois and as the Iroquois Five Nation Confederacy. After the Tuscaroras joined in the early eighteenth century, it was known as the Six Nations. The exact date of the founding of the league is unknown. Its purpose was to bring peace, to build strength, and to create goodwill among the five nations in order to protect them from both attack by external enemies and warfare within the group. The code of the league summarized the intent of Deganawida and the chiefs of the confederacy to establish "The Great Peace." It called for the creation of the Pine Tree Chiefs, who were chosen by merit rather than by heredity. Deganawida served as one of those chiefs.

A grand council of all the chiefs of the five tribes gathered at Onondaga, home of the most centrally located of the five tribes, to establish the laws and customs of the league. Each tribe had an equal voice in the council, although the number of chiefs representing each tribe varied. As the council developed over the years, it became deeply involved in matters of diplomacy, including war and peace in both its associations with other tribes and in its treaties with the European settlers on their borders. Deganawida is credited with the development of the advanced political system of the league, which was primarily democratic and also gave women a major role. Many of the principles, laws, and regulations of the league are credited to Deganawida. The Iroquois political system inspired many elements of the new U.S. government's structure some two centuries later. Before the American Revolution, Iroquois spokespeople counseled American leaders about the Five Nations' form of democracy. As the founding fathers sought to unite many states in liberty, they modeled their constitution, in part, around the Great Law of the Iroquois.

By 1677, the league was the most powerful of all the North American Indian confederations and consisted of approximately 16,000 people. The successful union begun by Deganawida flourished into the nineteenth century. After its peak of influence, the league began its collapse as a result of many factors, including the influence of outsiders, the supply of trade goods, the control of military posts, agreements with the whites, rivalries between warriors and chiefs, and structural weaknesses. However, the league owed its several centuries of influence to the leadership of Deganawida, especially his shrewd negotiations and his wisdom in framing the laws and principles that served as the basis for the entire structure of the league.

Further Reading

Graymont, Barbara, *The Iroquois in the American Revolution,* New York: Syracuse University Press, 1972.

Tooker, Elisabeth, "The League of the Iroquois: Its History, Politics, and Rituals," in *Handbook of North American Indians,* edited by William C. Sturtevant, Washington, DC: Smithsonian Institution, 1978.

Delaware Prophet

Delaware spiritual leader
Flourished 1760s
Also known as Neolin ("The Enlightened")

The time when Indians could have thrown out the whites or ignored them economically had clearly passed. Yet the Indians could still turn their focus inward, renewing traditional rituals and practices and restoring social order among themselves. The teachings of the Delaware Prophet supported such aims.

The Delaware Prophet is the best known of a number of spiritual leaders of the Delaware tribe who were prominent in the Ohio Valley between 1740 and 1760. He has held a lasting place in history partly because his teachings were so clear, and partly because he greatly influenced his most famous convert, the Ottawa chief **Pontiac** (see entry), who was to use the teachings of the prophet as the basis for the uprising he led against English forts in the Great Lakes region in 1763.

The nativist revival

The Delaware tribe, originally of the regions that became eastern Pennsylvania, New Jersey, and southeastern New York, had been trading with Europeans since the early seventeenth century. In this way they acquired blankets, household utensils, and firearms, among other goods, in exchange for furs. As increased trade led to the killing off of the animals they hunted to survive, and as lands were given up to European settlers, the Delaware were forced to leave their homelands and move westward toward the Ohio and Allegheny river valleys. During the mid-eighteenth century they became caught up in the French and Indian Wars, in which European powers fought for colonial empires in the Americas. The Delaware sided with the French, thus making enemies of the British.

These events may have created the conditions for the nativist revivalism (a movement to restore former beliefs and practices) that arose among the Delaware in the mid-eighteenth century. A major feature of the revival was the activity of the spiritual leaders, or prophets, who urged their people to throw off their dependence on whites and return to their traditional ways. Among those who came before or were contemporary with the Delaware Prophet were Papounhan, who preached a kind of pacifism, or nonviolence, that resembled that of the Quaker Christian sect; the "Old Preast," who carried an "Indian Bible" made up of pictures illustrating his teachings; and Wangomen, whose preaching was inspired by a vision in which the Great Spirit urged reconciliation of the Indians to their god. All of these religious figures urged a return to Indian traditions of earlier times, and each, with the exception of Papounhan, had an anti-European message.

By the time the Indian revival began, white Christian missionaries had been at work for some time among the Indians. Many historians have seen a parallel between the crusading Indian prophets and the activities of the missionaries. Some have pointed to the influence of the "inner light" of Quakerism, and others to the un-Indian nature of the chart or "Bible" some of the prophets used. Most believe that the missionaries had at least some influence on the development of Indian revivalism among the Delawares.

Neolin, the Delaware Prophet

It was in these circumstances that Neolin, who became known as the Delaware Prophet, rose to prominence in around 1762. The Delaware Prophet's authority was based on a religious experience. After a period of fasting, dreaming, and incantation (speaking or singing to produce a magical effect), Neolin undertook a spiritual journey; at its conclusion he went before the Great Spirit, or Master of Life, who gave him instructions for the betterment of the lives of Indians and for the proper means of worship.

The Master of Life indicated his displeasure that Indians let the white men—and the

English in particular—live among them, and that they had adopted many of the European ways. He blamed the declining fortunes of Indians on these circumstances, and he told the prophet that the way to win back his favor and once more find happiness and prosperity was to reject the ways of the English and their trade goods, especially guns and alcohol. He instructed Indians to hunt with the bows and arrows and stone-pointed lances of their forefathers and once more to dress themselves in skins. He also directed them to lift the hatchet—that is, make war—against the English, who, he said, had robbed them of their hunting grounds and driven away their game animals.

The French were not part of the Master of Life's condemnation of whites. "They are very dear to me," he was supposed to have said, "for they love the red men." The Master of Life concluded by giving the prophet some rules for a moral life-style, instructing Indians to marry only one wife, to deal with one another fairly, and to avoid excessive drinking and the practice of magic.

Following these teachings, the prophet traveled from village to village, preaching and distributing deerskins with charts on them. These charts illustrated Indians' path to heaven and showed how it was blocked by the whites. The Delaware Prophet was reportedly a powerful and emotional speaker; one observer remarked that he cried constantly as he preached to his listeners. His message met with widespread response, and Indians of many tribes traveled long distances to hear him. His deerskin charts, which were much copied and widely distributed, conveyed his message to those who were unable to hear him in person.

Alliance with Pontiac

While the Delaware Prophet pursued his mission among his people, the Ottawa chief Pontiac pondered the declining fortunes of Indians and their troubled relations with the British. Even as Pontiac was developing his plan to form a political and military alliance among Indians to drive the British from their fortifications along the Great Lakes, the words of the Delaware Prophet reached him. The prophet's message deeply inspired Pontiac, and the resulting alliance of the two leaders undoubtedly strengthened the authority of each.

Pontiac disagreed with the prophet on one important point, however: the use of guns by the Indians. He did not believe they could succeed in battle without firearms. At the great council that Pontiac called on the Ecorse River in April 1763 to rally support for his planned uprising, the chief made a persuasive speech full of references to the teachings of the prophet.

Pontiac's alliance with the prophet made the political and military mission of the nativist revival much clearer. In the months that followed the Ecorse council, Pontiac's military campaign ultimately failed, and so did the revival. The fortunes of the Delaware Prophet seem to have waned with those of Pontiac, but his career was not yet over. In fact, he continued to preach among his people during the years that followed Pontiac's decline and death. He was described by an observer in 1765 as "an Indian of good repute among the Delawares." After 1766, he disappears from recorded history.

The best known and most complete account of the Delaware Prophet's teachings and vision has come to us through the person who wrote down Pontiac's speech at the Ecorse River council. The identity of this scribe is unknown, but he is thought to have been a French priest. There has been much debate among scholars about whether Pontiac altered the words of the prophet to suit his political ends. Pontiac's plans to drive out the British required French help, and the message he attributed to the Delaware Prophet, in which the Master of Life makes a great distinction between the English and the French in relation to the Indians, was certainly helpful to his plans. However, the Indians had long enjoyed cordial relations with the French, while their dealings with the British had been tense. Furthermore, a number of manuscripts that have survived from the period detail the preaching of the prophet from firsthand observation, and they agree substantially with Pontiac's version.

Many historians question Pontiac's conversion. Some writers believe he adopted the prophet's teachings for purely political reasons, while others see Pontiac's vision of a united Indian effort to reclaim lost lands and traditions as the effort of a genuine convert. In the end, both the militaristic aspects of the revival and the prophet's preachings against trade with the whites failed. By the mid-eighteenth century, the Indians were thoroughly dependent on the goods they obtained from trade with whites, and the revival did not seriously affect that trade.

A lasting legacy

The scope and importance of the Delaware nativist revival go far beyond its association with Pontiac's military campaign. Arising out of conditions of economic hardship and social and spiritual chaos, it sought a new order to solve these problems. The time when Indians could have thrown out the whites or ignored them economically had clearly passed. Yet the Indians could still turn their focus inward, renewing traditional rituals and practices and restoring social order among themselves. The teachings of the Delaware Prophet supported such aims, addressing basic issues such as family structure, fairness, spiritual practices, and rules governing alcohol use and banning polygamy, or multiple marriage, as well as stealing, murder, and conflict between tribes.

In the years after the Delaware Prophet's heyday, the Delaware tribe reunified. A central organization replaced the former loose alliance of the three major divisions of the tribe. The spiritual foundation laid down by the Delaware Prophet became the basis of a national religion. This, in its turn, served as the spiritual basis of a national political unit with a principal chief and a national council for centralized decision making. What is more, his influence extended beyond his own tribe and his own time. The Delaware Prophet's teachings are reflected in the careers of later spiritual leaders such as the Shawnee Prophet Tenskwatawa and the Seneca leader **Handsome Lake** (see entry).

Further Reading

Dowd, Gregory E., "Thinking and Believing: Nativism and Unity in the Ages of Pontiac and Tecumseh," *American Indian Quarterly,* 16, 1992, pp. 309-35.

Peckham, Howard H., *Pontiac and the Indian Uprising,* Cambridge: Princeton University Press, 1947.

Wallace, Anthony F. C., "New Religions among the Delaware Indians, 1600-1900," *Southwestern Journal of Anthropology,* 12:1, 1956, pp. 1-21.

Ella Cara Deloria

Yankton Sioux ethnologist, linguist, and novelist
Born January 31, 1889, Yankton Sioux
　　　　Reservation, South Dakota
Died 1971, Vermillion, South Dakota

"I actually feel that I have a mission: To make the Dakota people understandable, as human beings, to the white people who have to deal with them."

Ella Cara Deloria was a well-known linguist (a scholar who studies languages), ethnologist (a scholar who studies the characteristics of the different human races), and novelist whose work is only recently being appreciated for its depth and volume of detail, as well as for its artistry. Her contributions to the field of Native American ethnography—the recording of culture—are vast and include translations of original sources, texts on Sioux grammar, and even a Sioux-English dictionary. These accomplishments had earned Deloria the reputation as the leading authority on Sioux culture by the 1940s. She wrote a popular book on Indians in general, *Speaking of Indians,* in 1944, and a novel about Sioux ancestral culture, *Waterlily,* which was published after her death in 1988.

Family history and education

Ella Cara Deloria was born into the prominent Deloria family in 1889 at White Swan, South Dakota, on the Yankton Sioux Reservation. Her brother, **Vine Deloria, Sr.** (see entry)—like their father—was a promi-
nent minister and leader in the community, and her nephew, **Vine Deloria, Jr.** (see entry), is a noted writer and lawyer. The Deloria family's involvement in the leadership of their community goes back a long way. In 1869, Deloria's grandfather, Chief François Des Laurias (a medicine man and leader of the White Swan band), called for the establishment of an Episcopal mission among his people.

Her father, Philip Deloria, was ordained an Episcopal priest in 1891. He was widowed by his first two wives and in 1888 married Mary Sully Bordeaux, a widow who also had children from a previous marriage. Mary, Ella Deloria's mother, was also a devout Christian, and though only one-quarter Indian, had been raised as a traditional Dakota. Thus Ella was raised in a home that valued Christian principles balanced with traditional Sioux ways; Dakota was more often than not the language spoken at home.

Deloria began her education at St. Elizabeth's School, attached to her father's church, St. Elizabeth's, on the Standing Rock Reservation in North and South Dakota. In 1902 she attended All Saints, a boarding school in Sioux Falls, South Dakota. In 1910 she was a student at Oberlin College, Oberlin, Ohio. She received a bachelor of science degree from Columbia University Teachers College in New York City in 1915. In the same year she returned to All Saints as a teacher and stayed until 1919, when she accepted a job that gave her the opportunity to travel extensively throughout the western United States. Her position as a YWCA health education secretary for Indian schools and reservations also put her in contact with many Indian groups.

In 1923 she became a physical education and dance instructor at the Haskell Institute, an Indian School in Lawrence, Kansas.

Affiliation with Franz Boas and ethnography

Deloria is held in high esteem as an ethnologist, but in fact she never studied anthropology (the study of human societies) in a university and made it known that she didn't wish to be an academic anthropologist. It was her knowledge of the Lakota language, as well as her general scholarly abilities, that attracted the attention of Franz Boas, a pioneer in the field of anthropology who taught at Columbia University from 1899 to 1942. Deloria was a student at Columbia Teachers College in 1915 when Boas hired her to work on a collection of Lakota texts (written materials) which had been assembled in 1887 by George Bushotter, a Sioux, under the supervision of Smithsonian Institution ethnologist James Owen Dorsey. She found the job of translating and analyzing language rewarding. Twelve years later, when Deloria was at Haskell Institute, Boas contacted her again, and work on the texts resumed. She translated additional texts as well, and in 1929 published her first work, an article on the Sun Dance, in the *Journal of American Folk-Lore.*

In 1928, Deloria moved to New York to work for Boas and at this time the anthropological study of her people became her primary occupation. While in New York, she met Ruth Benedict, a well known anthropologist who focused on American Indian groups. Benedict encouraged Deloria to focus on kinship, tribal structure, and the roles of women—issues Deloria handled skillfully in her novel *Waterlily.* Over the next 20 years, she worked closely with Boas and Benedict (until Boas's death in 1942 and Benedict's in 1948) and completed a body of work that added greatly to the field of Native American ethnography. She finished the translation of the Bushotter collection and translated manuscripts of the Oglala Sioux George Sword from around 1908, plus an 1840 text by the Santee Sioux Jack Frazier.

During this time she published several books, including *Dakota Texts, Dakota Grammar,* and *Speaking of Indians.* She also assembled a Sioux-English dictionary and amassed such a wide array of Lakota and Dakota texts, including conversations, autobiographies, stump speeches, and jokes, that no comparable body of written work exists for any other Plains tribe. In 1943 she was awarded the Indian Achievement Medal and was recognized as the foremost authority on Sioux culture.

After Boas's death, Deloria began analyzing the data she had collected. A manuscript, which she sometimes called "Camp Circle Society" and sometimes "Dakota Family Life," would later serve as the inspiration for her novel, *Waterlily.* The manuscript, which was never published, attempts to describe ancestral Sioux culture in all its aspects. It is full of personal impressions and quite idealistic, making the novel an appropriate way to present this vast, diverse material.

In a 1952 letter to H. E. Beebe, Deloria described her reason for preparing such a work: "I feel that one of the reasons for the lagging advancement of the Dakotas has been that those who came out among them to teach and preach, went on the assumption that the

Dakotas had *nothing,* no rules of life, no social organization, no ideals. And so they tried to pour white culture into, as it were, a vacuum. And when that did not work out, because it was not a vacuum after all, they concluded that the Indians were impossible to change and train. What they should have done first, before daring to start their program, was to study everything possible of Dakota life, to see what made it go, in the old days, and what was still so deeply rooted that it could not be rudely displaced without some hurt... I feel that I have this work cut out for me." Deloria's sense of mission and her personal stake in the material she collected undoubtedly made it difficult for her to be the kind of detached and objective observer the academic anthropologist was expected to be in the 1940s. She always favored a more subjective, or personal, approach.

From the time when she was a student at Teachers College of Columbia University, Deloria gave informal lectures and presented Sioux songs and dances at churches, schools, and civic organizations. She wished to bridge the gap of misunderstanding and ignorance that lay between Indians and whites in a way that scientific writings could not. In the letter quoted earlier she also asserted, "This may sound a little naive, Mr. Beebe, but I actually feel that I have a mission: To make the Dakota people understandable, as human beings, to the white people who have to deal with them." Her nontechnical description of American Indian culture of the past and present, *Speaking of Indians,* was assembled with this goal in mind. It was published by one of the organizations that invited her to speak, the Young Men's Christian Association (YMCA).

Publishes novel *Waterlily*

Boas's colleagues tended to search for nontechnical materials, perhaps even fiction, in order to present anthropological concepts to a general audience. Zora Neale Hurston, a well-known writer, was an anthropologist and follower of Boas's ideas who did just this to paint a picture in her novels of the life of African American women in the deep South. Similarly, Elsie Clews Parsons was a student and colleague of Boas who edited a book of fictional sketches of the Native Americans of the past, entitled *American Indian Life,* in 1922. Boas and Benedict believed that Deloria was eminently qualified for this kind of work and suggested that she write a novel about the life of a nineteenth-century traditional Sioux woman. That idea would become what is Deloria's best known work today, *Waterlily.*

In *Waterlily* Deloria mixed different aspects of her collected data and life experience, including the texts of George Bushotter and George Sword, interviews with living elders, and the stories and values of her own family. In many ways, the book is impossible to categorize. It is full of cultural details; it is a historical novel firmly grounded in its place and time; it is an essay on the social organization of a highly complex society; and it is a work of fiction with an intricate plot and well-developed characters.

Like Hurston's 1937 novel *Their Eyes Were Watching God, Waterlily* does not focus on the tragedy of an embattled and oppressed people, but chooses instead to celebrate a rich and healthy culture. References to the doom faced by *Waterlily*'s people are subtle, such as the happy chanting of the children: "While the buffalo live we shall not die!" The book was not published during the author's lifetime. Macmillan turned it down, as did the University of Oklahoma Press. Both publishers admired its extensive detail but feared the reading public would not buy it. It was finally published by the University of Nebraska Press in 1988.

In 1955 Deloria returned to her former grade school, St. Elizabeth's, to serve as director. She held that post until 1958. From 1962 to 1966 she continued her work at the University of South Dakota. She died at Vermillion, South Dakota, in 1971. Her work remains invaluable, both to academic linguists and anthropologists for her translations and research, and to the general reading public for the rich and polished *Waterlily.*

Further Reading

Deloria, Ella Cara, with Franz Boas, *Dakota Grammar,* Sioux Falls, SD: Dakota Press, 1941.

Deloria, Ella Cara, *Dakota Texts,* 1932; New York: AMS Press, 1974.

Deloria, Ella Cara, *Speaking of Indians,* 1944; Sioux Falls, SD: Dakota Press, 1979.

Deloria, Ella Cara, *Waterlily,* Lincoln: University of Nebraska Press, 1988.

Native American Women, edited by Gretchen M. Bataille, New York: Garland Publishing, 1993.

Vine Deloria, Jr.

Yankton Sioux writer
Born March 26, 1933, Martin, South Dakota

"One reason I wanted to write [Custer Died for Your Sins: An Indian Manifesto] *was to raise some issues for younger Indians which they have not been raising for themselves."*

V ine Deloria, Jr., of the Yankton Sioux, became a well-known political activist through his writings, which explained the goals of the Native American rights movement to the American public. His family heritage, combined with his academic training, gave his writings authority. Deloria was born in 1933, in Martin, South Dakota, the son of Vine and Barbara Eastburn Deloria.

He joined a distinguished family: his great-grandfather François Des Laurias ("Saswe") was a medicine man and leader of the White Swan band of the Yankton Sioux tribe; his father, **Vine Deloria, Sr.** (see entry), was the first American Indian to be named to a national executive post in the Episcopal church. His grandfather Philip was an Episcopal priest, and his aunt **Ella Cara Deloria** (see entry) gained recognition as an ethnographer, or scholar of the beliefs and customs of a people, who specialized in Indian life and language. From 1932 to 1982 the Indian Council Fire, an organization in Chicago, presented 54 achievement awards to recognize quality of Indian initiative and leadership. Of these awards, three went to

Vine Deloria, Jr.

members of the Deloria family: Vine, Sr., Ella, and Vine, Jr.

Deloria attended grade school in Martin, South Dakota, and graduated from Kent High School in Kent, Connecticut. He served in the Marine Corps from 1954 to 1956, then attended Iowa State University, where he received his bachelor's degree in 1958. He had considered following his father into the ministry, but seeing Vine, Sr.'s, frustrations convinced him that church work did not have the influence on Indian life that he wanted his career to have. Before he gave up the idea, however, he earned a theology degree at Augustana Lutheran Seminary, Rock

Island, Illinois, in 1963. The following year he was hired by the United Scholarship Service in Denver to develop a program to create scholarships for American Indian students in eastern preparatory schools (private high schools). He successfully placed a number of Indian students in eastern schools through the program.

He served as the executive director of the National Congress of American Indians (NCAI) in Washington, D.C., from 1964 to 1967, an experience he claimed was more educational than anything he had done in his previous 30 years. He was expected to solve problems facing Indian tribes from all over the country but found that certain dishonest people made the task impossible. He was frustrated by the feeling that the interests of tribes were often played against one other.

In addition, the NCAI had financial difficulties and was often close to bankruptcy, so that most of its time was spent dealing with money issues. Still, the organization was able to win a few policy changes in the government's Department of Interior, which deals with numerous issues facing Indians, including many environmental matters. Although Deloria felt the organization had been successful, especially because of the support and hard work of organization members, he knew he would need other tactics to further the cause of Indian rights.

Earns law degree

He decided to return to college and earn a law degree from the University of Colorado in 1970. This decision was influenced in part by success of the Legal Defense Fund of the National Association for the Advancement of Colored People (NAACP), which had been established to help the black community. He also realized that local Indian tribes did not have lawyers and knew little, if anything, about their rights. He received his law degree with the goal of starting a program to help smaller Indian tribes and communities to understand their basic rights.

Throughout his career Deloria's goal has been to support tribes through advocacy organizations—groups that do political and other work on their behalf—and to educate Native Americans on the law through teachings and writings. These educational efforts stress the historical and political relationships of Indians to other people. His role as an activist in the efforts of Native Americans to achieve self-government has focused on change through education rather than through violence.

From 1970 to 1978, Deloria was a lecturer in the ethnic studies division of Western Washington State University at Bellingham. He also worked with Northwest Coast tribes in their effort to protect their fishing rights, taught at the University of California at Los Angeles, and chaired the Institute for the Development of Indian Law, headquartered in Washington, D.C. For the 12 years after that very busy period, he served as a professor of American Indian studies and political science at the University of Arizona.

In 1990 he moved to the University of Colorado in Boulder to join the faculty of the Center for Studies of Ethnicity and Race in America. In addition to his teaching positions, Deloria served in leadership positions in several organizations, including the Citizens Crusade against Poverty, the Council on Indian Affairs, the National Office for the

Rights of the Indigent, the Institute for the Development of Indian Law, and the Indian Rights Association.

Publishes Indian activist views

Deloria may be best known, however, as a writer who has dramatically presented his case for Indian self-government. *Custer Died for Your Sins: An Indian Manifesto,* written while he was attending law school, captured the attention of reviewers and critics and gain increased recognition for Native American issues. Written at the time the American Indian Movement (AIM) was drawing public attention to the struggle, Deloria's book clearly presented the goal of most Native American activists: to become self-ruled, culturally separate from white society, and politically separate from the U.S. government.

While blasting America's treatment of Indian people, Deloria explained that policies such as termination are used by the U.S. government in order to break its agreement to respect tribal governments, taking away Indian rights and money. He also argued that a return to tribalism (strong loyalty to one's own group) represented the best hope for an Indian future.

Although Indian nationalism (emphasis on and promotion of one's own nation) grew at the same time as the civil rights movement of American blacks, Deloria wrote of important differences between black nationalism and Indian nationalism. He argued that since Indian civil rights issues were based on treaties—agreements between the U.S. government and Indian leaders—they had to be handled in a special way. Deloria explained his reasons for writing his book in its afterword: "One reason I wanted to write it was to raise some issues for younger Indians which they have not been raising for themselves. Another reason was to give some idea to white people of the unspoken but often felt antagonisms [feelings of opposition or hostility] I have detected in Indian people toward them, and the reasons for such antagonism."

Attacks Christianity

Deloria's second book, *We Talk, You Listen: New Tribes, New Turf,* also addressed the issue of tribalism and once again proposed a return to tribal social organization in order to save society. His third book, *God Is Red: A Native View of Religion,* captured the attention of readers across the nation. In it Deloria offered an alternative to Christianity, which he claimed had failed both in its theology—its definition of God and other spiritual matters—and its approach to social issues.

A 1992 edition of the book took these ideas even further. Admitting that even he found it hard to live without the conveniences of modern American life, Deloria proposed that religion in North America should follow traditional Native American ideals and seek spiritual fulfillment in terms of "space" by feeling the richness of the land. Most critics applauded his presentation of Indian religious practice but were offended by his attack on the Jewish and Christian traditions. His later book *The Metaphysics of Modern Existence* followed up on this theme by questioning non-Indian worldviews of modern life.

All of Deloria's writings emphasize the failure of U.S. treaties to provide for the needs of Indian people. Using his legal training, he has analyzed past relationships between the U.S. government and Native American groups and has argued the need to reopen treaty negotiations to allow Indians more control over their culture and government.

As an expert on U.S. Indian treaties, Deloria was called as first witness for the defense in the 1974 trial of **Russell Means** and **Dennis Banks** (see entries), who had been part of AIM's takeover of Wounded Knee, South Dakota. Later, Deloria blamed the failure of the Indian civil rights movement on the unwillingness of the American public to revise their ideas about Indians, which most whites had learned, he felt, from television. He attacked the American public for avoiding the real Indian world, noting that even as some sympathetic whites copied Indian fashions and bought books about Indian struggles, Native Americans were still being oppressed everywhere.

Deloria's books often try to combat stereotypes (overly simple and often ill-considered ideas or images of a group) that his white readers have developed so that they can begin to comprehend the issues from an Indian viewpoint. Not without humor, he frequently makes fun of white culture and then offers his alternative. He commented in an interview that Americans can be told the obvious 50 times a day without learning anything from it. He has also commented that white readers are often disappointed that he doesn't share mystical Indian secrets but instead talks tough about politics.

Another of Deloria's major themes has been concern for the natural environment. He blames modern society with its dependence on machines for destroying the earth, predicting the end of the planet if changes are not made soon to allow the natural environment to recover. He predicted in an interview with the magazine *The Progressive* that in 500 years "there will be fewer than 100,000 people on whatever this continent comes up as, there will probably be some Indians and all kinds of new strange animals—the Earth a completely different place, people talking about legends of the old times when iron birds flew in the air."

Further Reading

Bruguier, Leonard Rufus, "A Legacy in Sioux Leadership: The Deloria Family," in *South Dakota Leaders,* edited by Herbert T. Hoover and Larry J. Zimmerman, Vermillion: University of South Dakota Press, 1989.

Deloria, Vine, Jr., *The Aggressions of Civilization: Federal Indian Policy since the 1880s,* Philadelphia: Temple University Press, 1984.

Deloria, Vine, Jr., *American Indian Policy in the Twentieth Century,* Norman: University of Oklahoma Press, 1985.

Deloria, Vine, Jr., *Behind the Trail of Broken Treaties,* New York: Delacorte, 1974.

Deloria, Vine, Jr., *Custer Died for Your Sins: An Indian Manifesto,* New York: Macmillan, 1969.

Deloria, Vine, Jr., *God Is Red: A Native View of Religion,* Grosset, 1973; second edition, New York: North American Press, 1992.

Deloria, Vine, Jr., *The Metaphysics of Modern Existence,* New York: Harper, 1979.

Deloria, Vine, Jr., *We Talk, You Listen: New Tribes, New Turf,* New York: Macmillan, 1970.

Deloria, Vine, Jr., with Clifford Lytle, *American Indians, American Justice,* Austin: University of Texas Press, 1983.

Deloria, Vine, Jr., with Clifford Lytle, *The Nations Within: The Past and Future of American Indian Sovereignty,* New York: Pantheon, 1984.

Paulson, T. Emogene, and Lloyd R. Moses, *Who's Who among the Sioux,* Vermillion: Institute of Indian Studies, University of South Dakota, 1988.

Warrior, Robert Allen, "Vine Deloria Jr.: 'It's About Time to Be Interested in Indians Again,'" *The Progressive,* April 1990, pp. 24-27.

Vine Deloria, Sr.

Standing Rock Yankton Sioux minister
Born October 6, 1901, near Wakpala,
    South Dakota
Died February 26, 1990, Arizona

Though Vine Deloria, Sr., always felt that Native Americans should assimilate, or adjust to the norms of U.S. culture, he never lost sight of the importance of Indian culture and customs.

V ine Victor Deloria was born on October 6, 1901, at St. Elizabeth's Mission, near Wakpala, South Dakota. His grandfather, François Des Laurias ("Saswe"), the son of a French fur trader and Indian mother, was a leader of the Ihanktonwan (Yankton) Dakota half-breed band and was valued by federal officials because of his bicultural—that is, part-European—background.

Deloria's father, Philip Joseph Deloria, was first in line to take over as leader of the half-breed band and earned a position in the warrior society. However, he joined the Episcopal clergy to serve his people better in their process of adjusting to white society. Vine's sister, **Ella Cara Deloria** (see entry), became a well-known scholar, whose linguistics (the study of language) research drew attention to the importance of Indian studies. Deloria explored several career options before finally following his father's path in the Episcopalian ministry.

After his mother's death in 1916, Vine Deloria attended Kearney Military School in

Nebraska, attaining the rank of cadet colonel. From there, he moved to St. Stephens (Bard) College in New York and received his bachelor of arts degree. He enjoyed all sports, playing football, baseball, and basketball and coaching for a year at Fort Sill Indian School in Oklahoma. Between school semesters he worked in a coal mine. For a while, he considered becoming a carpenter.

Entered priesthood

In the late 1920s, Deloria's father became ill and expressed the wish that Vine follow him into the Episcopalian priesthood. Reluctantly, Vine completed the course at General Theological Seminary in New York City and was ordained as a minister in his father's church shortly before his father's death in 1931. Vine's first position was among his people at the Indian Mission in Pine Ridge, South Dakota. Next, he served on the Sisseton Reservation, Sisseton, South Dakota. The first 20 years of his career were spent serving Indian people in South Dakota. He made many visits to the Niobrara Deanery Convocations and often served as the voice for Indian Episcopalians to outsiders.

Deloria's success in the mission field led to his appointment in 1954 to the Episcopal National Council in New York City, where he was in charge of all Indian mission work as the Indian secretary for the Episcopal Church of America. Frustrated by efforts to improve Indian life through the church hierarchy, Deloria returned to local service. He spent two years in Iowa and then was appointed archdeacon of the Niobrara Deanery. Deloria served as archdeacon in Pierre, South Dakota, visiting as many as 87 churches throughout the state.

Deloria's interest in sports was evident throughout his life. He was proud of his own accomplishments on the football field for St. Stephens College, where he once completed a 55-yards pass. He often used sports comparisons in his sermons to make his ideas clear.

Seen as visionary

In 1968, Deloria retired as archdeacon, but served as priest at St. Paul's Episcopal mission in Vermillion, South Dakota, for two years. He then retired to Pierre with his wife, Barbara Sloat Eastburn, and he moved to Arizona in 1986. Though he always felt that Native Americans should assimilate, or adjust to the norms of U.S. culture, he never lost sight of the importance of Indian culture and customs. By the 1980s, he expressed disillusionment with Christianity, which he felt focused too much on the spiritual Christ and too little on Jesus the human being and therefore did not take a humanitarian approach to people around the world.

Deloria successfully ministered through the Episcopal church for 37 years. He was respected by Indians and non-Indians alike as an honest, hard-working friend. His influence was still evident at the 114th Niobrara Episcopal Convention at the Santee Agency in Nebraska in 1986. When it was proposed that mission land be sold to raise money, people waited expectantly for his opinion and followed his advice to keep the land.

Vine Deloria was considered a visionary (a person interested in long term, future issues) within the church, setting an agenda of Indian involvement at both the national and local levels. He died on February 26, 1990, leaving his wife, two sons, **Vine Deloria, Jr.** (see entry), and Sam, and one daughter, Barbara Sanchez. Vine Deloria, Jr., has carried on his father's fight for Indian rights as a political activist and writer. Sam has contributed to the field of Indian law.

Further Reading

Argus Leader (Sioux Falls, SD), March 6, 1990, p. C1.

Bruguier, Leonard Rufus, "A Legacy in Sioux Leadership: The Deloria Family," in *South Dakota Leaders,* edited by Herbert T. Hoover and Larry J. Zimmerman, Vermillion: University of South Dakota Press, 1989, pp. 367-378, 471.

Native North American Almanac, edited by Duane Champagne, Detroit: Gale, 1994, p. 1044.

Michael Dorris

Modoc writer, educator, and anthropologist
January 30, 1945, Louisville, Kentucky

Michael Dorris has shown the same remarkable energy and dedication as a parent and husband as he has as a writer and scholar.

Michael Anthony Dorris chaired the Native American Studies Department at Dartmouth College, has been a researcher, and is the author of best-selling novels, as well as an acclaimed children's book and numerous essays. He has shown the same remarkable energy and dedication as a parent and husband as he has as a writer and scholar.

He was born in Louisville, Kentucky, in 1945 to Mary Besy (Burkhardt), whose husband, Jim Dorris, was killed in World War II. Dorris was then raised by a household of women—his aunts and his grandmother, Alice Manion Burkhardt. A ferocious reader, he won prizes at his local library for finishing a book a day. He also exchanged long letters with pen pals in other countries. Educated in Catholic schools, he applied to Georgetown University to continue his study under Jesuit priests. In 1967, he graduated magna cum laude and Phi Beta Kappa, both high academic honors.

Under Woodrow Wilson and Danforth fellowships, he attended Yale University graduate school. After his first year there, he switched his major from the history of the theater to anthropology (the study of human societies) and earned a master's degree in 1971. He did his field research in Tyonek, Alaska, a fishing village on the west coast of Cook Inlet.

Single father adoption

Because of the loneliness he experienced in the far north, he decided to apply to a Catholic agency to adopt a child. Soon he was raising a three-year-old Lakota boy. The child, whom he named Reynold Abel, had been seven weeks premature. He was malnourished, and was soon diagnosed as mentally retarded. Yet Dorris was convinced that his problems could be solved through love and nurturing and would write about this undertaking later in his life. After a year teaching anthropology (the study of human societies) at Franconia College in New Hampshire, he was invited to found a Native American studies program at Dartmouth College in Hanover, New Hampshire, in 1972.

In 1974, Dorris adopted a second son, Sava, named after his deceased Alaskan

Michael Dorris

fishing partner, Sava Stephens. A daughter, Madeline Hannah, was adopted in 1976. In May 1979, he took all three of his children to dance at the annual Dartmouth powwow; there he met a former student, **Louise Erdrich** (see entry). Soon after the pow-wow, he and the children spent seven months in New Zealand, where Dorris—funded by a grant—did research on that country's native Maori people. While he was away, he and Erdrich sent their poetry back and forth with their letters, beginning their extremely successful literary partnership.

Literary collaboration and marriage

When Dorris returned to New Hampshire in 1980, Erdrich moved back there too, and they continued to collaborate on their writ-ing. Their literary relationship led to a deeply romantic one and in 1981 Dorris and Erdrich were married. The two writers worked together first on short stories. In 1982, a short story submitted to a magazine under Erdrich's name was judged the best of 2,000 entries. "The World's Greatest Fisher-man" became the first chapter of her novel *Love Medicine*. Dorris served as her agent, sending out chapters to magazines before selling the book to a publisher. He also sold the movie rights to the book, which won more awards than any other first novel in publishing history.

While they collaborated on short stories, Dorris and Erdrich used the pseudonym, or pen name, Milou North. Many of their early romantic tales were published by a British magazine, *Woman*. With the money from these stories, they were able to pay for repairs to the eighteenth-century farmhouse they bought in Comish, New Hampshire. The couple had four more children in addi-tion to Dorris's original three.

Dorris and Erdrich have an unusually close connection when it comes to writing their books. Their writing process begins with a first draft, usually written by who-ever had the original idea for the book—the one who will ultimately be considered the official author. But before and during the writing process they have constant discus-sions about the characters and the plot, and at times it is difficult for them to remember who contributed an idea that may have changed the course of the book. Although the author has the original voice and the final say, ultimately both Dorris and Erdrich are responsible for what the work becomes.

Award-winning achievements

In 1985, Dorris was awarded a Rockefeller Foundation research fellowship and became a full professor at Dartmouth. After receiving the Indian Achievement Award in Chicago, he was appointed delegate to the InterAmerican Indian Congress held in Sante Fe, New Mexico.

Dorris's novel *Yellow Raft in Blue Water* was published to good reviews in 1987. Each of its three sections deals with a different generation of the same family of courageous women. Beginning with Rayona, it moves backward into her mother, Christine's, life, and concludes with the life story of Ida—resolving some of the book's mysteries about family and identity. The book sold well, and John Sayles, an acclaimed film director, soon announced his intention to make a movie version.

Dorris's 1989 book, *The Broken Cord: A Family's Ongoing Struggle with Fetal Alcohol Syndrome,* is an autobiographical examination of the lives of children with fetal alcohol syndrome, a disease that begins in a child before birth when its mother drinks excessively while pregnant. Infants and children born with fetal alcohol syndrome often have quite severe birth defects, such as mental retardation, a lack of growth and development, or other defects of the skull, face, or brain. *The Broken Cord* won the National Book Critics Circle Award for best nonfiction, as well as earning the Christopher Award and the Heartland Prize. It was a Book of the Month Club selection and has been translated into eight languages. A film starring Jimmy Smits reached 30 million

viewers and won many prestigious awards. Dorris, personally committed through his own children's experiences, has been active in many aspects of infant and child health. He has been a member of the Research Society on Alcoholism and the National Organization for Fetal Alcohol Syndrome, a board member of the Save the Children Foundation from 1991 to 1992, and in 1992, a member of the U.S. Advisory Committee on Infant Mortality.

On the strength of *The Broken Cord*'s success, Dorris resigned from his full-time teaching to devote himself to writing. In 1991, *The Crown of Columbus,* a novel written jointly with Erdrich, also became a great popular success. The book marks the five hundredth anniversary of Spanish explorer Christopher Columbus's voyage to the Americas by questioning the meaning of that voyage for both Europeans and Native Americans. The novel, in which Native American college professor Vivian Twostar and her Euro-American academic lover Roger Williams search for a fabulous relic supposedly left by Christopher Columbus on his first landing in North America, was being filmed under the direction of Michelle Pfeiffer and Kate Guinzburg in 1995.

Also marking the anniversary of Columbus's voyage to the Americas is *Morning Girl* (1992), Dorris's first children's book. *Morning Girl* tells the story of two young Bahamians living in 1492. As Morning Girl (who loves the day) and Star Boy (who prefers the night) search for their own identities, Dorris evokes the natural world and its relation to the children's culture. The daily adventures of the young narrators are the focus of the novel, which ends as Christopher Columbus's crew lands on the island. *Morning Girl* received the Scott O'Dell Award for best historical fiction and was endorsed by *Horn Book* as one of the best books for young readers. Dorris plans to create more children's literature depicting Indian heritage.

Further Reading

Chavkin, Allan, and Nancy Feyl Jackson, *Conversations with Louise Erdrich and Michael Dorris,* Jackson: University Press of Mississippi, 1993.

Dorris, Michael, *The Broken Cord,* New York: Harper & Row, 1989.

Dorris, Michael, with Louise Erdrich, *The Crown of Columbus,* New York: HarperCollins, 1991.

Dorris, Michael, *Morning Girl,* New York: Hyperion Books, 1992.

Dorris, Michael, *Native Americans: Five Hundred Years After,* photographs by Joseph Farber, New York: Thomas Y. Crowell, 1977.

Dorris, Michael, *Paper Trail,* New York: HarperCollins, 1994.

Dorris, Michael, *Rooms in the House of Stone,* Minneapolis, MN: Milkweed Editions, 1993.

Dorris, Michael, *Working Men* (short stories), New York: Henry Holt, 1993.

Dorris, Michael, *A Yellow Raft in Blue Water,* New York: Henry Holt, 1987.

Rosenberg, Ruth, *Louise Erdrich and Michael Dorris,* New York: Twayne, 1995.

Frank C. Dukepoo

Hopi-Laguna geneticist
Born 1943, Mohave Indian Reservation, Arizona
Also known as Pumatuhye ("First Crop")

"I went back to bed and four days later, it started to come together and I said: Why not? Why not an Honor Society for Indian people?"

Frank C. Dukepoo was the first Hopi to earn a doctorate degree and was among the first American Indians of any tribe to earn one in the sciences. He gained national recognition as a motivator of Indian students by founding and coordinating the National Native American Honor Society in 1982. In addition, Dukepoo has conducted extensive research in many areas, including birth defects in Indians. The scholar is also an accomplished saxophone player and an amateur magician.

Dukepoo was born on the Mohave Indian Reservation in Arizona to Anthony Dukepoo, a Hopi laborer and house painter, and Eunice (Martin), a Laguna homemaker who took in laundry for additional income. Dukepoo was the fourth of 11 siblings. His older brother Freddie, who at one time worked as a lab technician, served as his childhood role model. Dukepoo credited his parents with creating in him the values of hard work, integrity, sharing, and caring. He went to school as a youngster in the Phoenix area, and he later noted that his high school counselor, Abraham Lincoln Herm, helped guide him toward college and success. His interest in genetics (the study of the inheritance of traits) also began at an early age. "As a child, I was obsessed with birth and the miracle of life as I watched hundreds of animals reproduce," Dukepoo said in an interview. "I even conducted a few controlled mating experiments with a myriad assortment of animals just to see what would happen."

In 1965 Dukepoo married, and he had two children, Christine and Andromeda Hope-Reminissa. In the meantime, he worked at the U.S. Department of Agriculture in Phoenix, Arizona, in 1965 and at Arizona State University, Tempe, as a teaching assistant in 1971. For the next two years, he served as a genetics instructor at Mesa Community College, Mesa, Arizona, and at Phoenix Indian School as a science and math teacher. In 1973, Dukepoo graduated from Arizona State University with a Ph.D. in zoology, or genetics. He credited one of his professors, Charles Woolf, with inspiring him to earn better grades. He raised his grade point average from 1.162 to nearly 4.0. "He pulled me through," Dukepoo maintained.

Dukepoo worked at the university as an assistant zoology teacher and as a laboratory instructor, and he taught at San Diego State University and Palomar Junior College, San Marcos, California. Dukepoo also held administrative executive positions with the National Science Foundation from 1976 to 1979. The next year he became assistant executive secretary for the National Cancer Institute.

Dukepoo also served as director of Indian Education at Northern Arizona University in Flagstaff. During this time, he headed a program supported by the National Science Foundation that earned a high rating because

Frank C. Dukepoo

100 percent of its Indian students completed the program. Dukepoo next became a faculty member in the biology department and special assistant to the academic vice president at Northern State University, where he started working in 1980.

Founds National Native American Honor Society

A true motivator, Dukepoo founded, incorporated, and coordinated the National Native American Honor Society in 1982. According to Dukepoo, the idea for this organization was given to him by the Great Spirit at precisely 4 A.M. in Flagstaff, Arizona, on a Sunday in October 1981. "I was in Flagstaff and I was laying in bed and I was aroused at 4 A.M. and something said to write this down: Happiness, education, achievement, Indians, success," he recalled. "I went back to bed and four days later, it started to come together and I said: Why not? Why not an Honor Society for Indian people?"

The program invites students from fourth grade through high school graduation, including professional school students, who earn a 4.0 semester at any time to be members. They receive a membership certificate and an eagle pin and are required to perform some type of community service; scholarships and awards are also offered. Dukepoo's long-term goals were to establish a scholarship program, to start up an Honor Society symphonic band, and to hold the First National Conference in 1999 with 19,999 to 29,999 in attendance. By identifying these exceptional students, the society works to promote positive and constructive values. In this way it hopes to serve as an example, inspiring in others the same pursuit of education and high self-esteem.

Meanwhile, Dukepoo also conducted research on birth defects in Southwest Native Americans, albinism (the absence of normal pigmentation), and inbreeding (intermarrying within a small group) among the Hopi Indians of northern Arizona. His work was made into three films and was considered for use in science instruction kits, especially in elementary schools.

The knowledge Dukepoo gained from these experiences prepared him for a position as a consultant to the Bureau of Indian Affairs, Department of Education, National Institutes of Health, National Science Foundation, Southwest Development Laboratory, and the Far West Laboratory. He gave training to teachers, Indian tribes, and the Department of Economic Security. Dukepoo has also been a member of scientific and educational societies and organizations. Commonly at the forefront of important programs and changes, Dukepoo was a founding member of the Society for the Advance of Chicanos and Native Americans in Science and the American Indian Science and Engineering Society.

Dukepoo's work has earned him a number of honors, including the John Hay Whitney Fellowship, Ford Foundation fellowship, Bo Jack Humanitarian Award, and Iron Eyes Cody Medal of Freedom Award. He also received the Outstanding Educator of the Year Award for the National Coalition of Indian Education and "Premier" status and "Exemplary" awards for the programs he created and directed while working with American Indian youngsters. In 1995 he was named Indian Man of the Year and inducted into the Indian Hall of Fame.

The scholar, however, is not always buried in books and research. Dukepoo's other interests include playing saxophone with various groups, including the Salt River Indian Band and a Latin orchestra. He is also an amateur magician who has performed "Mind, Magic and Motivation" shows around the country to audiences of youngsters and adults since in 1980. The shows incorporate the concepts of Eagle Force training, which is a course in communication, motivation, and self-esteem that he and Lee Cannon, a communications expert and Marine veteran, developed for Indian people.

Further Reading

Biographical Dictionary of Indians of the Americas, second edition, Newport Beach, CA: American Indian Publishers, 1991.

Johnston, Scott, "'Perfect' Students Attend Conference," *Arizona Daily Sun,* April 17, 1992.

Mickela, Paul, "Banquet Celebrates Outstanding Students," *Navajo-Hopi Observer,* May 2, 1990, p. 9.

Reid, Betty, "College Professor Magically Inspires Students to Learn," *Independent* (Gallup, New Mexico), September 27, 1991, p. 9.

Ryan, Steve, "Dukepoo Organizes Native American Honor Society," *Arizona Daily Sun,* April 22, 1990.

Dull Knife

Northern Cheyenne tribal leader
Born c. 1810, Rosebud River, Montana
Died 1883, present-day South Dakota
Also known as Tah-me-la-pash-me and Wo-hiev
("Morning Star")

The men moved forward through the windows with children under their arms, while the women followed, and once again Dull Knife and his band dashed for freedom.

B est known for leading his people in a courageous attempt to return from exile in Oklahoma to their Montana homeland in 1878, the Northern Cheyenne leader Morning Star was born in about 1810 on the Rosebud River. He was known mostly by his nickname of Dull Knife, given to him by his brother-in-law, who teased him about not having a sharp knife. A renowned Dog Soldier in his youth, Dull Knife became a member of the Council of 44 and in the 1870s was one of the four principal, or "old man," chiefs of the Cheyenne. These chiefs represented the mystical four Sacred Persons who lived at the cardinal points of the universe and were the guardians of creation.

Little is known of Dull Knife's early life. When he was a young man in the late 1820s, he went on a raiding party against the Pawnees. After he had captured a young Pawnee girl, he saved her life by asking that she replace a member of his family previously lost to the Pawnees. When he became a chief, Dull Knife made Little Woman his second wife, and the marriage produced four daughters. Dull Knife had two other wives, Goes to Get a Drink, with whom he had two daughters, and her sister Slow Woman, with whom he had four sons and another daughter.

Ambush on the Bozeman Trail

Dull Knife first became known to non-Natives in 1866, when he joined **Red Cloud** (see entry) and the Oglala Sioux in an ambush of U.S. soldiers marching under Captain William J. Fetterman. Frontiersmen, on their way to seek gold, followed the Bozeman Trail from Wyoming to Montana, cutting directly through Oglala Sioux land. The Cheyenne were allies of the Oglala in their successful attacks on U.S. miners and troops.

On May 10, 1868, at the end of the Bozeman Trail War, the Northern Cheyenne signed the Fort Laramie Treaty, in which they agreed to settle on a reservation. The U.S. government gave them the choice of joining the Crows in Montana, the Sioux in Dakota, or the Southern Cheyenne and Arapaho in Indian Territory (modern-day Oklahoma). To force an early decision, the government withheld supplies, and the Northern Cheyennes signed an agreement on November 12, 1874, to move to Indian Territory whenever the U.S. government saw fit.

Dull Knife

icine Lodge was present and died in combat against the Seventh Cavalry.

The pivotal battle for the Northern Cheyenne occurred on the morning of November 25, 1876, when General George Crook's force of 600 men of the Fourth Cavalry and about 400 Indian scouts surprised Dull Knife's camp on the Red Fork of the Powder River. Reportedly killed in the fighting were one of Dull Knife's sons and a son-in-law. The dead numbered around 40, but the destruction of the village and its contents sealed their doom. For all practical purposes, the campaign of 1876-77 ended the Indian wars on the Northern Plains.

Concern for their children caused Dull Knife and his people to surrender to troops under Crook in the spring of 1877. At Fort Robinson they learned that the government had decreed that all Northern Cheyenne would be sent to Indian Territory (now Oklahoma). Dull Knife and Little Wolf urged their tribesmen to obey the wishes of the government. The Northern Cheyenne people may have been led to believe that they could return to their tribal lands in a year if they did not like life in the south. A total of 937 Indians began the journey to Indian Territory on May 28, 1877. On August 5, 70 days later, they arrived at the Cheyenne and Arapaho Agency and selected a campsite.

A return to their homeland

Within a year, the Northern Cheyenne were ready to return to their homeland. Starved, ravaged by disease, preyed upon by white gangs of horse thieves, unwilling to farm, and with 50 of their children dead, they had had enough. So at 10:10 P.M. on September 9, 1878, a party of 353 Cheyennes—92

These arrangements were set aside, however, when the Black Hills gold rush led to war between U.S. troops and the Sioux and their allies. The Indians were ordered to return to agencies in South Dakota by January 31, 1876. The Bighorn expedition, intended to force the Indians back to their agencies, engaged the Sioux, Northern Cheyenne, and Northern Arapaho in several major battles, the most famous of which was General George Armstrong Custer's fight on the Little Bighorn in southeastern Montana, June 25 and 26, 1876. Dull Knife was not in the Indian village that day, but his son Medmen, 120 women, 69 boys, and 72 girls—quietly left the foreign place, leaving fires burning and lodge poles standing to fool distant military observers. The whites learned of their departure the next morning at 3:00 A.M. and began pursuit, eventually involving 13,000 men in three military departments.

Following the route of the Texas cattle trail from Oklahoma through Kansas, Dull Knife and Little Wolf, another Cheyenne war chief, and their followers skirmished with army units through September at Turkey Springs, Red Hill, Sand Creek, and Punished Woman Creek, each time eluding the troops and continuing north. On the journey, Little Woman was killed by a horse that stampeded through the camp. When the fleeing Cheyennes reached northeast Kansas, warriors roamed the countryside. They killed 40 male white settlers, some said in revenge for a mass killing of their kinsmen by whites in the area in 1875. In Nebraska, Dull Knife and Little Wolf separated, the former headed for Fort Robinson and Red Cloud Agency, the latter to the traditional Northern Cheyenne homeland in Montana.

On October 23, two companies of the Third Cavalry traveled up Chadron Creek and caught Dull Knife and his people. Taken to Fort Robinson, the Cheyenne learned on January 3 that the government had decided they must be sent back to Indian Territory. When they refused, the post commander, Henry Wessells, imprisoned the band in a cavalry barracks, cutting off heat, food, and water. Barricading doors and covering windows with cloth to conceal their movements, the captives tore up the floor and constructed rifle pits to command the windows.

At 10:10 P.M. on January 9, 1879, the Cheyennes began firing. The men moved forward through the windows with children under their arms, while the women followed, and once again Dull Knife and his band dashed for freedom. This time, though, they were not so fortunate. Soldiers sent volley after volley of bullets into the fleeing band. Twenty-two men, eight women, and two children died in the first attempt to leave, including Dull Knife's daughter, Traveling Woman, who was carrying her four-year-old sister on her back. The retreat continued for four miles in the darkness until the fugitives reached neighboring hills, where pursuit was no longer possible.

Stay alive by eating their moccasins

Twelve days later, four companies of soldiers caught the largest number of remaining Cheyennes. Twenty-three Indians were killed and nine captured, including two young girls, aged 14 and 15, discovered under the bodies of young men. The dead Indians were buried in the pit where they had hidden. In the meantime, Dull Knife, Slow Woman, and their remaining children had found a haven in the rocks, where they stayed for ten days, staying alive by eating their moccasins. After 18 days of wandering, they reached Pine Ridge, South Dakota, where they were hidden by Sioux relatives in a lodge under a little bluff on Wounded Knee Creek.

After wintering in a sheltered valley near the forks of the Niobrara River, Little Wolf and his followers headed north. On March 25, they surrendered to Lieutenant W. P. Clark on the Yellowstone River and were sent to Fort Keogh. In November, Indian Bureau officials permitted the Northern Cheyenne at Pine Ridge to transfer to Montana to join the rest. At the request of General Nelson A. Miles, Dull Knife was allowed to return to the valley of the Rosebud. An executive order of November 26, 1884, established a permanent home for the Northern Cheyenne in south central Montana, east of the Crow Reservation.

Dull Knife spent his remaining years embittered and grieving in the hills of southern Montana. Among the dead he had left behind at Fort Robinson were two daughters and a son; in a single year he had lost his wife, three sons, and two daughters. Dull Knife died in 1883 at his son Bull Hump's home. In 1917 the Cheyenne historian George Bird Grinnell had his remains and those of Little Wolf reburied in the cemetery at Lame Deer, where they are today.

Further Reading

The Dull Knife Symposium, edited by John D. McDermott, Fort Phil Kearny/Bozeman Trail Association, 1989.

Grinnell, George Bird, *The Fighting Cheyennes,* second edition, Norman: University of Oklahoma Press, 1956.

Powell, Peter J., *Sweet Medicine,* two volumes, Norman: University of Oklahoma Press, 1969.

Sandoz, Mari, *Cheyenne Autumn,* Hastings House, 1953.

Stands in Timber, John, and Margot Liberty, *Cheyenne Memories,* New Haven: Yale University Press, 1967.

Gabriel Dumont

Métis buffalo hunter and tribal leader
Born c. 1837, present-day Winnipeg,
       Manitoba, Canada
Died 1906, near Batoche, Saskatchewan

Although unable to read or write, Gabriel Dumont spoke perhaps as many as six Indian languages as well as French.

G abriel Dumont was a Métis buffalo hunter and military leader. During the mid- to late nineteenth century the Métis, natives of mixed French and Indian descent, roamed the Canadian prairie hunting buffalo. Their culture, a combination of Indian and French Canadian traditions, is considered by some to be the only culture truly indigenous to Canada. Dumont and the Métis played a major role in the 1885 Northwest Rebellion—also known as the Second Riel Rebellion—led by **Louis Riel** (see entry). Although greatly outnumbered, Dumont led a band of no more than three hundred Métis warriors and Indian allies against the Canadian militia and the North West Mounted Police on the Saskatchewan prairie. After the Métis were defeated at Batoche in May 1885, Dumont fled to Montana, where he remained for many years before returning to Saskatchewan.

Dumont was born in 1837 or 1838 in what is now Winnipeg, Manitoba. He was the fourth of eleven children—five girls and six boys—born to Isidore Dumont and Louise Laframboise. Isidore, the head of the Dumont band, had inherited the position from his

Semiannual buffalo hunt, the main event in the Plains Métis community

father Jean Baptiste Dumont, who had moved west from Quebec in the 1790s and married a Sarcee Indian woman. As a Métis leader, Isidore became famous for a peace treaty he negotiated with the Sioux. As a child, Dumont grew skillful with bow and arrow. His uncle gave him his first gun before he was ten, and Dumont was soon a skilled marksman. He fired his first shot in a battle against the Sioux when he was only 12 years old.

By the time he was 25, Dumont had been elected chief of the buffalo hunt, with about 300 Métis followers. Besides being a gifted leader, Dumont was an expert horse breaker, canoeist, camp doctor, and, unlike most Métis, swimmer. He also operated a ferry on the South Saskatchewan River at the place that came to be known as Gabriel's Crossing. He ran a store, farmed a small plot of land, and organized Métis labor crews, contracting for the construction of roads, trails, mail stations, and telegraph lines.

Although unable to read or write, Dumont spoke perhaps as many as six Indian languages as well as French. His knowledge of Indian languages and cultures made him valuable as an interpreter. Dumont also had the rare ability to "call" buffalo into a trap. As chief on the buffalo hunts he was a disciplinarian, allowing no violations of the Métis hunting code. He enjoyed horse racing, gambling, billiards, and drinking with his comrades, and he was known for his sense of humor. A generous person, he donated numerous buffalo to the poorer families in his camp. His wife, Madeleine Welkey, whom he married in 1858, was the daughter of a Scottish trader and his Indian wife. Madeleine taught school at Batoche, Saskatchewan, and accompanied her husband during the rebellion. She died of tuberculosis shortly after fleeing with Dumont to Montana in 1885. The couple had no children.

Métis buffalo hunts

The Métis society reached its peak just before the disappearance of the North American buffalo. During that period, almost 3,000 Métis hunters, their families, and their Roman Catholic priests ranged over the Canada, Montana, and Dakota prairies searching for buffalo herds. These expeditions were complicated financial enterprises and the economic backbone of Métis society.

Although the Métis did kill buffalo for their hides, it was pemmican (a food mixture with dried meat), an essential part of the transcontinental fur trade, that drove the campaigns. Pemmican is a combination of shredded, dried buffalo meat, hot tallow or buffalo fat, marrow fat, and, when available, berries. This mixture, while still hot, was poured into buffalo-hide bags capable of holding 100 pounds; the bags were then compressed as they cooled and sewn shut. Easy to transport and capable of lasting for years, pemmican could be eaten cold or heated and served as a stew.

The Métis hunters transported their buffalo hides, meat, and bags of pemmican on stable, two-wheeled Red River carts. These small, light, yet sturdy wooden carts with high wheels, drawn by a single ox or horse, were capable of carrying loads of up to 900 pounds. With their wheels removed, the carts could be turned into crude boats for crossing Saskatchewan's deep and treacherous rivers. Rolling across the prairie, accompanied by the shriek of their wooden axles, the carts could be heard for miles, announcing the arrival of the Métis.

Métis buffalo hunts were highly organized affairs, requiring firm, intelligent leadership. Governed by custom and tradition, the hunters elected officers to a general council, one of whom was in turn appointed to be chief of the hunt. It was a great tribute to Dumont's organizational and leadership skills that he was first named chief of the hunt when he was only 25. The chief commanded the officers, who maintained order and enforced the hunt's regulations. Leading expeditions of 200 to 300 hunters and their families was a difficult task, but Dumont excelled at it.

His reputation as a chief led to his being elected leader of a local council set up by the Métis in 1873. This council petitioned the Canadian government for recognition of their territorial claims, as had been awarded to the Manitoba Métis in 1870. The petition reflected the Métis' concern about a flood of white Protestant settlers encroaching on their Saskatchewan territory.

Recruits Louis Riel

By 1884 the Canadian government had still not addressed the Métis' demands to stem the tide of migration, and settlers continued streaming into Saskatchewan. That same year, Dumont and three other Métis traveled to Montana to ask Louis Riel to organize and lead a rebellion. Previously, Riel had led the Manitoba Métis in a campaign that culminated in the Canadian government's recognition of the tribe in 1870, but he was a different man in 1884. After leading the fight in Manitoba, Riel suffered a mental collapse; he spent time in Quebec insane asylums, where he had been diagnosed as suffering from delusions of grandeur. He had also become a fanatical Roman Catholic and believed he was a modern prophet. By the early 1880s he had moved to Montana, had started a family, and was teaching school. Riel reportedly believed the arrival of four Métis horsemen at his doorstep was a sign from God that it was his destiny to lead the rebellion.

Upon arriving in Saskatchewan, Riel became the leader of a provisional (temporary) government, with Dumont serving as its adjutant general. Dumont's loyalty to Riel was unconditional; he rarely challenged Riel's decisions, even after Riel began interfering in military matters. After Riel's attempts to negotiate a settlement with the Canadian government failed, violence broke out in Saskatchewan. In March 1885, at the Battle of Duck Lake, Dumont led the Métis in a guerrilla-style confrontation with a detachment of the Royal Canadian Mounted Police and civilian volunteers and soundly defeated them. The Métis suffered few casualties and they killed or wounded 25 percent of the Canadian force. However, one of the few Métis killed at the battle was Dumont's brother Isidore.

In April the Métis and their Indian allies were taken by surprise at the Battle of Fish Creek. Major General Frederick D. Middleton, commander of the Canadian militia, cornered Dumont and his men until 80 Métis from Batoche, led by Dumont's brother Edouard, arrived to fortify the beleaguered warriors. After inflicting minor casualties on the Canadians, the Métis withdrew to safety. However, the end for the Métis occurred one month later at their village of Batoche.

The Battle of Batoche

Batoche, located on the South Saskatchewan River between the present-day cities of Prince Albert and Saskatoon, was the center of Métis society. The Saskatchewan River Valley, home to the buffalo and Indians for centuries, had been occupied by Métis hunters since the late 1860s. In May 1885, at the Battle of Batoche, Dumont led fewer than 300 Métis and other Indian allies, low on ammunition, against 800 troops armed with cannon and a Gatling gun. The Métis steadfastly defended Batoche from rifle pits along the edge of the bush surrounding the village, holding off the Canadians for three days. Although Dumont wanted to wage a guerrilla attack on the Canadians using the hit-and-run tactics that had proved successful at Duck Lake, Riel insisted on defending Batoche by holding their present position. After running out of ammunition and having to resort to loading their rifles with nails and stones, the Métis surrendered on May 12, 1885. Both Riel and Dumont escaped.

After fleeing Batoche, Dumont searched for Riel among the scattered fugitives of the battle. He found Métis women and children everywhere, hidden in the brush and in caves carved into the coulees (small streams). In one of the caves he found Riel's wife and two children but did not find Louis. He discovered that Riel had already surrendered to General Middleton. Refusing to surrender himself, Dumont rode 600 miles, mostly at night, hiding during the day in canyons or in Indian or Métis camps. After two weeks of successfully evading hundreds of militiamen and police, he reached Montana.

While in exile in Montana, Dumont began to plot an elaborate rescue for the captured leader of the Métis rebellion. However, before he had the opportunity to carry out his plan, Riel was convicted of treason and hanged in Regina, Saskatchewan, on November 16, 1885. Dumont remained in Montana for several years after Riel's execution, traveling with William "Buffalo Bill" Cody's Wild West Show. He was billed as the "Hero of the Half-breed Rebellion," and using his rifle, "Le Petit," he demonstrated his marksmanship to admiring audiences. Although he was no longer a young man, Dumont also gave exhibitions of his riding skills for the Wild West Show.

The Canadian government granted Dumont a pardon in 1886, but he continued to travel with the show for several more years before returning to Saskatchewan in 1893. Dumont's travels during this period took him from French-speaking communities in the northeastern United States to Paris, France, where he told audiences his story of the Métis rebellion; he also dictated two memoirs of the conflict. Dumont died at Batoche in 1906 and is buried not far from Gabriel's Crossing, near the South Saskatchewan River.

Further Reading

Dumont, Gabriel, *Gabriel Dumont Speaks,* translated by Michael Barnholden, Vancouver: Talonbooks, 1993.

Harrison, Julia D., *Métis: People between Two Worlds,* Vancouver: Douglas & McIntyre, 1985.

Howard, Joseph Kinsey, *Strange Empire: A Narrative of the Northwest,* Westport, CT: Greenwood Press, 1974.

Charles A. Eastman

Santee Sioux writer and physician
Born 1858, near Redwood Falls, Minnesota
Died 1939
Also known as Hakada ("The Pitiful Last"),
    Ohiyesa ("The Winner")

"When I reduce civilization to its lowest terms, it becomes a system of life based upon trade."

C harles Alexander Eastman was born near Redwood Falls, Minnesota, of mixed Santee Sioux and white parentage. He was strongly influenced in his distinguished career as a writer, physician, and Indian spokesperson by his personal experiences in the last bloody Indian-white conflicts on the North American prairies and plains. Eastman was the first Native American physician to serve on the Pine Ridge Reservation and a prolific author of works about Indian life and culture. Eastman published two autobiographical accounts— *Indian Boyhood,* which recounts his youth, and *From the Deep Woods to Civilization,* which tells of his experiences as an adult Indian in U.S. society. He also wrote a series of novels and some historical nonfiction.

His parents were Jacob Eastman ("Many Lightnings"), a Wahpeton Sioux, and Mary Nancy Eastman, a mixed-blood Sioux who died when he was a baby. His maternal grandfather was the artist Seth Eastman. The youngest of five children, he was given the name Hakadah ("The Pitiful Last") because of his mother's early death. Eastman fled with his family from Minnesota to British Columbia, Canada, after the Sioux Indian uprising of 1862, when Minnesota Sioux attacked white settlements after nearly starving from a lack of supplies. Eastman's father was taken prisoner for his part in the uprising, and thereafter, Eastman was raised by a paternal grandmother, from whom he learned much about the old ways and practical things that hunters and warriors had to know.

In 1874 the family moved to Flandreau, South Dakota, and Eastman was enrolled in the Flandreau Indian School where he was introduced to U.S. culture for the first time. He went on to study at Beloit College, Knox College, Dartmouth College—where he earned a bachelor's degree in 1887—and Boston University, where he received his doctorate in 1890. In his position as government physician at the Pine Ridge Agency in South Dakota, he treated the survivors of the Wounded Knee Massacre, during which hundreds of Sioux were killed by the U.S. cavalry. There he also met—and the next year married—Elaine Goodale, a poet, educator, and reformer.

A series of positions followed with the Young Men's Christian Association (YMCA) and the Bureau of Indian Affairs (BIA), and he became known in America and England as an authority on Indian concerns. With his wife's assistance, Eastman began his career as an author in 1893 with a series called "Recollections of the Wild Life" in *St. Nicholas* magazine. Over the next 27 years he gained growing fame as America's distinguished Indian writer with many more articles and ten books, one written jointly with

Charles A. Eastman

Elaine. In addition to collaborating as writers, the couple had six children. In 1933, Eastman was recognized by the Indian Council Fire, a national organization, with its first award for "most distinguished achievement by an American Indian."

Eastman's reputation as a writer, speaker, and promoter of Indian rights had much to do with the fact that he had gone from the life of a traditional Sioux in the wilderness of Canada to the homes and lecture halls of white America. As a well-spoken and accomplished physician with a dynamic wife who spoke Lakota like a native, Eastman amazed readers of his books and audiences at his lectures. Even some congressmen were startled.

From 1897 to 1900, Eastman was a lobbyist for the Santee Sioux Tribe in Washington, D.C. After one presentation before a congressional committee, he was asked by representatives where he had received his education, and why there weren't more Indians like him.

Begins literary career with autobiography

Eastman's literary career began in earnest in 1902 with the publication of *Indian Boyhood,* dedicated to his son, Ohiyesa II. He had published a handful of short pieces in magazines, but his autobiography attracted a wide non-Indian public with its description of what he called "the freest life in the world." It consists of his earliest childhood memories as well as tributes to Uncheedah, his paternal grandmother, who had reared him, and to Mysterious Medicine, his uncle, who taught him the lore of a life lived close to nature. The book's moving conclusion tells of his father's return from the federal penitentiary at Davenport, Iowa.

Eastman had entered a new and shocking world when his father sought him out in Canada in 1873 and returned with him to the United States. They settled in Flandreau, Dakota Territory, where a group of Santees lived as homesteaders—people who had filed for a plot of land through the U.S. government's Homestead Act—among the whites. "Here," wrote Eastman, "my wild life came to an end, and my school days began." It was a strange reunion, because Eastman, thinking his father was dead, had sworn to take revenge on the whites for that death. Now he was living among them with his father and adopting their ways.

Eastman went on to publish *From the Deep Woods to Civilization,* the sequel to *Indian Boyhood,* in 1916. In this book, he deals with the painful realities faced by Indians as a result of white intervention. The innocent tone of *Indian Boyhood* is now replaced by one of frustration, and he observes that his training in white ways meant the replacement of a good kind of savagery with a bad kind. Above all, Eastman was deeply depressed by the failure of Americans to practice the Christianity that they professed, so that the meek might inherit the earth and "the peacemakers receive high honor." He wrote in *From the Deep Woods to Civilization,* "When I reduce civilization to its lowest terms, it becomes a system of life based upon trade."

Eastman wrote ten books, which established him as a powerful voice for his people. Among his other works are *Red Hunters and the Animal People* (1904), stories and legends for youth; *Old Indian Days* (1907), divided into stories about warriors and women; *Smoky Day's Wigwam Evenings: Indian Stories Retold* (1910), written with his wife Elaine; *The Soul of the Indian* (1911), the most fully developed statement of his religious beliefs; and *The Indian Today: The Past and Future of the First American* (1915), a review of Indian history, contributions, and problems. Eastman's last book was *Indian Heroes and Great Chieftains* (1918), a collection of short biographies of Sioux leaders written for young people.

Throughout their years together, Elaine Eastman served as her husband's editorial assistant, reading, criticizing, and often revising his work. Although Eastman resented some of Elaine's rewriting, she seems to have been essential to his publishing success, for after their separation in 1921 he published nothing more.

Serves Sioux people in many ways

In addition to writing, Eastman also served his people and the larger society in a variety of other roles. He served as a physician on the Pine Ridge Reservation from 1890 to 1893, in private practice in St. Paul, Minnesota from 1894 to 1897, and at Crow Creek Reservation in South Dakota from 1900 to 1903. While in St. Paul he began to work for the YMCA, organizing chapters around the country, and from 1897 to 1900 he lobbied the government on behalf of the Santee Sioux.

From 1903 to 1909 Eastman was engaged, at author Hamlin Garland's urging, in a BIA project to rename the Sioux, giving them legal names in order to protect their interests. In 1910 he began a lifelong association with the Boy Scouts of America, and from 1914 to 1925 he and Elaine operated a girls' camp near Munsonville, New Hampshire. In 1923 he entered the Indian service for the last time, working until 1925 as an Indian inspector on and off the reservations. Eastman devoted most of the last years of his life, until his death in 1939, to lecturing. Charles Eastman's most important contribution to American literature is as a writer of autobiography and as a preserver of Sioux Indian legends, myths, and history.

Further Reading

Copeland, Marion W., *Charles Alexander Eastman,* Boise, ID: Boise State University Western Writers Series, 1978.

Eastman, Charles, *From the Deep Woods to Civilization: Chapters in the Autobiography of an Indian,* Boston: Little, Brown, 1916.

Eastman, Charles, *Indian Boyhood,* New York: McClure, Phillips & Co., 1902.

Eastman, Charles, *Indian Child Life,* Boston: Little, Brown, 1913.

Eastman, Charles, *Indian Heroes and Great Chieftains,* Boston: Little, Brown, 1918.

Eastman, Charles, *Indian Scout Talks: A Guide for Boy Scouts and Campfire Girls,* Boston: Little, Brown, 1914.

Eastman, Charles, *The Indian To-day; The Past and Future of the First American,* Garden City, NY: Doubleday, 1915.

Eastman, Charles, *Old Indian Days,* New York: McClure Company, 1907.

Eastman, Charles, *Red Hunters and the Animal People,* New York: Harper & Brothers, 1904.

Eastman, Charles, *The Soul of the Indian: An Interpretation,* Boston: Houghton Mifflin, 1911.

Eastman, Charles, *Wigwam Evenings: Sioux Folk Tales Retold by Charles A. Eastman (Ohiyesa) and Elaine Goodale Eastman,* Boston: Little, Brown, 1909.

Eastman, Charles, with Elaine Goodale Eastman, *Smoky Day's Wigwam Evenings; Indian Stories Retold,* Boston: Little, Brown, 1910.

Meyer, Roy W., *History of the Santee Sioux: United States Indian Policy on Trial,* Lincoln: University of Nebraska Press, 1967.

Sister to the Sioux: The Memoirs of Elaine Goodale Eastman, 1885-91, edited by Kay Graber, Lincoln: University of Nebraska Press, 1978.

Wilson, Raymond, *Ohiyesa: Charles Eastman, Santee Sioux,* Urbana: University of Illinois Press, 1983.

Louise Erdrich

Chippewa novelist and poet
Born July 6, 1954, Little Falls, Minnesota
Also known as Milou North (joint pseudonym
   with Michael Anthony Dorris)

According to Erdrich, one of her novels "never seems to start in the beginning. Rather, it's as though we're building something around a center, but that center can be anywhere."

Louise Erdrich is known for her moving and often humorous portrayals of Chippewa life in North Dakota in poetry and prose. In her verse and in novels such as *Love Medicine, Tracks, The Bingo Palace,* and *The Beet Queen,* she draws on her years in North Dakota and on her German and Chippewa heritage to portray the great endurance of women and Native Americans in twentieth-century America. She has won an array of awards and substantial recognition for her novels, as well as for her short stories, poetry, and essays.

Karen Louise Erdrich was born in Little Falls, Minnesota, in 1954 and grew up in Wahpeton, North Dakota, a town on the border of Minnesota. Her father, Ralph Louis, was a teacher with the U.S. government's Bureau of Indian Affairs (BIA) at Wahpeton, and her mother, Rita Joanne Gourneau, was a BIA employee at the Wahpeton Indian school. The family lived in employee housing at the school, and Erdrich attended public schools and spent a few years at St. Johns, a Catholic school. She later noted that Catholicism—with its strong sense of ritual—had a powerful effect on her that remained a part of her even after she stopped practicing the religion.

Erdrich's German heritage comes from her father, and her three-eighths Chippewa heritage comes from her mother. She often visited her mother's people at Turtle Mountain Reservation, situated near Belcourt, North Dakota, when she was growing up. Her grandfather, Pat Gourneau, served as tribal chairman at Turtle Mountain for many years. She described him as having a clear understanding of—and involvement in—both Indian and Christian experience. Erdrich's admiration for her grandfather can be seen in several of the complex male characters in her writings.

Parents encourage her to become a writer

As a child, Erdrich's parents encouraged her to write. Her mother made little books with construction paper covers for Erdrich's stories, and her father paid Louise a nickel for each one she finished. Her mother found out about the Native American program at New Hampshire's Dartmouth College and helped Erdrich apply in 1972. Erdrich was in the first class at Dartmouth that accepted women in the previously all-male school. Several grants and scholarships allowed her to attend Dartmouth, and Erdrich, who majored in English and creative writing, won several writing awards. Finding that poetry came easily to her, she decided to pursue writing professionally.

After her graduation in 1976, Erdrich went back to North Dakota, telling herself, as she later related in an interview with

Joseph Bruchac, that she "would sacrifice all to be a writer." She took any job that gave her the opportunity to write. All in all, she reflected, "I think I turned out to be tremendously lucky." Back in North Dakota, she worked as publications director of a small press distributor, and served in the Poets in the Schools Program sponsored by the National Endowment for the Arts. She also worked on a film about the clash between the Sioux and Europeans in the 1800s for Mid-America Television.

Returning to the East, Erdrich received a master of fine arts degree in 1977 from Johns Hopkins University. While at Johns Hopkins, she began writing fiction. She then served as editor of the *Circle,* the Boston Indian Council newspaper. After a poetry reading she gave in 1980, Erdrich began a relationship with Michael Dorris, who had attended the reading and been interested in her and her work.

Dorris, who is three-eighths Modoc, had come to Dartmouth to found and direct the Native American Studies Program. Soon after meeting Erdrich, he left for New Zealand on an anthropology fellowship, and their relationship was put on hold until January 1981, when both returned to Dartmouth—he to resume his position in the Native American Studies Program and she as writer-in-residence. They were married in 1981, and Erdrich became the legal mother of Dorris' three Native American children, whom he had adopted and was raising by himself. They also have four children together, and live in Cornish, New Hampshire, where both Erdrich and Dorris devote themselves full-time to their writing and their family.

Louise Erdrich

First novel wins major literary award

With the help of Dorris, Erdrich gathered the stories she had published between 1982 and 1984 and made them into a novel called *Love Medicine* in 1984. The story is told through the voices of half-a-dozen characters, as though to someone listening to community gossip. Erdrich used this technique in several of her novels to portray the complicated relationships of the characters, many of whom appear from novel to novel. Scholars have devoted whole essays to the family histories of these characters. These works jump back and forth through time. In Erdrich's own words, a novel in this series "never seems to start in the beginning. Rather, it's as though we're building something around a center, but that center can be anywhere."

Love Medicine is set on the Turtle Mountain Reservation in North Dakota. Taking place between 1934 and 1983, the novel presents the story of Lulu Lamartine and Marie Kashpaw. Marie is married to Nector Kashpaw, but Nector desperately loves Lulu, who has had numerous husbands and romances resulting in many children. After Nector's death by some ill-fated "love medicine," Lulu and Marie unite and become tribal elders.

Love Medicine was an unqualified smash with judges of literature. The opening story, "The World's Greatest Fisherman," won the $5,000 Nelson Algren Award in 1982. The completed novel earned the National Book Critics Circle Award for best work of fiction, the *Los Angeles Times* Award for best novel of 1984, the best first fiction award from the American Academy and Institute of Arts and Letters, and several other honors. Erdrich later added some other stories to the book and published the new and expanded version in 1993.

Love Medicine, The Beet Queen, and *Tracks* encompass the stories of three interrelated families living in and around the reservation in the fictional town of Argus, North Dakota. As one moves through the novels, one repeatedly discovers surprising connections between the characters in the three books. For example, a character in the third novel, *Tracks,* turns out to be the mother of a woman who, in *Love Medicine,* was a grandmother.

The Beet Queen, published in 1986, takes place from 1932 to 1972 and explores Erdrich's German roots. Abandoned by her mother, Mary Adare comes to live with her cousin, Sita Koska, whose parents own the butcher shop. Mary becomes best friends with Sita's good friend, a mixed-blood girl, Celestine James. Celestine has a child by Mary Adare's brother, Karl, and the spoiled child—the Beet Queen—becomes the center of attention. Fleur Pillager, a major character in the novel *Tracks,* makes a brief appearance, healing Karl Adare after an accident. This work was named one of the best books of the year by *Publisher's Weekly.*

In *Tracks,* Erdrich's third novel, set from 1912 to 1919, the story is narrated by Nanapush, an elderly trickster, or spiritual comedian/con artist, who is the last of his family, and Pauline Puyat, a mixed-breed character whose Chippewa ancestors have been forgotten. She is so desperate to fit in that she renounces her Native American heritage to become an obsessed Catholic nun. Their stories revolve around a third character, Fleur Pillager, who possesses spiritual powers. Nanapush thinks the Chippewa nation can be saved by these powers, while Pauline sees them as evil and destructive. Erdrich's Catholic background is perhaps most strongly reflected in *Tracks,* which portrays the interaction of Native American spirituality and the views of the church.

Erdrich returned to the series with 1994's *The Bingo Palace,* the story of Lipsha Morrissey (Lulu's unacknowledged grandson, whom Marie raises). In this novel she not only brings together the families from the previous books but also looks toward the future. Lipsha's great-grandmother, Fleur Pillager, appears in the novel, forcing him to think about how to balance his Chippewa heritage with business plans, namely his Uncle Lyman Lamartine's plan to build a bingo palace on Fleur's property. A review in *Time* magazine found Erdrich "still a wry, intuitive, blood-related observer and a gifted writer," but found that her use of magic within the narrative had become so familiar over the course of the series that it had lost some of its power. Yet Erdrich's return to the series was inevitable; as she told an interviewer years earlier, "I can't stand not knowing what's happening...[because] there's an ongoing conversation with these fictional people. Events suggest themselves. You have no choice."

Collaborates with Dorris

Erdrich and Dorris collaborate on nearly all of their works. Each writes his or her own drafts after they discuss various aspects of the work, such as plot and character. They then carefully review the manuscript, publishing it only after they have agreed on every word. All of Erdrich's novels have been written in this way, as well as Dorris's *The Yellow Raft on Blue Water*, and his nonfiction book *The Broken Cord: A Family's Ongoing Struggle with Fetal Alcohol Syndrome*. Erdrich and Dorris coauthored the 1991 novel *The Crown of Columbus*, in which Native American college professor Vivian Twostar and her Euro-American academic lover Roger Williams search for a fabulous relic supposedly left by European explorer Christopher Columbus on his first landing in North America.

Erdrich has published two books of poetry, *Jacklight*, in 1984, and 1989's *Baptism of Desire*. The first book explores male-female relationships and, in sections such as "The Butcher's Wife" and "Old Man Potchiko," the author's German and Native American heritages. The first section of *Baptism of Desire*, meanwhile, draws on Erdrich's Catholic background, but also emphasizes Native American views and focuses on women's religious experiences.

A prolific short-story writer, poet, and essayist, Erdrich's work has appeared in numerous anthologies and such widely read magazines as the *New Yorker, Atlantic, Kenyon Review,* and *Ms.* Her achievements in this area made her a natural to edit the 1993 edition of the prestigious *Best American Short Stories* series. Culling 20 stories from 120 entries was a difficult task, requiring good judgement and great quantities of licorice. She notes in her introduction of the book, "If the story was strong enough to hold on to me, then I did not let go of it," she reports. In the end, she can "claim only to have done the best that can be done by one woman and a case of black licorice."

Throughout her work, Erdrich continues to provide a unique and loving perspective on what it means to be a person of mixed heritage facing the problems of Native American life today. Yet her appeal extends far beyond her cultural background. With her attention to physical detail, her belief in the possibility of magic in the everyday, and most of all in her compassion for even the most flawed characters, she creates enduring celebrations of humanity.

Further Reading

Bonetti, Kay, "An Interview with Louise Erdrich and Michael Dorris," *Missouri Review,* 11, spring 1988, pp. 79-99.

Bruchac, Joseph, "Whatever Is Really Yours: An Interview with Louise Erdrich," in *Survival This Way: Interviews with American Indian Poets,* Tucson: Sun Tracks and University of Arizona Press, 1987, pp. 73-86.

Erdrich, Louise, *Baptism of Desire* (poems), New York: Harper & Row, 1989.

Erdrich, Louise, *The Beet Queen,* New York: Holt, 1986.

Erdrich, Louise, *The Bingo Palace,* New York: HarperCollins, 1994.

Erdrich, Louise, *The Blue Jay's Dance: A Birth Year,* New York: HarperCollins, 1995.

Erdrich, Louise, *Jacklight* (poems), New York: Holt, 1984.

Erdrich, Louise, *Love Medicine,* New York: Holt, 1984; expanded version, 1993.

Erdrich, Louise, *Tracks,* New York: Holt, 1988.

Erdrich, Louise, with Michael Dorris, *Crown of Columbus,* New York: HarperCollins, 1991.

Howard, Jane, "Louise Erdrich," *Life,* April 1985, pp. 27-34.

Lambert, Pam, "Louise Erdrich: Sweet on Short Stories," *People,* November 15, 1993, p. 31.

Ruoff, A. LaVonne, *Literatures of the American Indian,* New York: Chelsea, 1991.

Billy Frank, Jr.

Nisqually activist
Born 1931, Washington

"We have to work together. There is no other way."

Billy Frank, Jr., is a Nisqually activist best known for his role in working out a peaceful settlement to 50-year-old fishing conflicts in Washington State and throughout the Northwest. After enduring numerous beatings and at least 40 jailings during the 1950s, 1960s, and 1970s for refusing to obey state laws restricting Native fishing rights, Frank directed his attention to reconciling the differences between the Nisqually people and state officials. From his post as chair of the Northwest Indian Fisheries Commission, which represents 20 Washington tribes in negotiating natural resource management plans with state and federal officials, Frank was instrumental in preventing further violence and conflict in the Northwest.

One of the originators of the concept of "cooperative management," a negotiating strategy that stresses common sense compromise rather than court intervention, Frank was awarded the prestigious 1992 Albert Schweitzer Award for Humanitarianism for his peacemaking efforts. Once known as "the last renegade of the Nisqually," Frank created a peacemaking program that has been the model for similar efforts in several states, producing solutions to numerous natural resource conflicts throughout the United States.

The son of Willy Frank—the last full-blooded Nisqually, who died in 1983 at the age of 104—Billy Frank, Jr., was born in 1931 on a Nisqually reservation located along the banks of the Nisqually River in Washington. Given a fervent pride in his Native heritage at an early age, he was first arrested at the age of 14 while fishing with his father in a restricted area. When Frank came of age, he continued his commitment to the rights of the Nisqually tribe, leading the Indian rebellion against state fishing authorities and a powerful sports fishermen's lobby during the salmon fishing wars of the 1960s and early 1970s.

Opponents of Frank and his supporters argued that Native Americans, like other citizens, had to obey state regulations while fishing off their reservations, although treaties signed in the mid-1880s had guaranteed Native rights to fish at "their usual and accustomed places." After a bitter struggle in which Frank was physically attacked and arrested numerous times, the treaty fishing rights were upheld by U.S. District Judge George Boldt of Tacoma, who ruled in 1974 that Native Americans were entitled to half of the harvestable catch of salmon and steelhead in Washington. Although the state and non-Native American fishing lobbies fought the ruling, the U.S. Supreme Court refused to overturn Boldt's decision.

Promotes negotiation rather than litigation

Although Native American rights were confirmed by the high court, Frank learned from his years of fighting the state that legal solutions, even when they resulted in a victory for his people, created bitterness between the opposing factions. Hoping to achieve a more lasting peace in the Northwest, Frank began bringing Native and non-Native Americans together, seeking solutions at the negotiating table rather than in the courtroom. "It's a new time of cooperation, a time of healing," Frank instructed a group of state legislators and tribal leaders from Wisconsin at a 1991 seminar. Agreements negotiated by the cooperative management principle, Frank argued, give both the state and the Native American community an incentive to adhere to the terms of a compromise because, in the long run, neither side benefits from a court decision. "We have to work together," Frank told George Rede of the *Oregonian*. "There is no other way."

Frank's commitment to Native American causes has not been limited to the fishing rights of the Nisqually people, but rather has been demonstrated through his work on a variety of environmental issues. In 1976, for instance, he began working with the Wash-

Billy Frank, Jr.

ington state government and the timber industry for reforms in logging and spraying practices that have seriously affected the bald eagle population in the Nisqually watershed (a region bounded by water that parts and then drains into another body of water). Eight years later, he helped to found the Northwest Renewable Resources Center, a nonprofit organization that helps to negotiate conflicts over natural resources in Washington and five other states.

For his humanitarian service, Frank was presented with the 1992 Albert Schweitzer Award, a $10,000 prize previously given to such notable individuals as former President Jimmy Carter, former U.S. Surgeon General C. Everett Koop, and Marian Wright Edelman, president of the Children's Defense Fund. As Roberta Ulrich of the *Oregonian* reported, the citation honored Frank's "achievements as a mediator between opposing interest groups and as a protector of the fragile cultural and environmental heritage that all humanity share." In receiving the prestigious award, Frank characteristically redirected the praise from himself to the tribes throughout the Northwest, viewing the award as a testament to the value of the Native American way of life.

Further Reading

Craig, Carol, "Wisconsin Delegation Visits Washington to Observe Co-Management Opportunities," *News from Indian Country,* September 15, 1991, p. 7.

"One Rebel's Reward," *Medford Mail Tribune,* May 14, 1992.

Rede, George, "'Last Renegade of the Nisqually' Will Receive Schweitzer Award," *Oregonian,* October 13, 1992.

Ulrich, Roberta, "Indian Rights Advocate Frank Wins High Honor," *Oregonian,* October 15, 1992.

Hanay Geiogamah

Kiowa/Delaware playwright, director,
    choreographer, and teacher
Born 1945

In Body Indian *Hanay Geiogamah tried to convey the Kiowa sense of humor, which he says is zany, raunchy, and sophisticated all at once.*

Hanay Geiogamah has become, through his theatrical productions, a virtual ambassador of Native American culture. His plays have toured the world presenting the vitality of Native American life.

He has also used the international language of dance to bring Indian culture to audiences at home and abroad. His scholarly work, meanwhile, has helped bring serious intellectual investigation of Native American culture into the university curriculum.

Creation of Native American Theater Ensemble

When he developed the Native American Theater Ensemble (NATE) in New York City in the early 1970s and served as its artistic director, Geiogamah gave American Indian performers a forum that had previously been lacking in American society, where they could professionally pursue their craft and express their creativity. The ensemble was the first professional acting company of American Indian performing artists, and its success quickly inspired many other Indian theaters to develop across the United States. Geiogamah also has been artistic director of the Native American Theater Ensemble in Los Angeles and of the American Indian Dance Theater, a national professional dance company.

In 1980 Geiogamah received his bachelor's degree in theater and drama from Indiana University in Bloomington, where he worked also as freelance director, producer, and instructor for American Indian communications and arts projects. From 1980 to 1982 he was the artistic director of Native Americans in Arts in New York City. Then, in 1983, he was visiting professor of theater and Native American Studies at Colorado College in Colorado Springs.

Geiogamah served as director of communications and then executive director of the American Indian Registry for the Performing Arts in Los Angeles from 1984 to 1988. The registry serves as an advocate for, and promoter of, American Indian actors, directors, producers, and technical personnel, who are entering mainstream professions in film and television. It has played a major part in changing the long-stereotyped and abused image of the American Indian in numerous feature films and TV series.

Dance troupe tours

From spring 1988 through January 1989, Geiogamah conducted tours of the American Indian Dance Theater in the United States and Europe, with a special eight-week engagement at the Casino de Paris Theater in Paris, France. The American Indian Dance Theater was formed in 1987 by Geiogamah, who is from Los Angeles, and a New York producer, Barbara Schwei. Its repertoire (works performed) includes the "Eagle Dance," the "Zuni Buffalo Dance," the "Apache Crown Dance," and a "Hoop Dance" that weaves together 20 hoops and was originated by a Cherokee, Eddie Swimmer. Each year members learn new dances. They recently performed Northwest Coast dances using raven, whale, and cannibal masks to represent Kwakiutl potlatches (gift-giving ceremonies). Appearances of the dance company sell out months in advance. The troupe has appeared twice on national television, and videotapes of their performances have become best-sellers.

In one interview, Geiogamah explained that normally each of these dances takes a number of days. Therefore, he stages only excerpts, or portions, and cuts down those selected episodes to heighten the dramatic interest. These short versions are really only the "appetizers" to the actual "feast" of the

Hanay Geiogamah

full dance. They can be enjoyed on the *Great Performances* series on public television.

Geiogamah as playwright

Geiogamah has also written a dozen plays, three of which have been published by the University of Oklahoma Press. In the early 1970s he worked at the Bureau of Indian Affairs (BIA) while writing his play *Body Indian*. He composed the play at the typewriter two days before the script was due in New York at Ellen Stewart's La Mama Theater. It premiered there with a cast from the American Indian Theater Ensemble in 1972.

In *Body Indian* he tried to convey the Kiowa sense of humor, which he says is

The American Indian Dance Theater performs an Eagle Dance

zany, raunchy, and sophisticated all at once. He claims that "Kiowas are always laughing." The time pressure under which he composed the play seems to have allowed this Kiowa humor come out clearly on the page. The anxiety he felt during rehearsals was relieved when, during the actual performances, the audiences laughed at the tragic, but at the same time comic, events on the stage. The Indians watching the play found humor in its portrayals of alcoholics taking advantage of each other. Geiogamah said that he had witnessed a great deal of such behavior at the BIA, where Indians sometimes were their own worst enemies.

The play *Foghorn* is about the 1969 occupation of Alcatraz Island, former site of a U.S. penitentiary. Eighty-nine Indians of various tribes "took over" the island to protest living conditions on reservations and other hardships, mocking Europeans' claims to Indian land by announcing they owned it "by right of discovery" and offering to buy it for $24.00 in glass beads and red cloth. Over the next 19 months about a thousand Indians moved in and out of the occupying group.

The first version of Geiogamah's play, which was later cut, projected on a screen a huge head that was gradually being lobotomized, or having its frontal lobe cut away. This surgical technique was once used to reduce what doctors and others thought to be violent tendencies, but in the play lobotomy serves as a symbol for social and political control. During rehearsals, the projection began to seem a silly device, so it was removed.

Wilfred Leach, the artistic director at La Mama, who was also a professor at Sarah Lawrence College, helped Geiogamah with the play's development. He taught him about the techniques of the left-wing German playwright Bertolt Brecht, who constantly struggled to keep the audience's attention on the message of the play rather than on the story. His tactics for achieving this were called alienation devices, because they distanced the crowd from the characters onstage and forced them to think more critically.

Geiogamah, who was still in his early twenties, absorbed what he could at the time, distracted as he was by the pressures of guiding his company for their appearance in Germany in 1973. While the group was in West Berlin, the Brecht Theater invited them to visit the Berliner Ensemble. *Foghorn* opened in West Berlin on October 18, 1973.

Geiogamah's troupe also toured reservations. His third play is called *49,* after the songs sung at the end of a powwow, or Indian ceremony. It is the most upbeat of his works. He has also written a musical comedy, *War Dancers.* His earlier plays used energetic, improvisational singing and dancing, and Geiogamah gives the members of his acting company the freedom to improvise (act spontaneously in their performance). In 1990, he wrote a teleplay based on **N. Scott Momaday**'s 1969 book, *The Way to Rainy Mountain.*

Geiogamah served as managing editor of the prestigious *American Indian Culture and Research Journal,* which is dedicated to advancing knowledge about Native Americans and is published by the Regents of the University of California. His teaching experience includes positions at Colorado College and at the Los Angeles campus of the University of California. He also does the choreography for the Thunderbird American Indian Dancers, a troupe based in New Jersey. The Thunderbirds meet on Tuesdays at the McBurney YMCA and hold an annual powwow in full regalia, or native costume, each July at the Queens County Farm Museum. The money it raises is contributed to a scholarship fund for promising Indian students. In 1993, Geiogamah—who has won many prestigious awards, honors, and grants over the past couple of decades— was among the recipients of the First Annual Totem Awards, presented to outstanding Native American artists in film, television, theater, and music.

Further Reading

Geiogamah, Hanay, *New Native American Drama: Three Plays* (includes *Body Indian, Foghorn,* and *49*), edited and introduced by Jeffrey Huntsman, Norman: University of Oklahoma Press, 1980.

Lincoln, Kenneth, "Indians Playing Indians," *PLUS,* fall 1989-1990, pp. 91-98.

Lincoln, Kenneth, "Interview with Hanay Geiogamah," *MELUS,* fall 1989-1990, pp. 60-82.

Dan George

Burrard Squamish actor and tribal leader
Born 1899, near Vancouver, British Columbia
Died September 23, 1981, Vancouver,
    British Columbia

*Dan George was always particularly
interested in changing the familiar
images of Native Americans in the
media, as well as the poor self-image
that many Indians had.*

Chief Dan George is most widely
known for his acting career, which
spanned the 1960s and 1970s. He is particularly recognized for his role as the Cheyenne
elder Old Lodge Skins in the 1970 film *Little Big Man,* which also starred Dustin Hoff-
man. Popularly known as "Chief," he came
to acting late in life.

Born and raised near Vancouver, British
Columbia, George worked as a logger, long-
shoreman, and musician before becoming,
in 1951, chief of the Tell-lall-watt band of
the Burrard Tribe of Coast Salish Indians
outside Vancouver. He later was named honorary chief of the Squamish and Sushwap
bands. Although he remained chief until
1963, he branched out into acting in 1959
when one of his sons, who happened to be
playing an Indian in the Canadian television
series *Caribou Country,* convinced the
director to give the chief a part. It was
George's later role in the 1969 Walt Disney
film *Smith* that attracted the attention of *Little Big Man*'s producers to him.

Stars in *Little Big Man*

Aside from its box office success, *Little
Big Man* set the tone for a number of 1970s
Hollywood films that strongly criticized U.S.
Indian policies. Unlike movies of the 1930s,
which tended to show Indians as ruthless
enemies of the white man and the cavalry,
these new films had scenes that portrayed the
army inflicting death and destruction on
innocent Native Americans. Attitudes surrounding the movie reflected civil rights concerns, opposition to U.S. involvement in the
war in Vietnam, and overall distrust of the
government. For his role in the film, George
was awarded the New York Film Critics
Award for best supporting actor and was also
nominated for an Academy Award.

Although George refused to endorse radical Indian political causes of the 1960s and
1970s, such as those promoted by the American Indian Movement (AIM), he eloquently
spoke for Native rights and the environment

throughout his career. He was always particularly interested in changing the familiar images of Native Americans in the media, as well as the poor self-image that many Indians had. His attempts to reach a broader audience included writing two books of prose-poetry, 1974's *My Heart Soars* and the 1982 collection *My Spirit Soars.*

Other movies in which he was featured include *Cold Journey, The Ecstasy of Rita Joe, Harry and Tonto,* and *The Outlaw Josey Wales.* In 1971, he received the Human Relations Award from the Canadian Council of Christians and Jews. Dan George was married and became the father of six children, Marie, Ann, Irene, Rose, Leonard, and Robert. George's wife, Amy, died as he was making plans to attend the Academy Award ceremonies in Hollywood. He died in his sleep at the age of 82 on September 23, 1981, in Vancouver.

Further Reading

Native North American Almanac, edited by Duane Champagne, Detroit: Gale, 1994.

New York Times, September 24, 1981, p. D23.

Geronimo

Bedonkohe Chiricahua Apache warrior,
    tribal leader
Born c. 1827, Arizona
Died February 1909, Fort Sill, Oklahoma
Also known as Goyathlay ("One Who Yawns")

It was Geronimo's belief that when Usen (the Apache word for God) created the Apaches, he also created their homes in the west. As more and more Apaches were removed from their homelands, Geronimo felt, they would sicken and die.

The world has come to recognize Geronimo as one of history's great warriors, and his larger-than-life image is probably the result of various film portrayals. Yet none of these versions accurately depicts the scope of his achievements. For in addition to being a husband, father, warrior, and medicine man, Geronimo was a respected leader who preserved Apache culture and traditions, as well as the right to live on the homelands that the Apache had occupied for generations.

Hundreds of books have been written about Geronimo's life; perhaps the most illuminating is the one that contains the story as he himself told it. Between 1905 and 1906, he related his life story to his second cousin, who in turn told it to S. M. Barrett, an education official who recorded it in 1906 as *Geronimo, His Own Story.*

Over the course of the 1800s, the Apaches fought off increasing attempts by migrating Europeans to seize their land. Their resistance included both isolated raids and armed

Geronimo

confrontation. Geronimo warded off intruders and soldiers until the mid-1800s, when the United States acquired southwest Apache lands from Mexico. Mexico claimed this territory through conquest, but it was the ancestral dwelling place of the Apache. Due to their attempts to defend themselves and their tribal lands, the Apaches were most often described by whites as savages who raided and killed innocent and unsuspecting settlers. But as Mexican and U.S. troops continued to invade and conquer Apache lands, the Apache's reaction was to fight back. And it was the savagery of Mexican soldiers that gave Geronimo a personal motive: revenge.

It was Geronimo's belief that when Usen (the Apache word for God) created the Apaches, he also created their homes in the west. As more and more Apaches were removed from their homelands, Geronimo felt, they would sicken and die. His strong conviction in this regard was apparent when he appealed vigorously to the "Great Father," U.S. President Theodore Roosevelt, to return the Apaches to their Native Arizona homelands to prevent their further destruction and death. His request was denied.

Early years

Geronimo's story begins somewhere around the 1820s; many historians believe that he was born in 1827. He himself claimed to have been born in June of 1829 in No-doy-ohn Cañon, Arizona. According to Geronimo, his tribe, the Bedonkohe, inhabited the region of mountainous country that lies west from the east line of Arizona, and south from the headwaters of the Gila River. Nearby there lived other Apache bands, such as the Chihenne (Hot Springs) Apaches, the White Mountain Apaches, the Nedni Apaches, and the Chokonen (Chiricahua) Apaches, whose chief was **Cochise** (see entry) and later his son, Naiche. Geronimo and Naiche were to become long-time companions both as warriors and prisoners of war.

The fourth child in a family of four boys and four girls, he was known as Goyathlay ("One Who Yawns") until his late teens. Goyathlay learned about tribal legends from his mother, Juana, and absorbed the discipline of praying to Usen for strength, health, wisdom, and protection. His father, Taklishim ("the Gray One"), told Goyathlay numerous tales of brave deeds by Apache warriors and described in depth the dangers and pleasures of warpath chases.

His paternal grandfather, Maco, was a Nedni Apache chief, but Goyathlay's father did not become a chief because he joined his wife's tribe and thereby lost his right to rule by heredity. Consequently, Goyathlay was not entitled to become a chieftain by hereditary right due to his father's marriage outside of the tribe. Mangas Coloradas instead succeeded Goyathlay's grandfather and became chief of the Nedni Apaches.

At the age of 17, sometime around the year 1846, Goyathlay was invited to join the council of warriors, and thus to share in the glories of the warpath and serve his people in battle. He was also able to marry a girl named Alope. Her father demanded many ponies in exchange for his daughter; once these were delivered, Geronimo took Alope and they went to live not far from his mother's tepee. No further ceremonies were needed, and Geronimo and Alope had three children. Geronimo eventually had four full-blood Bedonkohe Apache wives and four who were part-blood Bedonkohe Apache or of mixed Apache blood. Four of his children were killed by Mexicans and four were held in bondage by the U.S. government.

Mexican raids

During the summer of 1858, Geronimo suffered a great tragedy, which would affect his outlook on life and especially on people of Mexican heritage. While on a peaceful trip into Old Mexico to trade, he heard that a group of his people had been attacked by Mexican troops who had killed all the warrior guards, captured all the ponies, stolen their arms and supplies, and killed many of the women and children. During the aftermath, Geronimo discovered that his mother, wife, and three children had all been massacred by the Mexican soldiers.

Returning to Arizona quietly on the instructions of Mangas Coloradas, he vowed vengeance upon the Mexican soldiers. In the summer of 1859, Geronimo sought the assistance of other Apache, and at Arispe engaged Mexican soldiers in battle. While Geronimo could not bring back his loved ones, he claimed he "could rejoice in this revenge." The battle of Arispe is allegedly where Goyathlay acquired the name "Geronimo" from Mexican soldiers.

Geronimo sought to further punish the Mexicans, and embarked on a campaign of periodic raiding. In the summer of 1860, he convinced 25 warriors to join him in another battle; during this encounter he sustained head injuries that did not heal for many months and resulted in a scar that he wore for the remainder of his life. While the Apaches appeared to have won the battle, the losses were so great that no warriors would accompany Geronimo on such warpaths for at least another year.

During the 1860s, his raids became more successful, enriching the tribe and emboldening them to continue the fight. Even so, the number of warriors accompanying him varied greatly. Sometime around 1868, the Apaches fended off an attack by Mexican troops, not only protecting their own livestock but claiming animals belonging to their attackers. Geronimo later insisted that it was a long time before they ever went back into Mexico or were disturbed by Mexicans. Another Mexican attack occurred in 1873 in the Sierra Madre Mountains; it lasted only a few minutes and resulted in heavy losses for the Mexican troops.

In 1882, while in the Sierra Madre Mountains leading one of the bands on a raiding spree, Geronimo and his warriors were surrounded by U.S. General George H. Crook's troops and forced to surrender to government authorities. Though ordered by military authorities to remain on the San Carlos Reservation, Geronimo managed to escape. He returned with his group to San Carlos later, claiming to have come back not on military orders but to "get other Apaches to come with him into Mexico." During a period of disruption and fighting between the Indians and soldiers on the San Carlos Reservation, Geronimo acted on his elaborate plans to flee the reservation and travel to Mexico. During the battle that followed—the last Geronimo ever fought with the Mexicans—he received a total of eight wounds.

Encroachment of the white men

Around 1858, Geronimo heard about some white men coming to measure land to the south of his homelands. Accompanied by other warriors, Geronimo went to visit them. While not understanding one another's language, the two groups made a treaty with one another promising to be brothers. They even traded game, and the Apaches were given paper money for the first time. After this group of surveyors left, the Apaches did not see another white man for about ten years. Unfortunately, trouble later developed between the two groups, and thanks to the treachery of U.S. troops, the Apache decided never again to trust white soldiers.

In 1872 President Ulysses S. Grant sent General O. O. Howard to Arizona to make peace with the Apaches, and Geronimo said he traveled to Apache Pass to make a treaty with the general. According to Geronimo, General Howard kept his word with the Apaches and treated them as if they were brothers. He claimed he could have lived in peace forever with him.

Although U.S. officials described Geronimo as either living on or escaping from reservation lands, he did not believe his travels violated any laws. He was moving across Apache land, after all, and as food provisions or other necessary items depleted, it was only customary that the Apache would relocate to a bountiful area to replenish their stock or to visit their homelands. This conflict in the way they interpreted his actions continued between Geronimo and government officials until he was disarmed by U.S. soldiers and taken to headquarters, where he was tried by court-martial.

Sentenced to the guardhouse and put in chains, Geronimo demanded that his captors explain this treatment. He was told it was because he had left Apache Pass. He replied indignantly, "I do not think that I ever belonged to those soldiers at Apache Pass, or that I should have asked them where I might go." He was kept a chained prisoner for four months and then transferred to San Carlos. Upon his return, it appears that peace presided for a little over two years. In the summer of 1883, however, a rumor surfaced that officers were planning to imprison Apache leaders.

These rumors reminded the Apaches of past wrongs and made them wary of the officers' intentions. Fearing for themselves, they held a council meeting and decided that they would leave the reservation. Geronimo, on the other hand, believed it would be better to die on the warpath than to be killed in prison. He and another leader, Whoa, led 250 followers in battle with U.S. soldiers, who were unaccustomed to fighting on the rough terrain, while the Apaches were well equipped with arms and supplies they had accumulated while living on the reservation. The remainder of the provisions were supplied by the White Mountain Apaches.

Geronimo claimed that the Apaches roamed the area for one year and then returned to San Carlos, taking with them their cattle and horses, which were confiscated by General Crook upon their arrival. Upset with this action, Geronimo undertook plans to travel to Fort Apache. General Crook ordered officers and soldiers to arrest Geronimo, and to kill him if he resisted. Apaches informed Geronimo of General Crook's plans, and he prepared to head south to Old Mexico with about 400 Apaches.

Camping in the mountains west of Casa Grande, the Apaches were attacked by government Indian scouts. According to Geronimo, one boy was killed and nearly all of the

A later photograph of Geronimo

next year I put in a crop of oats, and when the crop was almost ready to harvest, you told your soldiers to put me in prison, and if I resisted to kill me." According to Geronimo, General Crook denied this allegation, saying he never gave any such orders and that the troops who spread these rumors at Fort Apache knew that it was untrue. The Apache warrior then agreed to return to San Carlos with the general.

Fearing further treachery and deceit, however, Geronimo decided to remain in Mexico with about 40 of his followers. General Crook then resigned and was replaced by General Nelson A. Miles. As Miles's territorial powers expanded to cover more of the western frontier, U.S. troops trailed the Apaches. Thinking that the troops had left Mexico, Geronimo and his followers returned there, attacking and killing every Mexican they found, since they believed the Mexicans had invited the U.S. troops. The Apaches discussed the situation and arrived at a grim decision: "Give no quarters to anyone and ask no favors."

After some time, the Apaches were reunited with their people in the Sierra de Antunez Mountains. Unbeknownst to them, the U.S. troops had not left Mexico and were soon trailing them closely. Mexican troops near the Apaches explained that they no longer wanted to fight and would welcome the prospect of a treaty. Claiming that the U.S. troops were the real cause of these wars, the Mexican troops agreed to stop fighting the Apaches if they would return to the United States. Agreeing to these conditions, the Apaches resumed their march northward, hoping to make a similar treaty with the U.S. soldiers upon their return to Arizona. Geronimo realized there was no other course to follow.

women and children were captured. Escaping to the foothills of the Sierra Madre Mountains, the remaining Apaches were soon attacked again by a very large army of Mexican troops. Recognizing the inevitable, Geronimo claimed it was "senseless to fight when you cannot hope to win."

While holding a council of war that night, Apache scouts reported that approximately two thousand soldiers were combing the mountains seeking them. General Crook had arrived in Mexico with his troops; upon Geronimo's arrival at Crook's camp, the general asked him why he had left the reservation. Geronimo replied, "You told me that I might live in the reservation the same as white people lived. One year I raised a crop of corn, and gathered and stored it, and the

Becomes a prisoner of war

Geronimo encountered Lieutenant Charles B. Gatewood near Fronteras. The Apache attempted to invoke peace terms he had established with General Crook, but was refused. He pleaded at last that his people be immediately reunited with their families and, after serving a two-year prison term in the East, be returned to the reservation. There are varying accounts of what followed.

Knowing that General Miles was in charge of the officers, Geronimo decided to negotiate only with him. He later changed his mind on the surrender conditions, provided the Apaches would be speedily reunited with their families. General Miles apparently agreed to this several days later, but the promise was never fulfilled. In a subsequent meeting with General Miles, Geronimo explained how he had been wronged and that he wanted to return to the United States with his people. General Miles responded by saying he was sent on behalf of the president of the United States, who had agreed to negotiate with the Apaches if they would agree to a treaty promising them land, livestock, and other amenities. Geronimo expressed disbelief at the general's words, but the general assured him that "this time it is the truth."

Geronimo agreed to make the treaty and placed a large stone on the blanket before himself and the general. The treaty was made before the stone and was intended to "last until the stone should crumble to dust," thereby "bounding each other with an oath." Geronimo gave up his arms and stated, "I will quit the warpath and live at peace hereafter." General Miles swept a spot of ground clear with his hand and said, "Your past deeds shall be wiped out like this and you will start a new life." Geronimo did not know that the start of his new life was also the beginning of his life as a prisoner of war.

Upon his final surrender—with his companion Naiche—on September 4, 1886, Geronimo and his followers were loaded onto the southern Pacific Railroad bound for San Antonio, Texas, where he was held to be tried for crimes committed. Narrowly escaping civilian trial for murder in San Antonio, Geronimo was hurriedly swept away to Fort Pickens in Pensacola, Florida. Apparently, the residents of Pensacola demanded that "the hostiles" be sent to Fort Pickens in hopes of aiding a lucrative tourist business.

Many of the Apaches sent to Florida died in that unfamiliar climate from tuberculosis and other diseases. In 1894, after the government rejected another appeal from the Apaches to return to their homelands, the former Apache foes, the Kiowa and Comanches, offered them a home on their reservation lands near Fort Sill, Oklahoma. Geronimo spent the remainder of his life on that reservation adapting to the white man's ways and economic system. Growing watermelons and selling his signature were his only sources of income. Although still under government protection as a prisoner of war, he was permitted to travel to numerous fairs and exhibitions at Buffalo, Omaha, and St. Louis, selling his signature and photographs—for twenty-five cents—to thousands of spectators.

Baptized

Attempting to understand the Christian religion, Geronimo questioned repeatedly the concept of a part of man that lived after death—the spirit—as he had never seen such a thing. However, believing that an association with Christians would help improve his character, Geronimo joined the Dutch Reformed Church and was baptized in the summer of 1903. It was reported that he regularly attended services at the Apache Mission at Fort Sill Military Reservation. He was later expelled from the church for incessant gambling.

Geronimo later fell off his horse into a creek bed and lay exposed for several hours. The resulting pneumonia took his life in February 1909. His place in history as a great warrior was assured, but his struggle for dignity and peace—and the reclamation of land and rights that had belonged to his people for generations—is equally important to understanding this momentous and complex figure.

Further Reading

Brown, Dee, *Bury My Heart at Wounded Knee,* New York: Holt, 1971.

Geronimo, *Geronimo, His Own Story,* edited by S. M. Barrett, introduction by Frederick W. Turner, III, New York: Dutton, 1970.

Nabokov, Peter, *Native American Testimony,* New York: Penguin, 1992.

Skinner, Woodward (Woody) B., *The Apache Rock Crumbles: The Captivity of Geronimo's People,* Pensacola, FL: Skinner Publications, 1987.

Tim Giago

Oglala Sioux publisher and author
Born July 12, 1934, Pine Ridge Reservation, South Dakota

"Not only did they desecrate our sacred land, they also memorialized four presidents who committed acts of atrocity against our people."

Editor and publisher of the largest independently owned American Indian weekly newspaper, Tim Giago has been outspoken in protesting American social trends that demonstrate a lack of respect for Native culture. He has criticized the tendency to make heroes of American historical figures who took part in the injustices committed against Native Americans, as well as the use of "Indian" mascots among university and professional sports teams.

Giago was born in 1934 on the Pine Ridge Reservation in South Dakota in a house with no electricity or plumbing. As a boy he attended Holy Rosary Indian Mission as well as a school run by Jesuits (Roman Catholic priests). "Our teachers told us our ancestors were heathens," Giago told *People* magazine. "It was a brutal way to be raised." He left the reservation after high school to join the navy; he served in the Korean War and was wounded in action. Afterwards, he attended San Jose Junior College in San Jose, California.

Giago told *People* that he held several odd jobs for about 15 years, and every summer he would return home, because "It was the only place I ever felt comfortable." He continued his education at the University of Nevada at Reno and later at Harvard University on a Nieman Fellowship from 1990 to 1991. He was the first American Indian to be accepted into this program. Giago was also awarded an honorary doctorate degree in humanities from Nebraska Indian Community College in 1993.

Ventured into journalism

His writing career began in 1979, when he became an Indian affairs columnist for the *Rapid City Journal* in Rapid City, South Dakota, earning $7.50 for each column. This opened the door to a position as a full-time reporter. In 1981, Giago founded what was to become the nation's largest American Indian newspaper, the *Lakota Times*, later renamed *Indian Country Today*. He began the newspaper with $4,000 borrowed from a boyhood friend, and it grew from a circulation of 3,000 free copies to 50,000 in paid subscriptions in 1991.

Giago has also written a weekly column about contemporary Indian issues, syndicated by Knight-Ridder News Service to 340 newspapers. His columns and public stands on issues have been uncompromising. During a celebration of the two hundred fifteenth birthday of the United States at Mount Rushmore, near Keystone, South Dakota, Giago strongly expressed his resistance to the veneration of George Washington, Thomas Jefferson, Abraham Lincoln, and Theodore Roosevelt—the U.S. presidents whose likenesses appear on the South Dakota monument—as heroes and defenders of justice. "Not only did they desecrate our sacred land," Giago was quoted as saying, "they also memorialized four presi-

Tim Giago

dents who committed acts of atrocity against our people."

Giago has also written articles about other Native concerns for *USA Today, New York Newsday, New York Times, Christian Science Monitor, Newsweek, Native Peoples* magazine, and the *Atlanta Constitution.* In a *Newsweek* article about the name of the Washington Redskins, Giago described the "largest protest by American Indians against a professional football team in the history of this country. Our complaint: very simply, Indians are people, not mascots." He wondered in the essay "why non-Indians find it hard to understand why we consider it insulting to be treated as mascots. If white and black America is so inconsiderate of its indigenous people that it can name a football team the Redskins and see nothing wrong in this, where has our education system gone wrong?"

Giago's opinions on Indian issues have been broadcast on numerous talk shows, including CBS's *Nightwatch* and the *Oprah Winfrey Show*. He has also written extensively on Indian culture in his books *The Aboriginal Sin* and *Notes from Indian Country, Volume 1*. Giago served as editor of *The American Indian and the Media Handbook*. In the summer of 1994, he was in the process of developing a new newspaper in Scottsdale, Arizona, *Indian Country Today Southwest*.

Giago's accomplishments and activism have won him several honors. In 1982, he was named Print Media Person of the Year at the National Media Convention at Albuquerque, New Mexico. In 1985 he received the South Dakota Newspaper Association best column by a local writer award, and in 1988 he was given a Civil Rights and Human Rights Award by the South Dakota Education Association. In 1989, Giago was the recipient of the National Education Association's Leo Reano Memorial Award for Civil and Human Rights for providing leadership in education to resolve social problems affecting Native Americans. Two years later, he earned a medal of honor for distinguished journalism from the University of Missouri School of Journalism. He also won the Harvard University Award for Contributions to American Journalism. Most recently, Giago was nominated for the South Dakota Hall of Fame's September 1994 inductions.

Further Reading

Chu, Daniel, and Bill Shaw, "About Faces," *People*, July 22, 1991.

Giago, Tim, *The Aboriginal Sin: Reflections on the Holy Rosary Indian Mission School*, San Francisco: Indian Historian Press, 1978.

Giago, Tim, "I Hope the Redskins Lose," *Newsweek*, January 27, 1992.

Giago, Tim, *Notes from Indian Country, Volume 1*, Cochran Publishers, 1985.

James Gladstone

Blood Blackfeet political figure
Born May 21, 1887, Mountaqin Hill,
 Northwest Territory, Canada
Died September 4, 1971, Fernie,
 British Columbia, Canada
Also known as Akay-na-muka ("Many Guns")

"My work will be aimed at improving the position of Canada's Indians, obtaining for them better conditions as they want them and are ready for them."

James Gladstone was the first Native Canadian to serve as a senator in the Canadian Parliament. During his 13-year career with the Senate, he defended the rights of the First Nations (a term used in Canada to describe the different groups of Native peoples) and fought to keep the traditions of his people alive.

Gladstone was born May 21, 1887, to the Blood tribe of Canada. Though born at Mountain Hill in the Northwest Territory, he spent his childhood on the Blood Blackfeet Reservation in Alberta, where he was called Akay-na-muka ("Many Guns"). Well known later for his role as a politician and as a voice for all Indian peoples, he did not find his way to this career early in his life. First, he attended Calgary Industrial School, then he worked briefly for the *Calgary Herald* newspaper as a typesetter. In 1911, the Royal Northwest Mounted Police asked him to be a scout and interpreter among his people. Around this time he married Janie Healy, with whom he had five children.

Gladstone was the first Indian on the Blood Reserve to have electricity or to use a tractor, and he readily took advantage of such modern conveniences to make his ranch of 800 acres as prosperous as possible. His excellent farming abilities won him the admiration of many, and, during World War I, he passed on his agricultural knowledge, helping the other Blood farmers to tend their cattle efficiently and to increase the yield from their crops.

Fights for his people as politician

Gladstone worked as many long, hard hours for his people as he did on his ranch. Like many members of Lakota and Blackfoot tribes struggling to govern themselves and keep their threatened languages alive, Gladstone fought for education and for treaty rights for his people. As a delegate to Ottawa, he repeatedly represented his people in discussions with the Canadian federal government concerning changes to the Indian Act. This act was a large-scale effort by the government, beginning in 1876, to define its relationship with Native people. In hearings held from 1946 to 1948, Gladstone led the fight against the revisions to the Indian Act because they "replaced provisions better designed for concentration

camps than for reservations," according to Olive Patricia Dickason in her book *Canada's First Nations.*

Still, the hearings of the Joint Senate and House of Commons Committee on the Indian Act marked the first time Canada had listened to the input of Native Americans at that level of government. The revised act was passed in 1951, and Gladstone can be credited in large part for fighting for the rights of Indians to govern themselves. Though his efforts on behalf of his people helped to make the act a reality, Gladstone would have preferred to abolish it altogether. He felt the act interfered with the Native nations' ability to govern themselves and hindered the cause of equality. Of the Indian Act, he once said: "Indians are the only ethnic group in Canada with a special act."

In addition to fighting for the rights of his people with the Canadian government, Gladstone also encouraged them to become involved in managing their own affairs. He among others, founded the Indian Association of Alberta in 1939 and served as president from 1948 to 1954, and again in 1956. In 1958, he was named honorary president.

Becomes first Native senator

In 1958, Gladstone was appointed as a senator to the Canadian Parliament; he was the first Native to serve as senator in Canada. In a gesture that demonstrated Gladstone's commitment to preserving the traditions of his people, he delivered his first senatorial speech to the Parliament in the language of the Blackfoot nation "as a recognition of the first Canadians." In the same speech, Gladstone said, "My work will be aimed at improving the position of Canada's Indians,

James Gladstone (left) talking with residents of the Blood Indian Reserve

obtaining for them better conditions as they want them and are ready for them. I'm particularly interested in seeing more encouragement given to Indians for individual, rather than collective effort."

Gets vote for his people

In 1959, Gladstone delivered on his promise. He was named co-chair of a joint Senate and House of Commons committee created to study the issues involving Canada's 170,000 Native Americans. In 1960, through his efforts, treaty Indians gained the right to vote in Canada's national elections. For this success and his other work, he was named Outstanding Indian of the Year in 1960's All-American Indian Days. In 1969, Gladstone traveled with Canada's delegation to Japan for the Moral Rearmament Asian Assembly. He supported a philosophy of tradition and progress for his people, who should "hold tradition with one hand and reach forward with the other." Gladstone died September 4, 1971, in Fernie, British Columbia.

Further Reading

Dickason, Olive Patricia, *Canada's First Nations,* Norman: University of Oklahoma Press, 1992.

The Native Americans: An Illustrated History, edited by Betty and Ian Ballantine, Atlanta: Turner Publishing, 1993.

Native North American Almanac, edited by Duane Champagne, Detroit: Gale, 1994.

Waldman, Carl, *Atlas of the North American Indian,* New York: Facts on File, 1985.

Carl Nelson Gorman

Navajo artist and lecturer
Born October 5, 1907, Chinle, Arizona
Also known as Kin-ya-onny beyeh ("Son
of the Towering House People")

Carl Nelson Gorman has emphasized his interest in all art forms, Indian and non-Indian, and his intention to help Native American art evolve.

T hough he was raised in a traditional Navajo life-style on the reservation, the prominent Navajo artist Carl Nelson Gorman has won acclaim as a pioneer of nontraditional Indian art forms, such as oil paintings and silk screening. His contributions to Navajo and Native American art and culture inspired the dedication of the Carl Gorman Museum at Tecumseh Center at the University of California at Davis.

Gorman was born in 1907 at Chinle, Arizona, to Navajo parents Nelson Gorman and Alice Peshlakai. His Navajo name is Kin-ya-onny beyeh, which means "Son of the Towering House People." His parents founded the Presbyterian Mission at Chinle in 1921. Through his mother's family, Gorman is a distinguished member of the Black Sheep clan. His father was a trader and cattleman, and his mother a weaver, who also translated English hymns into Navajo. Other members of his family were tribal leaders.

He spent his school years at U.S. government and Indian schools in Arizona and New Mexico, such as Rehoboth Mission. In 1928 he graduated from Albuquerque Indian School in Albuquerque, New Mexico. Two years later, he married Adella Katherine Brown, whom he divorced in 1945. The couple had one child, Rudolph Carl, the artist **R. C. Gorman** (see entry), born in 1932, who followed in his father's footsteps and became an artist respected in his own right.

Dreams of art

As a boy, Gorman dreamed of becoming an artist. He liked to draw horses even though his father discouraged him from pursuing his interest in art. Having never lost sight of his dream, Gorman not only has been recognized as a leading Native American painter, but has guided other Native artists into new directions. Gorman has said that he believes in blending traditional and modern ways of creating in all art forms.

Immediately after graduation from high school, Gorman went to work. He owned a trucking business with his brother, Wallace, until 1936, and later worked as a clerk, timekeeper, and range rider for the Land Management division of the U.S. Department of the Interior. From 1942 to 1945, he served in the Marine Corps on the Pacific islands of Guadalcanal, Tarawa, Saipan, and Tinian during World War II. As a "code talker" he used coded Navajo language to confuse the Japanese military. After the war, like many veterans, Gorman took advantage of the G.I. Bill, which provided funds for higher education to armed forces personnel. He attended the Otis Art Institute in Los Angeles and graduated in 1951.

Gorman first exhibited his art in 1947 and has continued to show his work extensively ever since in California, Arizona, and New Mexico, among other places. Gorman also began a career at Douglas Aircraft Company in Santa Monica, California, as a technical illustrator. At the same time, he founded his own silk screen design company, Kin-ya-onny beyeh Originals. In 1963, he left Douglas Aircraft and California.

Returning to Arizona in 1964, he managed the Navajo Arts and Crafts Guild and served as the director of the Navajo Culture Center at Fort Defiance, Arizona, where he demonstrated his deep concern for the Navajo people and reverence for Navajo culture. During this time he held a variety of positions on committees for Navajo festivals and tribal affairs. He even invented a new dance, the Navajo Gourd Rattle Dance, based on a blend of traditional elements. In 1973, Gorman became coordinator of the Office of Native Healing Sciences at the Navajo Health Authority, hoping to help the Navajo gain improved and coordinated health care coverage. He was also active in preserving traditional ways of healing until 1976.

Multiple art forms

Gorman experimented with a wide variety of art media that were not traditionally used by Natives, such as oil and watercolor paintings, ceramics, mosaics, textile and industrial designs, jewelry, and silk screens. He has received numerous awards for his work, but his greatest honor came in 1973 at the dedication of the Carl Gorman Museum at Tecumseh Center at the University of California at Davis, where he had served for four years as a lecturer in Native American studies. Gorman retired from the University of California-Davis in 1973. Three years later, he retired from Navajo Community College as Navajo cultural research coordinator and lecturer. He became a part-time instructor in Native American art and studio art in 1986 at the University of New Mexico in Gallup. Since retiring in 1992, he has been lecturing on Navajo history and culture as well as on the Navajo code talkers. Honored as an Arizona Indian Living Treasure in 1989, Gorman received an honorary doctorate in humane letters from the University of New Mexico on May 12, 1990.

He has emphasized his interest in all art forms, Indian and non-Indian and his intention to help Native American art evolve. Gorman has also expressed his hope that Indian artifacts would reach a wider portion of the art-buying public and has announced plans to publish a book of photographs and other cultural materials he has collected.

Further Reading

American Indian Painters: A Biographical Dictionary, compiled by Jeanne O. Snodgrass, Museum of the American Indian, Heye Foundation, 1968.

Greenberg, George, and Henry Greenberg, *Carl Gorman's World,* Albuquerque: University of New Mexico Press, 1984.

Wade, Edwin, L., and Rennard Stricklan, *Magic Images: Contemporary Native American Art,* Norman: University of Oklahoma Press, 1981.

R. C. Gorman

Navajo artist
Born July 26, 1931, Chinle, Arizona

"The reservation is my source of inspiration for what I paint; but yet I never come to realize this until I find myself in some far-flung place like the tip of Yucatan [Mexico] or where-have-you."

R. C. Gorman

Rudolph Carl Gorman is one of the most prominent contemporary Native American artists of the twentieth century. His art combines the traditional with the nontraditional in style and form. Like other innovative Indian artists, R. C. Gorman has at times faced criticism because his work has been considered "not Indian enough." While his subject matter and inspiration have been centered on the reservation, his style is unique and individual, and does not fit neatly into the conventional genres assigned to Native American art. Nonetheless, Gorman has received an extraordinary number of awards and honors, his work has been shown consistently and frequently in exhibits around the world, and he has remained one of the most hailed of all contemporary Native American artists.

Gorman was born in 1931 on a reservation at Chinle, Arizona, to the Navajo artist **Carl Nelson Gorman** and Adelle Katherine Brown Gorman. Like his father, he felt the desire to express himself through art from an early age and he was always encouraged to express himself through art. Gorman remembers making his first drawing at three

years old, tracing patterns in mud with his fingers at the base of the Canyon de Chelly in northeastern Arizona, a beautiful and famous Navajo landmark.

As a boy, Gorman lived in the *hogan,* the traditional Navajo dwelling, where he herded sheep with his grandmother. But his education exposed him to a wide variety of influences as a young man. He attended school at Chinle and St. Michael's and graduated from Ganado Mission High School in Arizona in 1950. He then attended Guam Territorial College, Arizona State College (now Northern Arizona University) at Flagstaff, and San Francisco State University, studying both art and literature. The Navajo Tribal Council awarded Gorman a

Moonrise, by R. C. Gorman

grant to study at Mexico City College (now University of the Americas), marking the first time such a grant had been awarded for study outside the United States. From 1952 until 1956, he served in the U.S. Navy.

Launches career as a painter

Though Gorman showed talent as a writer, he chose to pursue a career in art. He said in an interview, "The reservation is my source of inspiration for what I paint; but yet I never come to realize this until I find myself in some far-flung place like the tip of Yucatan [Mexico] or where-have-you. Perhaps when I stay on the reservation I take too much for granted. While there, it is my inspiration, and I paint very little, and off the reservation it is my realization." Yet Gorman is known for a cosmopolitan (having worldly sophistication) art style of considerable depth and range. Despite his sentiments about his Navajo background, some have accused him of not being in touch with the culture and affairs of his people.

Part of the reason that Gorman's work has been attacked by purists (strict followers of

Flower of Los Lunas, by R. C. Gorman

tradition) is that, though he often paints Native American subjects, his style is not traditionally Native. Gorman's work is usually highly abstract, more concerned with producing an effect of the paint on the canvas than with duplicating physical reality. Working in ink, oil, pastel, watercolor, and acrylic, Gorman often applies bleeding colors, washes (thin coats of paint), and fadeouts in his paintings, and he continually searches for innovative and original directions with his art. In addition to many group showings and exhibitions, his work has appeared in more than 60 national and international one-man shows, and five shows with his father.

Inclusion in Metropolitan Museum of Art show

One of Gorman's greatest achievements was realized in 1973 when two of his works were selected for the cover of the catalogue and for the show of the Masterworks of the Museum of the American Indian exhibit held at the Metropolitan Museum of Art in New

York City. He was the only living Native American artist included. In 1975, the Museum of the American Indian chose Gorman as the first artist featured in its series of solo exhibitions of contemporary American Indian artists.

In addition to his work as an artist and the many awards and exhibits that have accompanied his success, Gorman is the founder and manager of the Navajo Gallery in Taos, New Mexico.

Further Reading

Adams, Ben Q., and Richard Newlin, *R. C. Gorman: The Complete Graphics,* Taos Editions, 1988.

Gorman, R. C., *The Man Who Sent Rain Clouds,* New York: Viking, 1974.

Henningsen, Chuck, and Stephen Parks, *R. C. Gorman: A Portrait,* Boston: Little, Brown, 1983.

Wade, Edwin, L., and Rennard Strickland, *Magic Images: Contemporary Native American Art,* Norman: University of Oklahoma Press, 1981.

Graham Greene

Oneida actor
Born 1952, Six Nations Reserve near Brantford, Ontario, Canada

With his dry, understated manner, Greene has established himself as a powerful stage and screen presence; his most popular roles combine soft-spoken humor with intelligence and dignity.

Graham Greene, one of the most prominent Native American actors working on the stage and in film today, is probably best known for his roles in the films *Dances with Wolves* and *Thunderheart.* With his dry, understated manner, he has established himself as a powerful stage and screen presence; his most popular roles combine soft-spoken humor with intelligence and dignity.

Greene was the second of six children born on the Six Nations Reserve near Brantford, Ontario, Canada, to John, an ambulance driver and maintenance man, and Lillian Greene. At the age of 16, he dropped out of school and went to Rochester, New York, where he worked at a carpet warehouse. Two years later he studied welding at George Brown College in Toronto, Ontario, then worked in a factory, building railway cars. In the 1970s Greene worked as a roadie and sound man for Toronto rock bands and ran a recording studio in Ancaster, Ontario. He has also worked as a high-steel worker in the construction industry, a landscape gardener, a factory laborer, a carpenter, and a bartender.

Greene took his first acting role, playing the part of a Native American in 1974 as part of the now-defunct Toronto theater company, the Ne'er-Do-Well Thespians. In 1980 he played a Native American alcoholic in *The Crackwalker* by Judith Thompson, and in the 1982 theater production of *Jessica,* coauthored by Linda Griffiths, he played the role of The Crow. In the 1980s Greene worked with the Theatre Passe Muraille, acting in an "irreverent set of plays, *The History of the Village of the Small Huts.*" When not acting, he welded sets and worked lights in the theaters.

Ups and downs as film actor

Greene's first film role was in 1982's *Running Brave*; he played a friend of the Native American track star **Billy Mills** (see entry). Two years later, in 1984, he played a Huron extra in *Revolution,* a movie about the U.S. War of Independence that was shot in England and starred Al Pacino. In the meantime, Greene had a daughter by the Toronto actress Carol Lazare in 1981. The death of his father in 1984, however, started what Greene described as a wild, rough period. Moving to the country around the same time, Greene found himself out of work and selling hand-painted T-shirts in Toronto by 1988.

Events took another upward turn in 1989 when Greene played a cameo role as Jimmy, an emotionally disturbed Lakota Vietnam veteran, in the film *Powwow Highway,* an independent film set in the 1970s that shows that Indian culture and spirituality are necessary for Indian self-determination and survival. That same year Greene received the Dora Mavor Moore Award of Toronto for

Graham Greene

best actor in his role as Pierre St. Pierre in Cree author Tomson Highway's play *Dry Lips Oughta Move to Kapuskasing.*

Lands key role in *Dances with Wolves*

Greene's biggest break as a film actor arrived with the 1990 production *Dances with Wolves.* The role of Kicking Bird, a Lakota holy man who befriends the character played by the producer-director and star Kevin Costner, earned Greene an Academy Award nomination for best supporting actor in 1991. While he was on location for the movie in the Black Hills of South Dakota, Greene studied Sioux traditions and the Lakota language. He told a *Maclean*'s interviewer, "I still get a tingle up my back when I think about South Dakota. It's really a powerful spot." Meanwhile, Greene's personal life moved forward as well. While shooting *Dances with Wolves,* he married Hilary Blackmore, a Toronto stage manager.

As his film career took off, Greene continued his theater work, playing "a toothless, beer-guzzling Indian buffoon" in an all-Native cast of *Dry Lips Oughta Move to Kapuskasing.* The part could not have been more different than his role as the wise and dignified Kicking Bird; Tomson Highway said in an interview that "Graham has a chamelion-like ability to change himself into any character he chooses. And he's a master clown." Greene, who played the part of an Indian alcoholic in both *Dry Lips* and *The Crackwalker* has had his own struggles with alcohol. Asked if he minded playing the stereotypical role of the drunken Indian, Greene quoted a native elder named Lyle Longclaws in *Maclean's*: "Before the healing can take place, the poison must first be exposed."

In 1990 he made a couple of high-profile appearances on television as well, playing a Navajo lawyer on the popular series *L.A. Law,* and Leonard, a Native American shaman (a priest who uses magic to cure illness and control events), on the hit program *Northern Exposure.*

Apart from his supporting role in *Dances with Wolves* and his brief appearance in *Powwow Highway,* Greene is probably most popular for his role as the mystical, murderous Native activist Arthur in the 1991 Canadian movie *Clearcut,* which was based on the Toronto writer M. T. Kelly's novel *A Dream Like Mine.* In 1992 he played **Ishi**

(see entry), the last Native American in California to live completely apart from white culture, in the made-for-television movie *The Last of His Tribe.* The same year Greene gave a strong performance as a Lakota tribal policeman, Walter Crow Horse, in *Thunderheart,* a drama loosely based on events in Oglala, South Dakota, in which two FBI agents were shot and killed.

Greene has also appeared in, among others, the 1991 adventure movie *Lost in the Barrens,* the 1992 Turner Network Television (TNT) feature *Cooperstown,* the made-for-television children's production *WonderWorks—Spirit Rider, Huck and the King of Hearts,* a loose and modern adaptation of the adventures of Mark Twain's *Huckleberry Finn,* the thriller *Benefit of the Doubt* with Donald Sutherland, and the western comedy *Maverick,* starring Mel Gibson, Jodie Foster, and James Garner.

Greene's upcoming work includes roles in the film adaptation of Thomas King's *Green Grass, Running Water,* and in the television movie *The Broken Chain* with other Native actors Wes Studi, Eric Schweig, and Floyd Red Crow Westerman. Greene currently lives in Toronto with his wife and cat.

Further Reading

"A Filmmaker's Instincts: Costner's Dances with Wolves," *Commonweal,* January 11, 1991, pp. 18–19.

Johnson, Brian D., "Dances with Oscar: Canadian Actor Graham Greene Tastes Stardom," *Maclean's,* March 25, 1991, pp. 60–61.

Native North American Almanac, edited by Duane Champagne, Detroit: Gale, 1994.

Handsome Lake

Seneca spiritual leader
Born c. 1735, Conawagas, near Avon, New York
Died August 10, 1815, at the Onondaga Reservation, near Syracuse, New York
Also known as Hadawa'ko ("Shaking Snow"), Skaniadariio, Ganeodiyo, Kaniataro ("Beautiful Lake"), and Sedwa'gowa'ne ("Our Great Teacher")

The Code of Handsome Lake, published around 1850, played a large role in the preservation of the Iroquois cultural heritage and was revered throughout the Iroquois nations in Canada and in the United States.

Handsome Lake, a great leader and prophet, played a major role in the revival of the Senecas and other tribes of the Iroquois League or Confederacy (an alliance of the Mohawk, Oneida, Onondoga, Cayuga, and Seneca formed in about 1570). He preached a message that combined traditional Iroquois spiritual beliefs with elements from European-based religions. This message, eventually published as the Code of Handsome Lake, serves as the basis of a religion practiced by approximately half of the Iroquois people today.

Handsome Lake was born around 1735 in the Seneca village of Conawagas, located on the Genesee River near Avon, New York. Very little is known of his parents. He was born into the Wolf clan and was named Hadawa'ko ("Shaking Snow") but was eventually raised by the Turtle clan people. He was a half-brother to Cornplanter and an uncle of Red Jacket, both of whom were powerful Seneca tribal leaders. Born during the peak of the Seneca nation's prosperity, Handsome Lake participated in the French and Indian Wars that extended from 1689 to 1763, in which France and Great Britain and their Indian allies fought over North American territory. He also fought in the Ottawa chieftain **Pontiac**'s (see entry) war against the British, and in the American Revolution. As the eighteenth century drew to a close, however, Handsome Lake saw his people's society begin to fall apart.

The Iroquois' troubles had a number of causes. In the period after the American Revolution, Iroquois tribes lost most of their lands, and members were forced to live on reservations. The reservations had poor living conditions, and many Iroquois began to experience alcohol abuse, fighting, disintegration of family structure, and other hardships. The Iroquois social structure did not fit reservation existence, and traditional religious rituals alone could not improve the situation. As a result, the Iroquois began searching for new solutions.

Brings a message of *Gaiwiio* ("Good Word")

In 1799, after a period of illness due to many years of alcohol abuse, Handsome Lake had the first of a series of visions. In his first vision, three spiritual messengers warned him about the dangers of alcohol. They told him that witches were creating disorder and confusion within his tribe and that those practicing witchcraft must repent and confess. Handsome Lake was directed to reveal these warnings to the people. His nephew Blacksnake and half-brother Corn-

Handsome Lake Preaching, drawing by Jesse Cornplanter

planter were with him during this time and believed in the power of his visions. Shortly after Handsome Lake's first vision, he gave up alcohol.

When he regained his health, he began giving a message of *Gaiwiio* (the "Good Word") to his people. He preached against drunkenness and other evil practices. His message outlined a moral message that was eventually referred to as the Code of Handsome Lake. The code outlawed drunkenness, witchcraft, sexual promiscuity, wife beating, quarreling, and gambling. Handsome Lake warned his people that fire would destroy the world if his code were not obeyed.

Searches out witchcraft

Handsome Lake soon became obsessed with witch hunting and demanded confes-

sions from those he suspected of witchcraft; some of those who refused to confess were killed. His witch hunting nearly caused a war with another tribe when he accused a prominent young man of that tribe of being a witch and demanded he be punished. Gradually, the Iroquois people turned against Handsome Lake and what they considered his overzealous pursuit of witches. As a result he stopped his crusade against witches and for a time assumed a less prominent leadership role.

During the War of 1812 (an armed conflict occurring between 1812 and 1815 between the United States and Great Britain over shipping rights) Handsome Lake once again began to attract many new followers. In his second period as a prophet, Handsome Lake taught less about sin and destruction, and more about how to live a good life. Although not Christian, his code was inspired by Christian teachings, particularly those of the Quakers, whose missionaries were working among the Iroquois at the time. Along with other moral messages, Handsome Lake taught that husbands and wives should love each other and remain faithful, and they should treat their children with kindness. He urged compassion for the suffering and instructed his people to perform ceremonies in the longhouse (a place of worship). All were to revere the Great Spirit and all of Creation. His lessons formed a religion that became known as the Handsome Lake Church or the revitalized Longhouse religion.

Handsome Lake's religion was more successful than most during that time, apparently because his code combined traditional Iroquois religion with European Christian values. Without calling for the sacrifice of the Iroquois identity, it recognized the need to make adjustments in order to survive in the changing world. The Code of Handsome Lake, published around 1850, played a large role in the preservation of the Iroquois cultural heritage and was revered throughout the Iroquois nations in Canada and in the United States. Handsome Lake, referred to as Sedwa'gowa'ne, "Our Great Teacher," died on August 10, 1815, at the Onondaga Reservation, near present-day Syracuse, New York. His religious beliefs were carried on by Blacksnake and other disciples, and his teachings remain a compelling force among the Iroquois. The Longhouse religion is practiced only by Iroquois nations. Today perhaps half of the Iroquois people are followers of the Code of Handsome Lake.

Further Reading

Native North American Almanac, edited by Duane Champagne, Detroit: Gale, 1994.

Waldman, Carl, *Who Was Who in Native American History,* Facts on File, 1990.

Wallace, Anthony F. C., "Origins of the Longhouse Religion," in *Handbook of North American Indians,* edited by William C. Sturtevant, Washington, DC: Smithsonian Institution, 1978.

Chitto Harjo

Creek warrior
Born 1846, Arbeka, Oklahoma
Died 1911
Also known as Crazy Snake and Wilson Jones

The threat of jail did not stop Harjo from organizing further Snake opposition to allotment. He escaped arrest for ten months, but deputy marshals captured him in the spring of 1902.

The Crazy Snake movement of 1900 to 1909, named after its leader, Chitto Harjo, occured during an important period of change for the Five Nations (Cherokee, Creek, Chickasaw, Choctaw, Seminole). At this time the U.S. government tried to force the Creek to accept allotments of individual farms by breaking up their reservation land in Oklahoma. The *Snakes,* as Harjo's followers were called, demanded that the Creek National Council and the president of the United States enforce the Treaty of 1832, which guaranteed the Five Nations a specified amount of land in Oklahoma. Among the Creek, the name *Chitto Harjo* (chit-to ha-cho) symbolizes resistance to the forces of assimilation—or blending into mainstream cul-

Chitto Harjo

where Arbeka warriors guarded the Creek Confederacy against surprise attack. Runners warned people of danger by carrying the war whoop to other Creek towns. In the summer of 1900, when Chitto Harjo spoke against allotment—the breaking up of reservations into small farms "allotted" to individuals by the U.S. government—at Creek stomp dances, he fulfilled the traditional role of carrying the war whoop to his people.

Harjo is a common second name among Creeks, it means "recklessly brave, one who is brave beyond discretion." It is usually translated as mad or crazy. *Chitto* is a derivation of the Creek word *catto,* which means snake. Harjo's name communicated qualities of daring and courage, with a little rashness, to Creeks. He was known more intimately to family and friends as Bill Jones, Bill Snake, and Bill Harjo.

Formation of the Four Mothers Nation

The Creek were able to avoid the division of their land into allotted farms for 11 years after the government imposed the Dawes Act of 1887. The passage of the Curtis Act in 1898, however, dissolved tribal governments and blocked tribal efforts to escape allotment, terminating the tribal identity and authority of the Creek. In 1899, the majority of Creek people surrendered to the federally imposed division of their land and community; individual Creeks selected and registered their allotments. Pleasant Porter was elected principal chief of the Creek because he pledged to cooperate with the Dawes Commission.

Some Creek, however, opposed allotment because it violated previous treaties, especially the Treaty of 1832. They initially called

ture—in the twentieth century. But Harjo's resistance caused panic among the white settlers in Oklahoma. Because of fear of a Snake uprising in 1901, federal troops arrested and imprisoned Harjo, and the Snake movement was forcibly subdued.

Harjo was born in 1846 in Arbeka, a Creek town on the Deep Fork River in Oklahoma, the westernmost town in the Creek territory. Prior to the removal of the Creek from Alabama in the 1830s, Arbeka had been a sacred village located on the upper Coosa River in Alabama. It had legendary meaning as one of the four original Creek towns: known as "the gate of the Muskogees," it was themselves the "adherents of the Opothle Yahola Treaty." Chitto Harjo always referred to them as "Loyal Creeks." Local newspapers often referred to them as conservative full-bloods. Creek leaders called them the "ignorant class" of Creek people. Eventually, the dissenters were called "Crazy Snakes" after their leader, Chitto Harjo.

Creeks who protested allotment formed the core of the Crazy Snake movement. The majority of Snakes arrested by U.S. marshals in 1901 were Creek, but other tribes opposed allotment as well. Cherokees, Choctaws, Chickasaws, and Seminoles joined forces with Harjo. Tribal representatives attended Snake meetings and organized factions among their people. After Harjo's arrest in 1901, the Crazy Snakes rapidly grew into an intertribal movement against allotment. In 1908, the Snake movement inspired the formation of the Four Mothers Nation, an Indian organization for collective political action in the state of Oklahoma.

Organization of the Crazy Snake Movement

Hickory Ground was the center of Snake activity. Located 30 miles southwest of Checotah, it ranked eighth in size among 48 Creek towns with its population of 343. Hickory Ground residents retained many Creek attitudes from the period before their forced removal from their homeland, including a strong anti-American sentiment and distrust of kinsmen who cooperated with whites. The tribal conflict over allotment was rooted in centuries of hatred between Hickory Ground residents and pro-American Creeks.

The nature and history of the Creeks made feuding over allotment inevitable. Creek his-

tory is full of political differences between factions. Harjo learned from his parents about the trauma of removal from tribal lands. He was well aware of the differences—many directly related to the politics and wars of European settlers in the area—that led Creeks to fight against each other. Factions (interest groups) formed around local leaders whenever there was a major disagreement, particularly in relation to Anglo Americans. Snakes who opposed allotment resorted to the traditional Creek method of dissension (expressing opposing views).

Ignorance of Creek culture caused outsiders to misunderstand Harjo's role—he was not the initial leader of the opposition movement. In 1900 Lahtah Micco was the *micco* (head chief) of Hickory Ground. Harjo was his *henehu,* the eloquent speaker who made announcements and speeches for Lahtah Micco. Lahtah Micco held the power at Hickory Ground, but Harjo's speeches attracted a great deal of attention, making him the most visible of the dissenters to his white neighbors.

Harjo was elected micco of Hickory Ground in the spring of 1900. Illness had stranded Lahtah Micco in Washington, D.C., for more than six months after he led a delegation there to persuade the president of the United States to enforce the Treaty of 1832. The whole delegation, except Harjo, contracted smallpox. Harjo left the delegation quarantined (isolated to prevent spread of disease) in Washington and returned to Hickory Ground to organize Creek resistance to allotment. As the movement grew in size, settlers and government agents called its members "Snakes" after the charismatic (having a forceful personality) orator.

The Snakes, hoping to gain control of Creek affairs, elected Chitto Harjo as their principal chief. They adopted a code of laws for Creeks living in the Hickory Ground vicinity and erected a new tribal emblem in the Hickory Ground square. Harjo appointed a Light-Horse unit (police force). Finally, in a bold move, the Snakes claimed authority over Okmulgee, the site of the Creek Council House, where the National Council met in session.

Harjo imprisoned for Snake activity

Harjo and the Snakes were regarded lightly until the Snake Light-Horse unit started enforcing Snake laws. Public whippings and ear croppings generated fear among non-Creeks. After Snake leaders threatened to kill Principal Chief Porter, National Council members and Dawes Commissioners requested federal help to end the Snake resistance. Troop A of the Eighth United States Cavalry from Fort Reno and a dozen deputy U.S. marshals set up camp near Henryetta. A deadly confrontation was expected, but the arrest of Harjo and other Snake leaders was quick and bloodless. Ninety-six Snakes, ranging from 4 to 88 years old were arrested.

The Snakes appeared in the U.S. District Court of Judge John R. Thomas, where they pleaded guilty to four charges. Judge Thomas sentenced them to two years in prison at Leavenworth but suspended the sentences when the Snakes pledged to live in peace. He promised future imprisonment at Leavenworth if they continued their resistance. The threat of jail did not stop Harjo from organizing further Snake opposition to allotment. He escaped arrest for ten months, but deputy marshals captured him in the spring of 1902. He and nine others were imprisoned at the Leavenworth federal penitentiary in March 1902; there they served the remainder of their two-year sentence.

Appealed to the United States Senate

Harjo took his opposition directly to the United States Senate in the summer of 1906. A select Senate Committee traveled to Oklahoma to investigate matters related to the termination of the Five Nations. On November 23, 1906, Harjo attended the public hearing in Tulsa, Oklahoma. In traditional, eloquent Creek oratory, Harjo requested in a petition that the committee restore the Treaty of 1832. Unfortunately, Harjo's speaking style was difficult for the senators to understand, and his manner of address only showed how far apart Creek and U.S. customs and beliefs were. He did not persuade the senators to take action, but he embarrassed them by challenging the unclear legal status of Indians.

Tensions continued to mount at Hickory Ground. A large gathering of Snakes at the Hickory Ground Green Corn ceremony in the summer of 1908 scared citizens of Checotah and Henryetta. In addition—much to the displeasure of Henryetta citizens—Hickory Ground had allowed many displaced black families from Henryetta to set up a tent camp near the town. Unemployed and landless, the families were often forced to steal food in order to eat.

A posse (people assembled by a sheriff to enforce laws) from Henryetta rode to the tent camp and a shoot-out followed as they tried to arrest suspected thieves. The posse opened fire, killing several black men. Harjo was not at the camp but 20 miles away at his home. The sheriff, however, blamed Harjo for the incident and sent four deputies to arrest him. At sundown, March 27, 1909, as the officers approached Harjo's cabin, one of Harjo's friends shot and killed two officers. A bullet fired by one of the officers penetrated the cabin and struck Harjo in the leg, above the knee. This wound eventually proved fatal.

The killing of the two officers created a furor in Checotah and Henryetta. A larger posse returned to Harjo's home to find him gone. They shot at the women in the cabin, forcing them to flee, then burned all of Harjo's property to the ground. Vigilante groups roamed the area pillaging Snake farms in search of Harjo. Alarmed, Oklahoma Governor Haskell called out the state militia. The First Regiment of the Oklahoma National Guard occupied Hickory Ground with 200 guardsmen. They quickly restored order but did not capture Chitto Harjo. His disappearance inspired many legends about his death. He most likely died on April 11, 1911, at the home of his Choctaw friend, Daniel Bob. Snakes continued their efforts to block assimilation (blending into the dominant society) for many years after their leader's death.

A warrior-statesman

Today, the Creek Nation views Harjo as a sincere, honest warrior-statesman and a shrewd and charismatic leader. Views about Harjo were mixed in 1907, when Oklahoma became a state. Creek leaders and mixed-bloods considered him ignorant and an embarrassment to the tribe. Non-Indians labeled him the most dangerous Indian in Oklahoma because they thought he intended

to kill every white in the region. Other tribes considered him smart and eloquent, but many refused to follow him in the later years of the movement because they feared imprisonment.

Chitto Harjo did not stop the intrusion of white culture upon the Creeks. Yet his efforts to persuade the U.S. government to honor its pledges in the Treaty of 1832 were not in vain. Harjo's powerful message of cooperation between tribes sowed the seeds for an official political organization, the Four Mothers Nation, which has fostered intertribal political activism throughout the twentieth century.

Further Reading

The Native North American Almanac, edited by Duane Champagne, Detroit: Gale, 1994.

Joy Harjo

Muscogee Creek writer, educator, musician, and artist
Born May 9, 1951, Tulsa, Oklahoma

"The way I interpret feminism in my own work is the power of a woman to be a warrior—to recognize the warrior characteristics within herself, which include self-love, vulnerability, honesty, integrity, a sense of morals, and so on."

Joy Harjo is in the forefront of a group of Native American writers and artists who have gained international recognition over the past two decades. She is a screenwriter, a teacher, and a musician, but her reputation rests largely on her widely acclaimed poetry. Beginning with her first published collection in 1975, that poetry has developed into a solid and influential body of work that has earned her numerous important awards and ranked her among the major poets of the twentieth century. Established as a writer, Harjo has increasingly turned to music: she plays alto and soprano saxophone with a group appropriately named "Poetic Justice," and she makes recordings and personal appearances with that group.

Harjo's different activities as an artist— her early work as a painter, her later work as a poet, and her more recent interest in music performance—often blend. For example, for her 1985 Watershed recording *Furious Light,* Harjo read her own poetry to musical accompaniment and created the artwork on the front cover.

Harjo is strongly aware of her political and social position and is sensitive to how others view that position in terms of her work. "I am seen as a feminist poet," she told a *Poets & Writers* interviewer in 1993. "The way I interpret feminism in my own work is the power of a woman to be a warrior—to recognize the warrior characteristics within herself, which include self-love, vulnerability, honesty, integrity, a sense of morals, and so on."

Childhood and education

Joy Harjo was born in 1951 in Tulsa, Oklahoma, to Allen W. and Wynema Baker Foster. She is the oldest of four children; her parents divorced when she was eight years old. As a young child she became involved in a local church, where her own passionate sermons made a deep impression on the children of her neighborhood. At this time Harjo's constant urge to travel made her want to become a missionary. But all thoughts of formal religion and missionary work ended when Harjo saw the local minister embarrass two Mexican girls who were noisy in church and told them to leave. Harjo left too—for good.

One of the most important moments in Harjo's life occurred when, at the age of 16, she went to boarding school at the Institute of American Indian Arts in Santa Fe, New Mexico (she would return to the same school in 1978 as an instructor). For the first time in her life she found her talents appreciated and encouraged in a school. Working with other Native American students was especially important to her development. She was further stimulated by her studies at the University of New Mexico at Albuquerque, where she earned her bachelor's degree in 1976. There she continued the painting she had begun in Santa Fe.

In her early twenties, Harjo sought out another painter in the family, her great aunt, Lois Harjo Ball, for guidance. She received the direction she needed, and as she told Susan Lepselter in 1989, her great aunt "was very connected to what I call the dream world." It was also at the Indian school that Harjo met such Native American writers as **Leslie Marmon Silko** (see entry) and Simon Ortiz and heard them read their work. These readings were a turning point for Harjo: she decided to give up painting and devote her energies to poetry. In 1993, she told *Poets & Writers* magazine that a reading by the Irish American bard Galway Kinnell had been especially influential for her, as had the work of a Ugandan poet, Okot p'Bitek, and the writers Audre Lorde, Gwendolyn Brooks, and **N. Scott Momaday** (see entry).

While she was living in Santa Fe, Harjo became pregnant with her son, Phil. Before the birth of that first child in 1968 (her second child, a daughter named Rainy Dawn, was born in 1973), she moved back to Oklahoma, where she held various jobs, including that of a nurse's assistant in a local hospital. Her genuine feeling for the work led to an assignment in the maternity area, where the closeness to the basic events of life and death deeply affected her. These experiences are expressed in her 1991 *Ms.* magazine article, "Three Generations of Native American Women's Birth Experience."

Two years after completing her bachelor's degree, Harjo earned a master of fine arts degree from the University of Iowa. She also studied filmmaking in 1992 at the Anthropology Film Center. By 1985 she was teaching at the University of Colorado, and from 1988 to 1990 she was with the University of Arizona. In 1991 she became a full professor at the University of New Mexico.

Early published poetry

Harjo's first collection of poetry was the 1975 chapbook (poetry collection) *The Last Song,* which includes material inspired by her early life and adolescence in the Southwest. Titles such as "Isleta Woman Singing," "Too Far into Arizona," and "For a Hopi Silversmith," offer important insights into some of the wellsprings of Harjo's creative imagination. All of the material in *The Last Song* reappears, along with 48 new poems, in her second collection, *What Moon Drove Me to This?,* published in 1980.

Joy Harjo

The poet's dissatisfaction with her early work is evident in a comment she made to *Poets & Writers* magazine. Speaking of the poems in *What Moon Drove Me to This?* Harjo concluded: "It was a very young book. There are probably only two good poems in it—poems that showed promise. It was a painful book, written during a difficult period in my life. You could see the beginnings of something, but it wasn't quite cooked."

Throughout this period, Harjo was also a writer-in-residence at Navajo Community

College, in Tsaile, Arizona (1978); the New Mexico Poetry in the Schools Program (1974-1976, 1980); and the State Arts Council of Oklahoma (1980-1981). She also served on the Native American Public Broadcasting Consortium, an organization devoted to supporting and encouraging Native work in television, video, and motion pictures, and the National Endowment for the Arts. In 1983, Harjo published *She Had Some Horses,* a volume that made the poet's work more widely known; more than a decade after its publication, the book was still in print and widely used in college literature courses. Its title poem is perhaps Harjo's single most famous poem—and the one she does not wish to discuss. "She Had Some Horses" presents the horse as a vision that shows human nature as a part of, and at the same time apart from, the world of nature.

Additional poetry and screenwriting

The world of nature, particularly the environment of the Southwest of her childhood and youth, became the subject of Harjo's 1989 *Secrets from the Center of the World,* a book of prose poems and accompanying photographs by Stephen Storm. The combination of Harjo's and Storm's surreal images evokes a special mood and suggests relationships among people, landscape, and history.

Throughout the 1980s Harjo had been working steadily on screen projects for various broadcasting outlets. She worked on screenplays for *The Gaan Story* and *The Beginning,* among several others, and produced a series of eight 20-minute scripts for Nebraska Educational Television under the title *We Are One, Umonho.* Harjo wrote poetry for a PBS film, *American Indian Artist Series II,* and worked as a production assistant on the project. Perhaps the most noteworthy moment on screen for Harjo herself occurred in 1989, when she appeared on the Bill Moyers PBS series *The Power of the Word.* Harjo was interviewed by Moyers and read selections from her own poetry, notably a lengthy section from *She Had Some Horses.*

Awards

In 1990 Harjo published her most critically acclaimed poetry collection to date, *In Mad Love and War.* It includes autobiographical themes, meditations on music, and explorations of the personal, social, and political implications of the power of love. The book was immediately well received; less than a year after its publication, it earned the writer both the William Carlos Williams and Delmore Schwartz awards for poetry. Harjo also received important recognition for her work during the earlier part of her career, including a first place award from the Academy of American Poetry in 1976 and a first place prize in poetry from the Writers Forum at the University of Colorado the following year. She received another first place award in poetry at the Santa Fe Festival in 1980 and a Pushcart Prize in 1988.

Another of Harjo's important publications was her 1994 volume of poems *The Woman Who Fell from the Sky.* The poems in this book return to some of the poet's earlier concerns, among them music, storytelling, the land and the human spirit, and female individuality. Speaking of the book in the publisher's fall 1994 catalogue, Harjo said: "The word *poet* is synonymous with the word *truth teller*. So this collection tells a bit of the truth of what I have seen since my coming of age in the late sixties." The book is accompanied by an audiocassette of Harjo performing her own work to music.

In addition to the publication of her own poetry, Harjo has been actively involved in the placement of the work of other writers. She has served as poetry editor for the *High Plains Literary Review* and as contributing editor for the journals *Tyuonyi* and *Contact II*. She has also been on the steering committee for the En'owkin Centre International School of Writing and has been a member of the National Third World Writers Association.

Harjo is a writer at once mystical and modern, a teacher whose greatest influence on students often takes place outside the confines of the classroom, and a visionary who not only takes us toward the future but also reminds us of our common past. Just as an artist may leave a native country but still work in the tradition of that country, Harjo's poetry explores many aspects of the modern world while constantly calling upon the symbols and traditions of her Native American experience.

Further Reading

Bell, Dan, "Ode to Joy," *Village Voice Literary Supplement,* April 2, 1991.

Bruchac, Joseph, "An Interview with Joy Harjo," in *Survival This Way: Interviews with American Indian Poets,* Tucson: Sun Tracks and University of Arizona Press, 1987.

Lepselter, Susan, "Spinning Dreams into Words" (interview with Joy Harjo), *Tucson Weekly,* December 27, 1989.

Smith, Stephanie Izarek, "Joy Harjo" (interview), *Poets & Writers,* July-August 1993, pp. 23-27.

Books by Joy Harjo:

Fishing (chapbook; originally published in *New York Times,* June 21, 1991), Minnesota: Ox Head Press, 1991.

In Mad Love and War, Middletown, CT: Wesleyan University Press, 1990.

The Last Song (chapbook), Las Cruces, NM: Puerto del Sol Press, 1975.

Secrets from the Center of the World (with photographs by Stephen Storm), Tucson: Sun Tracks and the University of Arizona Press, 1989.

She Had Some Horses, New York: Thunders Mouth Press, 1983.

What Moon Drove Me to This? New York: I. Reed Books, 1980.

The Woman Who Fell from the Sky, New York: Norton, 1994.

Elijah Harper

Cree provincial legislator
Born 1949, Red Sucker Lake, Manitoba, Canada

"But who's going to speak for us? We've been shoved aside."

Manitoba provincial legislator Elijah Harper is well known for his successful efforts to prevent the passage of the Meech Lake Accord in Canada. The accord was a 1990 federal proposal to amend (change) the Canadian Constitution in response to the province of Quebec's demands for home rule. Harper objected to the accord because the document did not deal with Native concerns. By preventing the passage of the Accord, Harper, the sole aboriginal

Elijah Harper

(native) member of the Manitoba legislature and former chief of the Red Sucker Lake Indian band, placed aboriginal issues at the top of Canada's constitutional agenda. In 1990 Harper was awarded the Canadian Press Newsmakers of the Year Award and, in 1991, the Stanley Knowles Humanitarian Award.

Harper, who was born in northern Manitoba near the community of Red Sucker Lake, left home at the age of eight for residential school. After completing high school, he attended the University of Manitoba in Winnipeg from 1970 to 1972. Along with studies in anthropology (the study of human cultures and beliefs), Harper helped establish the university's Native students' association with two other future Native political leaders, Ovide Mercredi and Phil

Fontaine. In 1973, Harper married Elizabeth Ann Ross; the couple have four children.

Political career begins as band chief

After returning to Red Sucker Lake and working on several community development projects, Harper began his political career in 1977. In that year he was elected chief of the Red Sucker Lake band; he served as band chief from 1977 until 1981. In 1980 and 1981 Harper traveled to London, England, where he participated with other Indian leaders in efforts to reform new constitutional proposals, which made no provisions to protect Native rights. At this time Indian groups were allowed to participate in constitutional reform discussions in Parliament only if the issue directly affected them. Upset because aboriginal people were not recognized in the new Canadian Constitution, Harper refused an invitation to attend its signing by the queen in 1982.

In 1981, Harper was elected to the Manitoba legislature (lawmaking body); he was reelected in 1986, 1988, and 1990. While serving in the legislature, Harper was legislative assistant to the minister of Northern affairs and cochair of the provincial cabinet's Native Affairs Committee. He was appointed as the minister responsible for Native affairs in 1986 and a year later became minister of Northern affairs. In 1990 Harper attained national recognition for his rejection of the Meech Lake Accord.

Stops Meech Lake Accord

Canada's constitutional crisis came to a head in June 1990. Although all of the other provinces agreed to support the Meech Lake Accord, Prime Minister Brian Mulroney feared that Manitoba would not. Attempting to pacify Manitoba's Native leadership, the prime minister offered to appoint a royal commission to investigate Native affairs and presented several other incentives. But Harper, with the support of Manitoba's Native leaders, prevented the legislature from ratifying (formally approving) the accord before the June 23 deadline. Commenting on his position in the *Globe and Mail, A Constitutional Primer,* Harper said: "It was not easy for me to make this decision.... But who's going to speak for us? We've been shoved aside." He added that his actions were meant "to symbolize that aboriginal people are not being recognized as the first people of this country and not being recognized as founders of this country."

Backed by the Assembly of Manitoba Chiefs, Harper blocked the accord's passage in the Manitoba legislature on June 22, 1990. Harper's vote, in addition to ending hopes for the accord and a new constitution for Canada that year, helped Canadian Natives to gain political power. Harper's stand captured the public's attention, and the Native legislator from Manitoba became a Canadian folk hero.

The standoff also convinced Canadian political leaders that Native concerns had to be addressed. By August 1990, both the provinces of British Columbia and Saskatchewan were reevaluating their Native policies. And as the 1990s progressed, other provinces followed. The affair gave Canada's aboriginal people political influence they had not had in centuries. Harper's stand and the public's reaction to it brought Native groups all across Canada together in a triumphant display of pride and determination. Not since the late 1960s had Canada's First Nations been so united. The image of Harper, standing in the Manitoba legislature, holding an eagle feather in one hand while quietly saying no to the prime minister, became a symbol of Native peoples' triumph in Canada.

Further Reading

Miller, J. R., *Skyscrapers Hide the Heavens: A History of Indian-White Relations in Canada,* revised edition, Toronto: University of Toronto Press, 1991.

Native North American Almanac, edited by Duane Champagne, Detroit: Gale, 1994.

Platiel, Rudy, "Canada Reconsidered: Aboriginal Rights," *Globe and Mail, A Constitutional Primer,* January 11, 1992, p. 7.

Sweet Promises: A Reader on Indian-White Relations in Canada, edited by J. R. Miller, Toronto: University of Toronto Press, 1991.

LaDonna Harris

Comanche political activist and economic developer
Born February 15, 1931, Temple, Oklahoma

LaDonna Harris has indicated that she sees her many roles as extensions of the traditional roles of Comanche women.

L aDonna Harris is one of the most widely involved activists for Native American economic development and human rights. An outspoken feminist and defender of

LaDonna Harris

The responsibility of raising young LaDonna fell to her full-blooded Comanche grandparents in Cotton County, Oklahoma, near her birthplace of Temple. Her grandfather, a former Indian scout at Fort Sill, Oklahoma, followed the traditions and established customs of his people and was an Eagle medicine man. Harris's grandmother was a Christian, but her grandparents' loving marriage was based on their mutual respect for each other's beliefs. Raised largely in the Comanche tradition, Harris spoke only her tribal tongue until she entered public school at the age of six. It was there that she first fully experienced the discrimination Native Americans faced in Oklahoma, even though the state had the largest and most tribally diverse Indian population in the country.

The senator's wife

In high school, Harris met her future husband, Fred Harris, who planned to study law and eventually run for elected office. Although hoping to work for the equality of Native peoples, Harris nevertheless put her goals on hold in order to help put Fred through college and later law school. The couple had three children, Kathryn, Byron, and Laura. In the years to come, Fred in turn supported Harris's ambition to help her fellow Native Americans. He had been a sharecropper's son who grew up in extreme poverty, so, although not a Native American, he understood some of the difficulties that many indigenous (original people of a region) people faced; he did not turn his back on them when he was elected to office. First serving as a state senator, then moving on to the United States Senate, he worked on human rights issues and helped Harris

the rights of children and the mentally ill, she has been recognized both nationally and globally throughout the last three decades for her humanitarian efforts on behalf of oppressed and poverty-stricken peoples.

Harris learned about the effects of racism against Native Americans early in her life. Her Comanche mother and Irish American father separated soon after her birth on February 15, 1931. According to the family, the discrimination her parents faced as a racially mixed couple was more than her father could endure. He moved to California, where he kept up a correspondence with his daughter, but he never returned to see her.

gain experience and make political connections that would aid her activist efforts in the future.

In 1965, the southern United States was embroiled in the struggle for African American civil rights, and much of the conflict involved laws segregating (separating) whites and blacks. At that time Harris, too, was working against segregation: that of the Southern Plains Indians in Lawton, Oklahoma. Her efforts included assembling representatives from nearly all of Oklahoma's tribes, and from one of these conferences emerged Oklahomans for Indian Opportunity. This organization, which was the state's first association to draw members from all of its 60 Native American tribes, linked the achievement of equality with economic stability, which had been sorely lacking in most Oklahoma tribes since the days of the Trail of Tears (the forced removal of thousands of Indians from their homelands in the Southeast to Indian Territory in present-day Oklahoma in 1838). Her work on this project earned Harris the title "Outstanding Indian of the Year" in 1965.

National prominence

Suddenly, Harris was a national figure, much sought after for service on public issues task forces, steering committees, and pilot projects. She became involved in policy issues related to children's rights and mental health, drawing on the skills and judgment she had developed in her work on behalf of Native Americans. The late 1960s, with its turbulent social and political climate, saw her working with such groups as the National Rural Housing Conference, the National Association of Mental Health, and the National Committee against Discrimination in Housing and chairing the Health Task Force of the National Steering Committee of the Urban Coalition.

In 1967, President Lyndon B. Johnson recognized Harris's work by appointing her to chair the National Women's Advisory Council of the War on Poverty. Johnson's administration had begun the "Great Society" programs aimed at fulfilling the promise of equal rights for all Americans through fairness in housing, employment, health care, and education. Again, Harris approached the task with tremendous energy and a positive outlook, so impressing Johnson that he named her to the newly created National Council on Indian Opportunity, a branch of the Office of Economic Opportunity.

Johnson was succeeded as president by Richard M. Nixon, who ushered in an era of "mixed signals" for Native Americans. His administration would ultimately prove sympathetic to religious and land rights for Native people, but reforms identified as "civil rights" were sometimes slow in coming.

Harris's appointment to the National Council on Indian Opportunity in 1968 was a good example of the Nixon administration's mixed signals on Indian issues. She had resigned as founding director of Oklahomans for Indian Opportunity to work with the national organization, but its first meeting was not held until January 26, 1970. The council was the responsibility of Vice President Spiro Agnew, but it was only at Harris's frustrated urging that the group was called together at all. After dealing for a while with the administration's contradictory attitudes, Harris left the position and again focused on grass-roots Native American movements and on women's issues. She became a founding member of the National Women's Political Caucus and, in 1970, founded Americans for Indian Opportunity (AIO).

Global advocate

During these years, Harris, still a caring mother and involved senator's wife, reached out to indigenous people the world over. She became interested in the Peace Corps and how its projects could promote local development for aboriginal (native to an area) groups. Traveling to such faraway countries as Mali, Senegal, the former Soviet Union, and numerous nations in Central and South America, she served as a representative of the Inter-American Indigenous Institute, a group formed by the Organization of American States.

Bestowed with awards and honors

Harris, a well-known activist, an insider on Capitol Hill, and a frequent official visitor to the White House, divided her time between national and international work, always keeping Americans for Indian Opportunity at the center of her plans. Already well connected on the rights of Native Americans, children, and the mentally ill, she was also emerging as a national figure in feminism. To encourage her efforts, President Gerald Ford named her to the U.S. Commission on the Observance of International Women's Year. She also received human rights awards from the National Association for Education and Delta Sigma Theta Sorority. Even though she had not attended college, she received three hon-

orary degrees, including a Doctor of Laws from Dartmouth College. Dartmouth had been founded for the purpose of providing higher education for Native Americans, so this honor was very special to Harris.

Although proud of her recognition by the Ford administration, she once again tired of the political bureaucracy (levels of organization) in Washington, which often caused long delays in carrying out national initiatives. Furthermore, her husband was finishing his senatorial term and wanted to return to the Southwest. The Harris family chose to settle in New Mexico, and Americans for Indian Opportunity relocated with them in 1975. Although directing most of her efforts to AIO, Harris nonetheless remained active in international affairs. Secretary of State Cyrus Vance offered her a position on the Board of Directors of UNESCO, and she accepted, blending her international work with her responsibilities in tribal development projects.

At the request of President Jimmy Carter, Harris served as a special adviser to Sargent Shriver, director of the Office for Economic Opportunity. Through this venture, she was able to achieve a long-held dream, that of creating an Indian version of the Peace Corps. Called the "Peace Pipe Project," this program trained Native North Americans to serve as local organizers and developers, assigning them to indigenous communities elsewhere in the hemisphere. The host communities felt more at ease working with other Indians, and the Peace Pipe workers learned skills they could apply when they returned to tribal or urban Indian communities. Although limited in actual application, this project would become the basis for another of

Harris's initiatives, the sometimes controversial Council for Energy Resources Tribes. This council's mission was to establish the fair development (or nondevelopment) of natural resources on Native American land, with an eye toward employment and an equitable (fair) market price for coal, oil, natural gas, and uranium, among others.

Carrying on Comanche tradition

Harris has indicated that she sees her many roles as extensions of the traditional roles of Comanche women. They all focus on methods for retaining Comanche values, while still equipping the next generation to survive in a changing world. Certainly her teaching post at the Washington School of the Institute for Policy Studies shows this, as does her service as a U.S. delegate to Women for a Meaningful Summit's international assembly in Greece.

Harris keeps busy at her continuing post as executive director of Americans for Indian Opportunity and her board memberships with the National Organization of Women, Save the Children, Common Cause, and the National Urban League, to name just a few. She is justly proud of her children: Kathryn Harris Tijerina, president of the Institute of American Indian Arts; Byron Harris, a filmmaker; and Laura Harris Goodhope, a Senate staffer. Her husband actively supports her work and has himself served on the President's Commission on Civil Rights, chaired the Democratic National Committee, and has twice run for presidency.

With all her accomplishments, it is easy to see why *Ladies Home Journal* named Harris one of their "Women of the Year and of the Decade" in 1979. Her tireless work on behalf of Native peoples continues today.

Further Reading

Biographical Dictionary of Indians of the Americas, Newport Beach, CA: American Indian Publishing, 1983.

Contemporary American Indian Leaders, edited by Marion Gridley, New York: Dodd Mead Publishing, 1972.

Native American Women, edited by Gretchen Bataille, New York: Garland Publishing, 1993.

Vogel, Virgil, *This Land Was Ours,* New York: Harper, 1972.

Ira Hayes

Pima military hero
Born January 12, 1923, Sacaton, Arizona
Died January 24, 1955, in the Arizona desert

"Sometimes I wished that guy had never made that picture."

Ira Hamilton Hayes is best remembered as one of the marines who helped raise the U.S. flag on Mount Suribachi, Japan, during the Battle of Iwo Jima (an island in the Pacific Ocean) in World War II. This brave action was captured in one of the most famous photographs to come out of the war, making Hayes and the other surviving members of his group instant national heroes. They received a hero's welcome from President Franklin Delano Roosevelt at the White House on

Ira Hayes

troops entered a fierce battle with the occupying Japanese forces for control of the island.

After fighting foot by foot to establish a secure beachhead where the rest of the Allied troops could land, the marines in effect declared victory over the Japanese by planting the American flag on Mount Suribachi, a small rise on the island. This effort—under fierce enemy fire—cost the lives of three of the six marines who planted the banner. The photographer Joe Rosenthal was present to capture the heroic moment on film, although some people believe that he actually restaged the event for the camera several hours later. In any case, the now-legendary photograph caused a sensation in the United States, and Hayes and the other surviving Marines became national heroes.

A hero's welcome

Hayes and the other two survivors of the flag raising were immediately called back to the United States, where they were received by President Roosevelt and reassigned to participate in the campaign to sell war bonds, investment certificates that helped finance America's involvement in World War II. This noncombat assignment, the constant public attention, and the fact that the three marines who died at his side while raising the flag were not similarly honored greatly disturbed Hayes. Because he felt he had done no more for his country than any other soldier who had died or who was still fighting in the war, he considered himself undeserving of his fame. Everywhere the war heroes traveled, they were honored at parades and other gatherings and enjoyed the goodwill of countless grateful civilians, who often wanted to buy them a drink.

their return home from combat, were immortalized in a larger-than-life bronze statue in Washington, D.C., and were honored with a commemorative postage stamp. Unfortunately, Hayes's later life was troubled, and he died in obscurity. "Sometimes I wished that guy had never made that picture," he reportedly once said.

Hayes was born to Joe E. and Nancy W. Hayes on the rural Pima Gila River Reservation in Sacaton, Arizona. Little is known about his life before he joined the marines to fight in World War II. Hayes served without attracting recognition until he participated in an Allied (including the forces of the United States, Britain, and the Soviet Union) invasion of the small Japanese-held Pacific island Iwo Jima. On February 23, 1945, Allied

While the war bond drive continued, the image of the flag raising over Mount Suribachi was becoming a national symbol. The government issued a postage stamp in honor of the event and appointed an artist to create an enormous bronze statue to be placed on display in Washington, D.C. Becoming increasingly dissatisfied with his duties, Hayes asked permission to return to active combat. By this time, however, the war was nearly over. Eventually, Hayes completed his tour of duty and left the marines, hoping to settle down to a peaceful life on the Pima reservation.

A troubled life after the war

Returning to the reservation turned out to be much more difficult than Hayes had imagined. By now, he was used to receiving public notice, although he remained humble. Life in the rural Sacaton community seemed very quiet and isolated, and Hayes began to feel that he did not belong there. He had never married, and with other relatives to look after his aging parents, he felt no obligation to stay. He began drifting around the country, trading on his name to get odd jobs, a place to sleep, and free drinks. During this period, Hayes became an alcoholic and started getting into trouble with the law.

Over the span of 13 years, Hayes was arrested more than 50 times, and most of these incidents were alcohol-related offenses. His inability to translate his fame into a stable place in life made him feel even more like an outsider. He moved from city to city and returned to the Pima Reservation once in a while with the desire to improve his life. But rural life eventually started to bore him each time. Never able to regain control of

his life, Hayes died of exposure in the Arizona desert on January 24, 1955, apparently after a drinking binge. He was buried alongside many of his fallen comrades in Arlington National Cemetery, not far from the bronze statue capturing the most famous moment in the life of this reluctant hero.

In 1961, a cleaned-up version of Hayes's life was portrayed in the film *The Outsider,* in which the actor Tony Curtis played Hayes. In 1965, the singer-songwriter Bob Dylan wrote a far more realistic account of the alienated hero in his song "The Ballad of Ira Hayes." For a generation of young Native Americans who came of age during the rise of Indian activism and the Vietnam War protest in the late 1960s and early 1970s, Ira Hayes became an important figure for different reasons. He was held up as the ultimate symbol of the wronged Indian warrior, one who fought for the United States and gained celebrity, but who died lost and in obscurity.

Further Reading

Dockstader, Frederick J., *Great North American Indians,* New York: Van Nostrand Reinhold, 1977.

Vogel, Virgil, *This Land Was Ours,* New York: Harper and Row, 1972.

William L. Hensley

Inuit leader
Born June 17, 1941, Kotzebue, Alaska
Also known as Iggiagruk ("Big Hill"
      or "Little Mountain")

The AFN lobbied in Washington for Eskimo land claims, and as a result of their efforts, the Alaska Native Claims Settlement Act of 1971 was passed in Congress, granting nearly $1 billion and 44 million acres of land to 80,000 Alaskan Natives.

W illiam L. Hensley has been a leader in the Alaskan community since he graduated from college in 1966. He was a cofounder of the Alaska Federation of Natives, which successfully lobbied the federal government for the settlement of land claims, and also served in the Alaska State Senate.

Hensley was born to John ("Aqpayuk") and Priscilla ("Naungiagak") Hensley on June 17, 1941, in Kotzebue, Alaska. His family was made up of hunters and fishermen who spoke Inupiaq, the native language of the Inuit (formerly called Eskimos). After attending elementary school in Northwest Alaska, Hensley, like most Native children, had to go away to receive further education. He attended a boarding school in Knoxville, Tennessee, where he graduated from high school. Hensley attended several colleges before receiving his bachelor's degree in political science and economics at George Washington University in Washington, D.C., in 1966. In 1974, Hensley married Abbe Ryan and they had four children, Priscilla, Molly, James, and Elizabeth.

Begins a life of public service

While attending college in Washington, D.C., Hensley wondered why his people did not have much representation in Congress. The Inuit faced poor living conditions and low employment, and most of the villages had no electricity. "It was a very tough life hunting and fishing," Hensley said in an interview. "I just had to do something." When he returned to Alaska after earning his degree, Hensley took a constitutional law class at the University of Alaska in Fairbanks. It proved to be a major turning point in his life. He wrote a paper entitled "What Rights to Land Have the Alaskan Native?" that presented a detailed account of the historical and moral obligation of the U.S. government to resolve the Alaskan land claim issue.

In 1966, Hensley was one of the founders of the Alaska Federation of Natives (AFN), representing 200 villages, 12 regional corporations, and 12 regional non-profit social service organizations. The AFN lobbied in Washington for Eskimo land claims, and as a result of their efforts, the Alaska Native Claims Settlement Act of 1971 was passed in Congress, granting nearly $1 billion and 44 million acres of land to 80,000 Alaskan Natives. Hensley served as executive director, president, and co-chair of AFN, and was instrumental in the passage of the land claims act.

Hensley was appointed by President Lyndon B. Johnson in 1968 to the National

Council on Indian Opportunity, and he was invited to an international meeting in Paris to speak on the future of the Eskimo tribes. Hensley also received the John F. Kennedy Memorial Award and was awarded a scholarship to study living conditions in Poland and the Soviet Union. He had been studying the Russian language at that time and was interested in seeing how the Russian people lived.

He served in the Alaska House of Representatives for two terms from 1966 to 1970 before being elected an Alaska State Senator in 1970. Hensley served one four-year term, then was appointed to the position again in 1986 and served two more years when the presiding senator became ill. Hensley has received several awards for his role in public service, including the National Public Service Award from the Rockefeller Foundation in 1980 and the Governor's Award for Alaskan of the Year in 1981. Also in 1981, Hensley received an honorary Doctorate of Laws from the University of Alaska in Anchorage.

Hensley has remained active in public service. He has worked to increase public awareness of many issues, including problems in Alaskan schools, suicide rates, and alcohol abuse. He has served as chair of numerous committees, including the Senate Special Committee on School Performance and the Senate Special Committee on Suicide Prevention from 1986 to 1988. He has also been involved with fish and game management and rights.

Active in Alaska Native issues

Hensley has played an active role in Alaska Native issues since the late 1960s. Besides his work with AFN, Hensley was

William L. Hensley

involved with the Alaska State Rural Affairs Commission and directed the Land Claims Task Force. While senator, his district covered over 150,000 square miles and a population of almost 20,000 people, most of whom were Inuit. He was founding president for the Alaska Village Electric Cooperative in 1967, which was a joint effort between the Rural Electric Company and the Office of Economic Opportunity. Through these efforts, 50 villages received electricity for the first time.

Hensley also served as chair of the Federal Subsistence Board, which establishes hunting and fishing regulations for over 200 million acres of land. He was vice-chair of Charter College and a member of the Pacific Region Council of the American Red Cross. He has served as chair of the Democratic Party in Alaska, as a National Committeeman, and as a member of the Clinton Transition Staff in Little Rock, Arkansas, after President Clinton's election in 1992.

Hensley founded the Northwest Alaska Native Association (NANA) Regional Corporation in Anchorage, and he has served as executive director, chair, and senior vice president. The corporation is Inupiat Eskimo-owned and employs 1,000 people. It is a diversified company with interests in natural resource development, tourism, food and janitorial contracting, electric power production, and security services. In 1989, Hensley was instrumental in developing the Red Dog Lead-Zinc Mine in Northwest Alaska, working on local, state, and federal levels. This zinc mine is the second-largest in the world with 85 million tons of reserve.

Further Reading

Biographical Dictionary of Indians of the Americas, Newport Beach, California: American Indian Publishers, 1991.

Native North American Almanac, edited by Duane Champagne, Detroit: Gale, 1994.

Hiawatha

Mohawk or Onondaga tribal leader
Flourished fourteenth century
Also known as Aiowantha

The five member tribes adopted the Great Tree of Peace as a symbol for the Iroquois Confederacy. According to legend, it was planted at the beginning of the new alliance with its roots pointing in four directions. The idea was that other nations, when they saw the roots, were to follow them to their source at the Great Tree, where they would discover Deganawida and Hiawatha's Great Law.

Hiawatha is the cultural hero from Iroquois mythology credited with founding the Iroquois Confederacy, the alliance of five Indian nations—the Oneidas, Cayugas, Onondagas, Senecas, and Mohawks—that came about in the fifteenth century. He is generally thought to have been Mohawk, but some versions of the legend have described him as an Onondaga.

Due to the various theories of his tribal origin, it is probable that the legend of Hiawatha does not stem from a single person in history. Instead, he was probably a combination of two or more figures from the northern Iroquoian tribes who worked to form the confederacy, and most likely brings together the best qualities of each. The time period during which Hiawatha's actions are generally believed to have taken place is the mid- to late-1400s, although the exact beginnings of the confederacy have long been the subject of debate.

Hiawatha, a painting by Jules Turcas

Confusion by Longfellow

Perhaps the most important thing to mention before beginning the actual story of Hiawatha and his accomplishments is the misuse of his name by the nineteenth-century American poet Henry Wadsworth Longfellow. Longfellow's poem, *The Song of Hiawatha* (1855) actually tells the tale of an Algonquian mythic hero named Nanabozho. In his researches, Longfellow was led to believe that Hiawatha and Nanabozho had similar stories. He may have decided to use the name Hiawatha thinking that it would be more pleasing to the Western ear than Nanabozho. In any case, the immensely popular poem has confused readers ever since about the identity of the real Hiawatha.

The legend of Hiawatha

According to legend, the Mohawk of a certain village at the conjunction of the Mohawk and Hudson rivers were particularly warlike. They continually sent out war parties to raid neighboring villages, hoping to weaken and ultimately defeat the surrounding tribes. Among the Iroquois chiefs was one named **Deganawida** (see entry), who was sickened by his tribe's constant fighting. During the council gatherings, he often spoke out against warfare between villages and tribes, warning his tribesmen that they might all die in such pursuits. Nevertheless, the aggressive young warriors rejected Deganawida's advice and, tired of cautioning the Iroquois tribes about their actions, Deganawida finally moved west to avoid the conflict.

During his journey, Deganawida came to the shore of a lake where he lay down to rest.

As he lay meditating, he heard the sound of a paddle in the water of the lake and looked out to see a man leaning over the edge of his canoe, dipping a basket into the shallow water. When he raised the basket, Deganawida saw that it was full of shells from the periwinkle, a creature related to the snail. The man then paddled his canoe to shore, where he lit a fire and sat stringing the shells into wampum belts. As he finished each string, he would touch the shells and talk. Deganawida watched as the strange man finished many strings in this fashion and then rose to his feet to make his presence known.

After the man from the canoe had introduced himself as Hiawatha, Deganawida asked to know the meaning of the strings of shells that he had made. Hiawatha replied that they were the rules of life and good government, and that the string made up of only white shells was the sign of truth, peace, and good will, while the string of all black shells represented hatred, war, and a bad heart. The string that alternated black and white, however, showed that peace should exist between nations, while the string with white on either end and black in the middle signified that wars must end and peace be declared.

Deganawida saw the wisdom of Hiawatha's words and realized that the warring Iroquois could benefit from such advice. Further, Deganawida recognized that all those who spoke one tongue should stop fighting and instead join forces to strengthen their position against other tribes. Hiawatha said that he had tried to share such ideas with Tadadaho of the mighty Onondaga nation, but the uncooperative chief had driven him away, so he had journeyed to this far lake where he could make laws that should govern all men. The strings of shells which he used to represent these laws would remind men for all time of the law and its meaning.

Deganawida invited Hiawatha to return with him to his village, where he called a council of all the chiefs, warriors, and women so that Hiawatha could explain his laws. The people were deeply impressed with these laws and agreed to live by them. Deganawida and Hiawatha also journeyed to the Oneida and the Cayuga nations so that they might tell them, too, of the laws, and both tribes agreed to abide by them. Then Deganawida and Hiawatha turned to the Onondaga and the mighty Tadadaho.

When Tadadaho learned that the Mohawk, Oneida, and Cayuga nations had united and that the two messengers of peace wanted the Onondaga to join as well, he ran from the village into the woods. The evil spirits that had lived inside him became serpents and sprouted from his head in a weaving mass, much like the snakes in the hair of the witch Medusa in Greek mythology. Despite Tadadaho's terrible transformation, Deganawida did not fear him, and he again asked the Onondaga chief to join the confederacy of peace and friendship.

Tadadaho continued to rage until Hiawatha approached him and combed the serpents from his head. He also told Tadadaho that he would be named the head chief of the confederacy as long as he promised to govern it according to the established laws. Upon hearing this condition, Tadadaho agreed to join the union, but asked why the mighty Seneca, who numbered more than any of the other tribes, had not been visited and asked to join the confederacy. Taking Tadadaho's concern seriously, the delegates visited the Seneca as well as other tribes to the west, but only the Seneca agreed to live by Hiawatha's laws.

Legend and history

Many parts of this legend fit with what is known today about the founding of the Iroquois Confederacy. Prior to the union, there had been a great deal of warfare among all of the tribes. Around the mid- to late-1400s, there is evidence that the five northern Iroquoian speaking tribes—the Mohawk, Oneida, Cayuga, Onondaga, and Seneca—came together to form an alliance based on their mutual needs for defense and economic stability.

With the arrival of French traders in the St. Lawrence Valley (in what is now Canada) around this time, the Indians may have seen the wisdom of facing these potential trading partners or enemies with a united Iroquois front. Also, the Iroquois nations probably recognized the advantages of defending themselves against their common enemies such as the neighboring Algonquian tribes, as well as providing a strong economic agreement that would assist any one of the member tribes in the event of a bad harvest or some other disaster. Most of all, the Iroquois probably felt that such a large alliance would give the five member tribes an edge over other groups—both Indian and European—in the economic and political issues that affected the region.

Tadadaho's selection as the Chief of the Chiefs of the Iroquois Confederacy in the Hiawatha legend may also be based in fact. Tadadaho was considered to be one of the most powerful witches among the Iroquois, and was both feared and respected not only by his followers, but by the other tribes as well. Therefore, in order for the Iroquois Confederacy to become a reality, it was necessary to deal with him. According to available historical records, the stubborn chief kept Hiawatha from talking to the Onondaga council three times, so Hiawatha finally left to speak to the Mohawk. They in turn joined up with the Oneida and Cayuga people to stand up to Tadadaho. Between this united front and Hiawatha's flattering request that the chief head the confederacy, Tadadaho was persuaded to support the union.

Another interesting part of the Hiawatha legend is the story of the Seneca woman Ja gon sah sa. Ja gon sah sa was believed to have met and fallen under the influence of Deganawida and Hiawatha when they visited the Seneca on their mission to assemble a confederacy. According to the legend, Ja gon sah sa played a vital part in convincing the Seneca to join the alliance, a role which proved crucial to the success of the whole undertaking. As a result of her contribution to the project, she was given the name of Ja gon sah sa, which means Lynx, to remind the member tribes of her importance. She is said to be buried at the present site of Ganondagan State Park near Rochester, New York.

The five member tribes adopted the Great Tree of Peace as a symbol for the Iroquois Confederacy. According to legend, it was planted at the beginning of the new alliance with its roots pointing in four directions. The idea was that other nations, when they saw the roots, were to follow them to their source at the Great Tree, where they would discover Deganawida and Hiawatha's Great Law. An eagle on top of the Great Tree represented the need to be alert to any approaching threat to the confederacy. Thus,

the five tribes sought to extend their ideas to surrounding groups and eventually bring peace and prosperity to much of the area.

The Confederacy as a longhouse

The symbolic political structure of the confederacy was set up in the form of the longhouse, which is, as its name implies, a long narrow dwelling in which an extended family would live. Longhouses could be ten to 15 feet wide and up to 250 feet in length. There was a door on either end of the dwelling, and two or more shelves ran down either side from one end to the other. Families lived in separated areas in the longhouse, each two families having their own fire in the center aisle and using the side shelves as sleeping and storage areas.

In setting up the confederacy, the founders saw the new political system as a large longhouse encompassing the territory of the five tribes. The Mohawk, being the easternmost people, were seen as keepers of the eastern door of the longhouse. The Seneca, the westernmost group, acted as keepers of the western door. The Onondaga, centrally located, served as keepers of the central fire of the longhouse, and their territory was where all formal confederacy meetings were to be conducted.

These three nations were considered the older brothers of the confederacy. As keepers of the doors at either end of the longhouse, the Seneca and Mohawk were expected to be the guardians. They officially greeted any visitors approaching the confederacy from their direction, and they warned the member tribes of any danger which might be approaching from their borders.

How the Confederacy was ruled

The governmental structure of the Iroquois Confederacy was made up of the Grand Council of Chiefs, which included 49 chiefs from the member tribes, plus the Chief of the Chiefs. The council had nine chiefs from the Mohawk, eight from the Oneida, fourteen from the Onondaga, ten from Cayuga, and eight from the Seneca. When the Tuscarora nation joined the confederacy at the invitation of the Oneida sometime after 1717, they were allowed no chiefs, but the Oneida represented them in council. Thereafter, the Five Nations of the Iroquois Confederacy became known as the Six Nations. All decisions of the confederacy were to be made by a unanimous vote of the chiefs, meaning they all had to vote the same way. If this didn't happen, they could "cover the fire," meaning that the nations agreed to disagree on that subject and the individual nations were free to act on their own.

In order to assure peace and an end to the warring and feuding among the five nations, the Great Law established rules for settling blood disputes. For example, an arbitrary price of ten strings of wampum, each at least a cubit (18-21 inches) in length, was determined as the value of a human life. Wampum was made from the shell of the quahog, or round clam, and shaped into a bead about an inch long. In the case of a murder, the victim's family was to be offered not only the price for their own lost member, but also the price for the murderer, who under the law must forfeit his or her life to that family. As a result of these rules, the sometimes generations-old cycle of feuding between Iroquois families and tribes was gradually resolved.

Hiawatha's legacy

Hiawatha held a position of great importance and authority after the Iroquois Confederacy had been founded. As one of the founding chiefs, he was given the high office of Keeper of the Wampum, in which he was responsible not only for the wampum which represented the Great Law and the confederacy itself, but also for all of the wampum belts which were later given great symbolic meaning by the Grand Council of Chiefs.

The names of Hiawatha and Tadadaho have held an esteemed place in the long tradition of the Iroquois Confederacy. To the present day, when a new leader is selected to be the Chief of the Chiefs of the grand council, he assumes the name of Tadadaho; likewise, a chief who is chosen to be Keeper of the Wampum takes the name of Hiawatha. These are titles of respect which serve to remind each member of the Iroquois Confederacy of the origins of its alliance and of its founding fathers. And the founding fathers of another confederacy—the United States of America—borrowed a number of ideas about governmental structure from the Iroquois organization, including political equality and freedom, separation of powers, and checks and balances between different parts of government.

Further Reading

Frederick Webb, *Handbook of North American Indians North of Mexico,* New York: Rowman and Littlefield, 1965.

Longfellow, Henry Wadsworth, *The Song of Hiawatha,* Boston: Ticknor and Fields, 1855.

Parker, Arthur C., *Seneca Myths and Folk Tales,* Volume 27, Buffalo Historical Society, 1923.

Wallace, Anthony F. C., *The Death and Rebirth of the Seneca,* New York: Knopf, 1970.

Jamake Highwater

Blackfoot (Blood) writer
Born February 14, c. 1942, Montana
Also known as Piitai Sankomaapii ("Eagle Son")

"The idea of life as art is part of being Indian. It's not quaint or curious or charming. It's fundamental, like plowing a field. There's great beauty in plowing a field."

Among American Indians the teller of stories is a weaver," writes Jamake Highwater in *Anpao,* his award-winning first novel. "His designs are the threads of his personal saga as well as the history of his people." Highwater's contribution as a literary "weaver" has been profound; triumphing over a difficult youth, he has become an internationally celebrated novelist, poet, and nonfiction writer. He has won numerous honors but has always viewed his role as a modest contribution to the survival of Native American tradition. "When I write, I go away for hours at a time," he told an interviewer, Jane B. Katz, in an exchange published in her book *This Song Remembers: Self-Portraits of Native Americans in the Arts.* "I don't know where I've been or who does the writing. I have to give myself up to it entirely. I'm a technician. I used a typewriter. But I can't take credit for my work. In some way I feel I'm just a conduit."

Highwater was born in Montana to Jamie Highwater, a rodeo clown and motion picture stuntman, and Amana Bonneville Highwater sometime in the early 1940s. He has never had access to accurate records about his birth. His father suffered from alcoholism, and both parents struggled to raise him against overwhelming odds, but had put him up for adoption by the time he was about six. Even so, he has always remembered Amana's lessons in Indian culture and credits her storytelling talents as the source of his own literary abilities. Though she was of mixed Blackfoot (Blood) and French Canadian heritage, his mother emphasized the attributes of Native American tradition. Unfortunately, Jamake's last exchange with his father was a bitter one, and Jamie Highwater died in a traffic accident before they could resolve their differences.

Troubled upbringing

Highwater was adopted by a white couple, Alexander and Marcia Marks, at a time when adoption enjoyed less public approval than it does today. He went to live with the Marks in their home in California's San Fernando Valley but was never given a house key; his adoptive parents furthermore would not discuss his birth parents with him, and he had to see Amana secretly. He acted up in school, often getting into fights with white kids who taunted him for being an Indian. He did, however, form a powerful bond with the Marks' youngest daughter. The two became so close that when she married and moved away, Jamake was devastated. "It took me years to recognize that as a child without a history or life of my own, I had wanted to live out my existence through my sister's life," Highwater commented.

When he couldn't unlock the door to his own parents' home—he was forced to wait until they returned from work—he was allowed to wait in the home of his neighbors, the Dorrs. Their collection of music and literature stimulated him, as did the encouragement of his teacher Alta Black. She gave him a typewriter and said she'd dreamed that he would be a writer; the desire to earn her approval motivated him to become an excellent student. Highwater stayed in touch with Alta Black until shortly before she died when she was in her nineties. The writer recalled later, "'As long as I am alive,' I promised her, 'you too will live. And as long as my books survive, you will survive with them. That I swear. I will breathe life into you with every word I write.'"

Jamake Highwater

Enjoyed San Francisco's "counterculture"

Highwater struggled to pay for a college education. He tried community college and even the Reserve Officers Training Corps (ROTC) but was unhappy with both. Eventually, however, he earned a doctorate degree and taught at New York University and Columbia University. In between, he moved to San Francisco and became a dance instructor. He helped start a small dance troupe and even took it on tour. San Francisco in the 1960s was very much to his taste. He found the city's counterculture (segment of a society whose customs and values differ from the majority) "remarkably similar to Native American values in some of its viewpoints and visions." His involvement with the "hippie" movement there led him to writing about rock music, and he authored a book about Mick Jagger, lead singer for British superstars the Rolling Stones. The book—which, like his other early work, was published under the pen name "J Marks"—received mixed reviews but was translated into several languages.

The increase in Native American political activity in the late 1960s also increased Highwater's interest in his heritage. This led to his first book dealing with these issues, and the first to bear his real name. *Indian America: A Cultural and Travel Guide* appeared in 1969. Two years later, he was offered a unique opportunity by Fodor Travel Guides, the company responsible for publishing some of the world's most popular tourist handbooks. Fodor "appointed me editor and writer of a student guide to Europe," Highwater once noted, "which gave me virtually unlimited access to the entire world, all expenses paid!" While in Europe working on the guide, he began writing *Anpao*. This tale of a youth who goes on a quest to gain the sun's permission to marry his beloved was often tagged as "children's literature," but Highwater insisted that the label didn't apply. As he explained, however, "in the mysterious world of American publishers, fantasy is usually kid stuff."

Given Indian name

In 1978 *Anpao* won the Newbery Honor Award, the *Boston Globe/Horn Book* Award, and the American Library Association's Best Book for Young Adults award. It also earned the admiration of a great many critics and other readers. Highwater insisted that it merged themes common to a vast number of tribes, though it emphasized the stories of Northern Plains and Southwestern people. He was also at pains to remind readers that "the diversity of Indians is great." His writings would henceforth explore various corners of Indian life, with special attention to art. He wrote about Native American painting, music, and dance, interviewing artists and doing extensive research.

One of the key events in Highwater's life occurred in 1979: a Blackfoot ceremony in which he was given a new Indian name. He became Piitai Sahkomaapii, which means "Eagle Son." This honor was the tribe's way of saluting his literary efforts to support Indian culture. Highwater continued this work in later years, writing—among other works—a novel about the decline of Aztec civilization; two scripts for public television, including the ACE award-winning *The Primal Mind;* several books of poems; and a cycle of novels (a series of works which are all related to each other) known as the "Ghost Horse" series that included *Legend Days, The Ceremony of Innocence, I Wear the Morning Star,* and *Kill Hole.* The "Ghost Horse" series incorporated autobiographical elements to tell the story of an Indian family's descendants over several centuries.

Diverse writings

Highwater's diverse work is not limited to recording and describing Native American culture. He has written on literature, music, and other topics for publications as varied as the *New York Times, Esquire,* and *Stereo Review* and was classical music editor for the *Soho Weekly News* for several years. For a 1988 audiovisual package called *Dogsong,* he lent his services as narrator. His 1994 nonfiction work *The Language of Vision: Meditations on Myth and Metaphor* used a deck of Tarot cards as a way to discuss differences between "Western" and "primal" ways of thinking about the universe, and he contributed an essay on sacred architecture to *Omni* magazine.

He has also worked on the art task force of President Jimmy Carter's Commission on Mental Health, as well as committees for the New York State Arts Council and many other organizations. He was the general director of Rice University's 1986 Native Arts Festival and of the Celebration of Multicultural Mythologies in the Arts in Philadelphia in 1991. He has been presented with scores of honors, notably the choice of his *Song from the Earth* as one of one hundred books representing America at the Moscow International Book Fair and an honorary doctorate from the Minneapolis College of Art and Design.

Highwater has long claimed that art is not mere recreation or diversion in Indian culture. "The idea of life as art is part of being Indian. It's not quaint or curious or charming. It's fundamental, like plowing a field.

There's great beauty in plowing a field." In his "Storyteller's Farewell" at the end of *Anpao,* he asserts his belief "in the existence of some sort of transcendent Indian sensibility, and I believe that its power and its truth can be expressed in modes typical of our day as well as in the venerated, old style of the traditionalists."

Further Reading

Chricton, Sarah, "PW Interviews: Jamake Highwater," *Publishers Weekly,* November 6, 1978, pp. 6-8.

Katz, Jane B., editor, *This Song Remembers: Self-Portraits of Native Americans in the Arts,* Boston: Houghton Mifflin, 1980, pp. 171-77.

Books by Jamake Highwater:

Anpao: An American Indian Odyssey (novel), illustrated by Fritz Scholder, New York: Lippincott, 1977.

The Ceremony of Innocence (novel), New York: Harper, 1984.

I Wear the Morning Star (novel), New York: Harper, 1986.

Kill Hole (novel), New York: Harper, 1993.

The Language of Vision: Meditations on Myth and Metaphor (nonfiction), New York: Grove/Atlantic, 1994.

Legend Days (novel), New York: Harper, 1984.

Many Smokes, Many Moons: A Chronology of American Indian History through Indian Art (nonfiction), New York: Lippincott, 1978.

(As J Marks) *Mick Jagger: The Singer Not the Song* (nonfiction), New York: Popular Library, 1974.

Rama: A Legend, New York: Harper, 1994.

(As J Marks) *Rock and Other Four Letter Words: Music of the Electric Generation* (nonfiction), New York: Bantam, 1968.

Shadow Show: An Autobiographical Insinuation, Alfred Van der Marck, 1986.

The Sun, He Dies: A Novel about the End of the Aztec (novel), New York: Lippincott, 1980.

Ishi

Yahi (Southern Yana) survivor and research informant
Born c. 1862, northern California
Died March 25, 1916, San Francisco, California

For most Americans Ishi is a romantic symbol of the last unspoiled Native, but to many Native Americans in California, he represents a terrible era of genocide and cultural devastation.

Often identified as "the last wild Indian" in North America, Ishi was the last known survivor of the Yahi tribe of northern California. His ancestors were the victims of 25 years of brutal violence at the hands of white settlers and prospectors following the California Gold Rush, during which the Native American population of the state was reduced from about 100,000 to only 20,000. In 1911 Ishi emerged alone from the forest and spent the remainder of his life in the urban world of San Francisco, protected by a group of academics who respected—and wished to learn about—his heritage and benefited from his friendship. For most Americans Ishi is a romantic symbol of the last unspoiled Native, but to many Native Americans in California, he represents a terrible era of genocide and cultural devastation.

Yana history and culture

In 1961 Theodora Kroeber compiled a composite picture of Yana life and history from traditional sources and the words of

Ishi

Ishi himself. She believed a full understanding of the group would come only with a grasp of "the land and people of Indian California." Apparently, the Yana population never exceeded two or three thousand people; they existed in what is now northern California for a period of between three and four thousand years. The range of activity of the Yana was probably confined to an area stretching 40 by 60 miles. There were four subgroups, each with a distinct dialect; the Yahi was the southernmost of these.

Generally the groups remained apart, living in small settlements, searching for food, and gathering together only in the autumn in large encampments. In the winter they reviewed the meaning of the yearly reunions, transmitted tribal legends and history, studied the pattern of the skies, and found meaning in personal dreams. The Yana had generally been unaffected by the Spanish and Mexican presence in California—and the missions they established to convert the Indians to Catholicism—during the late eighteenth to mid-nineteenth centuries. Sonoma, the northernmost mission, was still out of range of these Native peoples. But the Mexican land grants of 1844 and the gold rush at the end of the same decade resulted in a nearly complete destruction of the Yana by 1872.

Policy of extermination

Violent racism, combined with occasional murders of whites by Yana, led people in California to carry out a policy of extermination (to get rid of completely, generally by killing) of Indians. Beyond this violence, thousands of Native Californians were subjected to servitude and prostitution. Streams were polluted by the mining process and natural survival became more difficult. Theodora Kroeber analyzed the mental condition of the whites who arrived in California after a perilous journey from the East. She believed they often arrived in a "dehumanized" state and added that the lust for gold seemed to destroy the human mind and soul. Although there are "inconsistencies and gaps in the record" it is clear that a pattern of total suppression of the Yana started by 1850. A military removal and reservation plan at Nome Lackee failed from 1859 to 1861.

Ishi was probably born in 1862, at the beginning of the most intense extermination period. Not only were random Indians who remained in the wild killed, but even indentured men, women, and children were put to death by angry settlers. These stray people had gained the name "the Mill Creeks," which perhaps explains the intense attack on a group of Yahi on Mill Creek where Ishi's father was probably killed. Ishi and his mother were among the few survivors.

Another group of Yahi were massacred in a cave by a group headed by a man named Kingsley.

A people in hiding

Ishi apparently went into hiding at about the age of ten. During the years from 1872 to 1884, he and his people had to stay completely out of the sight and hearing of white people. An earlier effort by the Yahi to negotiate a peace settlement was ignored by the settlers. Theirs was to be a virtually noiseless world, and no foot prints could be left to reveal their existence. But Ishi and his family and associates were able to keep both their identity and their culture.

In 1884 desperate conditions made it necessary for the Yahi to raid settlers' homes for food and supplies. Ishi and three others were actually caught in the act as they exited a cabin window. Because they had only taken clothing in this case, a surprisingly tolerant owner let them go free. The grateful escapees later returned to the cabin and left a gift of two baskets.

The most permanent of Ishi's hiding places was a concealed area called the Grizzly Bear's Hiding Place. It was occupied by Ishi, his mother, a sister, and two men. Their solitude ended in November 1908 when two engineers scouting the area to build a dam for electrical power happened upon Ishi while he was fishing with a harpoon. According to their report, he fiercely scared them away. Shortly thereafter, a party of surveyors located the abandoned Grizzly Bear site. Ishi's sick mother was still there, wrapped in a blanket. All useful items, including food and implements, were taken by the white men. The dying woman was left behind. Ishi returned to move his mother, but she died a few days later. The others in the small group had disappeared. Ishi was totally alone for a period of nearly three years.

Confronts civilization

Ishi finally entered the "civilized" world, turning up in Oroville, California. He was the last survivor of his tribe. Under the circumstances, Ishi's survival and the events that followed were the one good thing to come from this otherwise tragic history of the end of a people. If Ishi had emerged from the wilderness at a different location in the summer of 1911 he might have been killed. Instead, the sheriff put him in the local jail cell for the insane. Newspapers quickly labeled him the "Wild Man of Oroville."

Within a few days, anthropologist Thomas Talbot Waterman travelled the 50 miles from San Francisco to bring Ishi to a new location. He soon gained Ishi's confidence by demonstrating his awareness of the Yana language. Soon "the Stone Age Man" encountered modern transportation: a train, a ferry boat, and a San Francisco trolley car. He was fascinated by the experience. His new home was the museum of the anthropology department of the University of California. It was located in Parnassus Heights, near Golden Gate Park in San Francisco. The department, which had been established in 1901, and the museum, scheduled to open to the public only two months after Ishi's arrival, were made possible by the support of Phoebe Apperson Hearst, mother of publishing tycoon William Randolph Hearst, who needed a home for her personal anthropological collection.

At first Ishi was quite timid and was easily startled by loud and unfamiliar noises. He shared the museum with two caretakers. Alfred Kroeber became his second significant friend. Because of public pressure, Kroeber gave him a name: "Ishi"—the Yahi name for "man." He never revealed his real name, or repeated the one the whites invented for him.

Because Ishi's state of mind is probably the most interesting part of this unusual story, the observations of Kroeber's wife, Theodora, about Ishi are important. He was shy and blushed frequently, she said, but kept his dignity. "He was no king's jester: no one ever laughed at him." He was amiable and had great curiosity. "To be sure, he would sit, unbored, dreamy, and withdrawn into his own mystic center, but only if there was nothing to do, no one to talk to.... He was interested, concerned, amused, or delighted, as the case might be, with everything and everyone he knew and understood."

Naturally there were those who wished to exploit Ishi. Among those who showed interest were promoters of vaudeville circuits, exhibitors for carnivals, and commercial phonograph producers. But Alfred Kroeber never allowed these intrusions. Kroeber helped Ishi establish an independent way of life. He was made a junior janitor at the museum with a $25-per-month salary. His formal public appearances in the museum were limited to two and one half hours on Sunday afternoons. Ishi showed great interest in learning people's names and was able to make distinctions between ethnic groups and the distinct classes of San Francisco society.

Ishi was most overwhelmed by the *number* of people he encountered in his new environment. Before his appearance near Oroville he had probably never seen more than 40 or 50 people at one time. When he attended a vaudeville show he was much more impressed by the audience than the performance. At the same time he felt uncomfortable in large groups of people. He compared the odor of sweating crowds to that of old deer hides. When he was taken to the beach for the first time to see the Pacific Ocean his first impression was not of the water but the masses of people on the beach: "Hansi saltu, hansi saltu!" ("Many white people, many white people!")

Before long he became increasingly independent, doing his own shopping and preparing food in the museum kitchen. He considered matches more interesting than gas or electricity. He walked to Golden Gate Park, where he first saw a buffalo, and travelled alone to the University of California campus in Berkeley. New items, such as ice cream, became part of his diet. On a daily basis he found new things that intrigued him—glue, roller shades on windows, kaleidoscopes.

In part because of his close friendship with a local doctor, Saxton Pope, Ishi spent much of his time at the hospital located next to the museum. He visited and showed great concern for patients; he detected that there were more male than female patients and concluded that this was because the men spent too much time indoors. He even watched actual operations, was distressed by anaesthesia (believing that artificially induced sleep resulted in the removal of the soul from the body), and concluded that tonsillectomies were unnecessary, since he had his own special cure.

Return to the wilderness

As many as 1,000 visitors would gather on Sunday afternoons to observe Ishi's unique skills as a craftsman. Supplies of special woods, obsidian, flint, and other items were delivered to him. He prepared hunting implements and shaped nearly perfect arrowheads. In May 1914 Ishi had the unanticipated, and unwanted, opportunity to use his survival skills in his former environment. Kroeber, Waterman, and Pope pushed Ishi into joining them on a month-long camping expedition in the region where Ishi had lived his solitary existence only three years before. The scholars believed that the journey would help them learn much more about Ishi's culture.

The troop, which also included Pope's 11-year-old son, took a Pullman sleeping car to Oroville. Ishi casually tipped the porter upon their departure from the train. Soon he was riding a horse for the first time and upon reaching his wilderness home, he abandoned his formal attire for a breechcloth. Once in his former setting he accepted the mission of this grand anthropological venture and became a perfect host for his amateur "primitives." Theodora Kroeber claims he also had "a sudden comprehension of a sense of history." Much of the summer activity was recorded in photographs. A return visit to the region in the autumn was cancelled because of the beginning of World War I.

Ishi's journey ends

The Bureau of Indian Affairs (BIA) showed a brief interest in Ishi and offered him the option of going to a reservation. His reply to the California Special Agent was: "I will live like the white man for the remainder of my days. I wish to stay here where I am now. I will grow old in this house, and it is here I will die." A formal reply from the BIA accepted his decision and concluded, "Owing to his previous manner of life, his mental development as far as understanding of our manner of life was concerned, was not beyond that of a six year old child." Kroeber replied with civility: "Ishi has taken readily to civilization ... his mental development was by no means stunted or sub-normal."

Kroeber, in fact, told his wife that Ishi "was the most patient man I ever knew." She added comments about Ishi's orderliness and observed, "The impulse of any sort of exhibitionism was totally foreign to him.... Affectionate and uncorrupt, he was denied the fulfillment of wife and children, or of any sex life whatever." However, Ishi was to fall victim to another element of civilization—tuberculosis. He developed a severe cough in December 1914 and soon required medical care. After some time in the nearby hospital, and as a guest in Waterman's home, a major exhibit was removed to give him a special room in the museum. It was there that he died on March 25, 1916.

Because of a European sabbatical, Kroeber was not with him in his final months, but he communicated by mail two or three times a week. The day before his death Kroeber sent an urgent message not to violate his body in any way. An autopsy would be a sacrilegious ending for the Yahi. "If there is any talk about the interests of science, say for me that science can go to hell." But the message was not received in time and Ishi's brain was removed. Consistent with Yana custom, his body was cremated. The ashes, and some of his artifacts, were buried in the

Mt. Olivet Cemetery in the small town of Colma, near San Francisco. He left an estate of $523 in cash.

Waterman blamed himself for pushing Ishi too hard during the summer of 1915. During that period, he worked daily with the great language specialist Edward Sapir. Fifteen hundred feet of valuable documentary film of Ishi was lost because of improper preservation, but fortunately about 400 wax-cylinder sound recordings survived. Waterman wrote to Kroeber that Ishi "was the best friend I had in the world." Pope added his own epitaph: "And so, stoic and unafraid, departed the last wild Indian of America. He closes a chapter of history. He looked upon us as sophisticated children—smart, but not wise.... His soul was that of a child, his mind that of a philosopher."

The image remains

Kroeber was so disillusioned that he abandoned his profession for a time and studied psychoanalysis. He chose not to write the story of his friend and Ishi's story might have been lost had not his wife decided to write a book nearly a half century later. Theodora Kroeber's 1961 biography, published by the University of California Press, created a general public awareness of the life of Ishi again. In a 1976 edition, she reveals the remarkable reaction to the book 15 years before: "I could not know that ahead of me lay the real experience of Ishi: the greatest human experience of my life.... All sorts of people came, wanting sometimes to question, more often to talk, to express complex reactions, to philosophize, to wonder, even to cry—shamelessly, men and women—to put into words their feeling for Ishi's humanity."

Three years later Theodora issued a fictionalized account of his life. Nearly 30 years after the initial publication, during a wave of interest in Native American life, her novel was made into a film with **Graham Greene** (see entry) in the title role. A documentary film about his life, in "The American Experience" series, was also completed. In 1966 a monument was dedicated near Oroville by the white man who first saw Ishi in 1911. Conservationists have also been active in preserving an Ishi Wilderness in the region of his original home.

Further Reading

Ishi: The Last Yahi; A Documentary History, edited by Robert F. Heizer and Theodora Kroeber, Berkeley: University of California Press, 1979.

Kroeber, Theodora, *Ishi in Two Worlds: A Biography of the Last Wild Indian in North America,* Berkeley: University of California Press, 1961.

Kroeber, Theodora, *Ishi: Last of His Tribe,* Berkeley: Parnassus Press, 1964.

Meyer, Kathleen Allan, *Ishi: The Story of an American Indian,* Minneapolis: Dillon Press, 1980.

INDEX BY
FIELD OF ENDEAVOR

Volume number appears in **bold**.

FEB   2001

REF 970.004 NAT v. 1
Native North American
33292004112003   PA